STUDENT WRITERS AT WORK

617

STUDENT WRITERS AT WORK

The Bedford Prizes

Edited by

Nancy Sommers & Donald McQuade

foreword by Edward P. J. Corbett

A Bedford Book
ST. MARTIN'S PRESS · NEW YORK

Library of Congress Catalog Card Number: 83–61616
Copyright © 1984 by St. Martin's Press, Inc.
All Rights Reserved.
Manufactured in the United States of America
8 7 6 5 4
f e d c b a
For information, write St. Martin's Press, Inc.,
175 Fifth Avenue, New York, N.Y. 10010
Editorial offices: Bedford Books *of* St. Martin's Press
165 Marlborough Street, Boston, MA 02116

ISBN: 0–312–76938–5

Typography: Anna Post
Cover Design: Richard S. Emery

Acknowledgments

Page 163: Writing assignment from Sylvan Barnet and
Marcia Stubbs, *Barnet and Stubbs's Practical Guide to Writing:
Fourth Edition with Additional Readings,* p. 55. Copyright ©
1983 by Sylvan Barnet and Marcia Stubbs. Reprinted by
permission of Little, Brown and Company.
Page 166: Gift of the Frederick J. Kennedy Memorial
Foundation. Courtesy, Museum of Fine Arts, Boston.
Page 167: Courtesy, Museo del Prado.

PUBLISHER'S NOTE

The Bedford Prizes in Student Writing was a nationwide contest for essays written for a freshman composition class in 1982. It was sponsored by Bedford Books, an imprint of St. Martin's Press.

The contest drew over 1200 entries from over 500 colleges and universities in 48 states. All the entries were read at least twice by a panel of experienced composition instructors, and this preliminary screening produced the essays sent to the eight contest judges for a final reading. In neither the preliminary nor the final judging were the readers aware of the students' names or schools.

The 31 winning essayists come from 29 two- and four-year schools in 20 states across the country. They and their instructors received cash awards as well as hand-lettered certificates. We congratulate them, their instructors, and their writing programs. We also thank everyone who entered the contest for helping to make it a success.

We are grateful to the distinguished judges—Wayne Booth, Edward P. J. Corbett, Ellen Goodman, Maxine Hairston, Donald McQuade, Nancy Sommers, Alice Trillin, and Calvin Trillin—for their enthusiastic support for and participation in the contest. To Donald McQuade and Nancy Sommers—who were not only judges but also contest coordinators and co-editors of this anthology—we offer special thanks for their high standards and hard work, for their belief in the worth of the contest and their vision of the potential of this book.

The Bedford Prizes in Student Writing will be offered again. A formal announcement together with the new contest rules will be sent out early in 1984. Anyone wanting information on the new contest can also write to Bedford Books of St. Martin's Press, P.O. Box 869, Boston, Massachusetts 02117.

FOREWORD

by Edward P. J. Corbett

Those of us involved with the Bedford Prizes in Student Writing had little idea of what to expect from the contest. A nationwide competition open only to essays written for freshman composition had never been conducted before, and thus neither the sponsors nor the judges could predict what the response would be. How many entries would be received? Where would they come from? What would they be like? The answers to these questions were both surprising and gratifying.

To everyone's delight, the contest proved to be truly nationwide: Over 1200 essays arrived from over 500 schools in 48 states. Even more delightful, the entries were of very high quality. As a contest judge I saw only those essays that had survived a preliminary screening (really a secondary screening, considering that the submitting instructors had first chosen which essays to enter), but the pervasive excellence of the writing I read was still astounding. As I commented when I submitted my ranking of the essays, "One of the best ways to silence those who perennially lament about the miserable state of student writing in this country would be to invite those people to read some of the essays submitted to this contest."

The winning essays provided another pleasant surprise. The judges did not know the names of the student writers or the schools they attended. Judging the essays solely on their merits, we ended up selecting work from large schools and small schools, from four-year universities and two-year community colleges, from tax-supported schools and private, religious-affiliated schools, from schools in large cities and schools in small towns, from schools with highly selective admisssions and schools with open admissions. We hear enough about the bad writing being done everywhere; it was gratifying to see that good writing is also being done in all kinds of institutions in all parts of the country.

As significant as I find the contest and as remarkable as I find its results, the book in which the winning essays appear seems to me even more extraordinary. When it was announced in the contest rules that the winning essays would be published by Bedford Books in early 1984, I assumed the book would be a simple celebratory volume presenting the student essays, with perhaps a brief preface commenting on the quality of the writing. I should have known that Nancy Sommers and Donald McQuade would not be content with just that. What they have produced instead is probably the most process-oriented reader ever published for college writing courses. Its many unique features, detailed in the preface that follows, make it a uniquely useful textbook for anyone working with student writing or considering doing so.

I salute Bedford Books for sponsoring the Bedford Prizes in Student Writing. I commend Nancy Sommers and Donald McQuade for having treated the student writing in this book with great seriousness and dignity and for having produced such an original and valuable teaching tool. I hope that both the contest and this book will be around a long time.

PREFACE

Student Writers at Work celebrates the writing of students and particularly the accomplishments of the thirty-one winners of the Bedford Prizes in Student Writing. But the book is more than merely celebratory. It accords students' writing the attention and respect it deserves, not only by publishing it, but also by subjecting it to critical attention like that brought to bear on professional essays in the typical composition anthology. And it explores the composing processes of the writers, letting them speak in their own voices about their purposes and strategies, their problems and rewards. The book is designed to serve either or both of two functions in the classroom. First, it provides a compact and inexpensive anthology of accessible essays, representing attainable models, to be used in place of or along with a collection of professional essays. Second, it provides an instructional resource when the primary focus of a course is on the writing of students in the course.

The anthology portion of *Student Writers at Work* is in some ways similar to the typical composition reader and in other ways very different. On the one hand, the essays are as diverse as any group of professional essays would be: The writers vary widely in age, background, and experiences; each of their voices is distinctive; their subjects include science, social issues, and literature as well as personal experience; and their purposes range from expressive to explanatory to argumentative. On the other hand, the material surrounding the essays is unprecedented in a reader. Because the contest rules stipulated that all entries be accompanied by preliminary notes and drafts, and because all the winning essayists and their instructors completed detailed questionnaires, the headnotes and discussion questions on the essays can explore the writers' composing processes as well as their finished product. The headnotes provide not only biographical information on the writers but also quotations from them about their intentions and their writing habits. The questions after

the essays fall into three groups. Those on reading address the standard concerns of content and form; those on writing suggest related topics for students'
own essays. The third group focuses on revision in one of two ways: either by
highlighting the writer's strategies and choices as revealed in his or her questionnaire responses or preliminary notes and drafts; or by posing "What if?"
questions that invite students to consider the effects of further changes in the
essay. Together, the questions are intended to encourage students to read critically and to evaluate the relative success of various writing strategies in particular circumstances.

Though the anthology is the heart of *Student Writers at Work*, it is not all
the book offers. Also included are four unique sections designed to help students in their own writing and in working with their fellow students' writing:

Students on Writing. This introduction provides an overview of the writing
process through the voices of the winning essayists. They discuss their satis-
factions and frustrations as writers and their specific strategies for getting started,
writing, and revising.

Two Student Writers at Work. In this part students have an opportunity to
witness the composing processes of two of the winning essayists. Guided by
editorial comments, students first examine the complete notes for and the
rough and final drafts of one of the winning essays, along with the writer's
own explanations of her intentions. Then, guided by questions, students analyze the choices made by another of the winning writers as her essay developed
through two preliminary drafts to a final version.

Peer Editors at Work. This part prepares students to be effective peer editors
and to respond as writers to the editing of their peers. After an explanation
of the principles and procedures of peer editing, students see the comments of
four composition students on one of the winning essays. Students are then
invited by questions both to analyze the peer editors' comments and to evaluate
the essay themselves. The writer of the essay then responds to the peer editors'
comments and revises her essay, and students are again invited by questions
to examine this stage of peer editing. Exercises in peer editing, including work
on another of the winning essays, conclude the part.

The Professional Editor at Work. The final part demonstrates what happens
to writing when it is prepared for publication. After an introduction explaining
the goals and procedures of editing, a professional editor offers specific recommendations for two of the winning essays, with particular emphasis on
improving communication between the writer and the reader. Each writer then
revises his essay and comments on the revision and on the experience of being

edited. Students are guided by questions to examine the editing of both essays and the writers' responses to it.

Each of these unique parts receives special attention in the complimentary instructor's manual prepared with the help of Miriam Baker of Dowling College. The manual discusses each part as well as each essay thoroughly and offers teaching suggestions, discussion questions, and writing topics. It also provides a syllabus with ideas for using *Student Writers at Work* throughout a semester and a detailed arrangement of the essays by elements of composition.

In conceiving and developing *Student Writers at Work*, we have been influenced by nearly two hundred members of the Council of Writing Program Administrators who responded to a survey on the uses of student writing in the classroom. Among many other ideas, the respondents shared their almost unanimous belief that student writing should be the primary text in the composition class; as one administrator put it, no book can replace "the living, breathing student in the class who is there to speak up, to argue, to defend, to explain, to accept, and to reject." *Student Writers at Work* does not attempt such replacement. Instead, it offers a collection of essays that are both worthy of emulation and possible to emulate. And it supplements the work of students in the class with the work of their peers across the nation, giving them an opportunity to sharpen their critical skills without risk of offending classmates, to study how successful writers make the composing process work for them, and to see themselves as members of a community of writers that extends well beyond the classroom walls.

Acknowledgments

Sherwood Anderson once said that "the whole glory of writing lies in the fact that it forces us out of ourselves and into the lives of others." Behind the publication of *Student Writers at Work* stands an unusually large number of colleagues and friends who graciously allowed us into their already crowded lives to seek advice and encouragement.

Before there was a book, there was a contest. And before there was a contest, there were rules to be written. For their counsel during this phase of the project, we would like to thank A. Harris Fairbanks (University of Connecticut), and Hans Smit, Esq. Most importantly, we would like to acknowledge both the instructors across the country who supported the contest by entering their students' work and the 1200 students who wrote essays worthy of submission.

We are indebted to the kind people who kept track of the essays as they were submitted and who prepared them to be read anonymously: Matthew Evans, Tim Evans, Hugh Gabrielson, Bob Gustafson, Jeanne Hillson, Todd Macalister, Keith Powers, and Teresa Venditto. Judson Evans helped with these tasks and with mailing and statistical analysis of the entries. And surely not to be overlooked are the efforts of John Ryle of the U. S. Postal Service, who hauled the thousands of essays and pieces of contest material through Boston's distinctive brand of snow, sleet, and rain.

We are grateful to the writers, editors, and teachers of writing who served as judges in the first reading: Carla Asher, Arnold Asrelsky, Regina Barreca, Philip Beitchman, Donald Billiar, Alan Coes, Jacqueline Costello, Robert DiYanni, Alan Dubrow, David Gibson, Lesley Hansen, George Held, Freda Hepner, Dexter Jeffries, Virginia Johnson, Kathleen Kier, Mitchell Levenberg, Elaine Levy, Norman Lewis, Nancy Perry, Charles Piltch, Ziva Piltch, John Pufhal, Lesley Robins, Lillian Rossi, Sid Shanker, Rockwell Stensrud, Ely Stock, Susan Stock, Amy Tucker, Robert Webb, Peter Weiss, Gordon Whatley, John Wheeler, Norman Will, Marcie Wolfe, Patricia Zaccardo, Kathleen Zane, and Robert Zweil. Special thanks to Deborah Asher who helped recruit many of our first-round judges, and to Sue Shanker who also helped recruit the judges and then trained them and adeptly choreographed the multiple readings of each essay.

For their advice on the book, we'd like to thank Deborah Asher, Robert DiYanni, Ed Dornan, Betsy Kaufman, Elaine Maimon, Mimi Schwartz, and especially Judith Stanford. We are indebted to Jane Aaron, who in addition to being an eloquent and encouraging voice in the "Professional Editor at Work" section, has most generously contributed to the planning and development of virtually every phase of this book. We are particularly grateful to Miriam Baker (Dowling College), a first-rate teacher and writer, for her help in preparing the *Instructor's Manual*.

We would like to acknowledge our colleagues in England and the United States whose work helped shape the section on peer editing: M. L. J. Abercrombie, Lil Brannon, John Clifford, Richard Gebhardt, Thom Hawkins, Edwin Mason, Stephen Tschudi, and especially Ken Bruffee, Rosemary Deen, and Marie Ponsot. For their help on this section we would also like to thank the student writers and peer editors at the University of California at San Diego: Suzanne Bastien, Becky Bloom, Claudia Carpenter, Craig Cuthbert, Julie Dalton, Chris Knigge, Susan Mackey, Margaret Miller, Greg Nakahira, Bethany Ogden, Samantha Roby, Lisa Shives-McCrea, Kim Strub, D'Arcy Swartz, Paula Thomas, Peter Wertheimer, and with special thanks to David Caldwell, Angela Didio, Jo-Ellen Fisherkeller, and Dan Martin. Their intelligence, energy, and eagerness to learn made a working community of writers both possible and productive. Thanks also to Gerry McCauley, who helped at both ends of this project.

For the elegant look they gave us, we thank Anna Post, who designed the contest poster and the book, and Dick Emery, who designed the book's cover. Barbara Flanagan has been an outstanding copyeditor.

Finally, our greatest thanks go to the staff of Bedford Books. Karen Henry, editorial assistant, coordinated the complex administrative work of the contest with great skill and intelligence. Nancy Lyman, editorial assistant, contributed to every phase of this project with uncommon energy, skill, and irrepressible good humor. Sue Warne, Managing Editor, graciously—and seemingly effortlessly—helped us through what appeared to be a maze of production problems. Joan Feinberg, Associate Publisher, gave us generous, rigorous comments on the manuscript and encouraged us throughout the project. She is the kind of editor every writer hopes to work with and the kind of reader every writer hopes to write for. And Chuck Christensen, Publisher, who enticed us with the idea of the Bedford Prizes, has offered wise and genial support and shown ample confidence in his authors. *Student Writers at Work* has been a truly collaborative enterprise.

Judy and Amanda Myers gave us time to work, and Hans Dieter, Sarah, and Amelia Batschelet welcomed weary travellers in search of a place to work. Throughout this project, our families have supported us in innumerable ways. We can only hope that in this sentence Patrick and Rachel Hays and Susanne, Christine, and Marc McQuade will now know how much they have helped us and how much their help has meant to us.

Nancy Sommers
Donald McQuade

CONTENTS

From sweat running down his face to blood running in his shoes, a paramedic recounts all the drama and tension surrounding the treatment of a gun-shot victim.

In a powerfully moving narrative, Barrus writes about the death of her child.

Baby sitting isn't what it used to be. Bean humorously recounts her experiences with today's sophisticated children.

Do businesses have an obligation that goes beyond making money? Boxerman argues forcefully against Milton Friedman's ideas on corporate social responsibility.

Steve
2b

STUDENT WRITERS AT WORK

STUDENTS ON WRITING

Part I

ONE OF THE MOST reassuring discoveries that any student of writing can make is that there is no single way to write, no fail-proof formula to produce successful essays. Anyone seriously interested in learning to write can benefit from listening to what other writers have to say about the challenges and pleasures of the composing process. The pages that follow will give you a special opportunity to examine the writing process from the point of view of student writers. The thirty-one winners of the Bedford Prizes in Student Writing explain their successes and frustrations as writers as well as their particular methods of composition. From their detailed responses to a questionnaire on their specific habits and goals, their strategies and concerns as writers, we have drawn insightful and practical information on many aspects of writing—from how these student writers search for an idea and then develop it in a first draft to how they revise and then prepare that idea for presentation in a finished essay.

What do these student writers talk about when they are invited to discuss writing? Like all writers, they invariably speak of the problems and the pleasures of struggling to convey a clear sense of their ideas. They also talk about the purpose and structure of their essays and their use of language and relation to an audience. They frequently touch on their respect for and anxiety about mastering the skills required to write good prose. And they describe in detail the distinctive ways in which they compose: how they go about generating ideas for a paper, how they get started on their first drafts, how they contend with the procrastination and the dead ends that threaten their progress, how they revise, and how they determine when their essays are finished and ready to be submitted to their instructors. Given the academic context within which they work, they also discuss their concern about grades and their perceptions of the place of writing in their career goals.

The perspectives these thirty-one writers present on the composing process are as varied as their ages and backgrounds. But the procedures they follow when writing can be grouped into three general phases: getting started, writing, and revising. Writers usually go about getting started by searching for and then deciding on a subject to write about, developing their ideas about the subject, clarifying their purpose in writing, organizing their thoughts, and considering the audience to be addressed. In the writing phase, they usually carry out their detailed plan in a first draft. And in the revising phase, they study what they have written and determine how they can improve their first draft. These designations are not a lock-step series of discrete stages that writers work through in exactly the same manner each time. They are simply patterns of activities that describe what happens when writers write. As any writer knows, at least intuitively, writing is not a linear but a recursive process. Writing rarely proceeds neatly from one phase to the next. Rather, the phases frequently overlap, making the process often appear messy. Many writers, for example, revise what they have written as soon as the word or the sentence appears on the page. Each writer participates in the writing process in a different way, at a different pace, and with a different result. Tracing the exact movements of a writer's mind at work on an idea is as difficult as charting the precise flight path of a bird of prey as it swoops and circles, soars and glides, hovers over and then clutches its quarry. It is possible to discover and describe patterns in each, but the specific circumstances and the particular moves are never exactly the same every time.

Yet reading what other students have to say about writing should assure you that all writers—whether they are professionals, prize-winning student essayists, or classmates—grapple with many of the same basic problems. You may be surprised—and pleased—to learn that in many instances the solutions and observations of the prize-winning student writers are similar to those you may have developed in your own writing. If not, these prize-winning student writers may offer new solutions and suggestions that can help you improve your writing. Recognizing both the unique and the shared elements of the writing experience will enable you to place yourself in the company of other writers and to distinguish your own voice from others'. What follows is not a comprehensive survey of every facet of the writing process but a detailed report on what happens when successful student writers are productively at work.

GETTING STARTED

In the first of the three phases of the writing process a writer usually chooses a subject to write about if one has not been assigned, discovers a purpose for writing about the subject, generates a thesis or a controlling idea about the subject, considers the audience to be addressed, and then develops that idea in an outline or some other form that will be the basis of a first draft of an essay. This is the most difficult phase of writing for most people. And because they usually face so many problems and obstacles here, most writers seem to have more to say about it than any other phase.

Perhaps the single most common obstacle the prize-winning student writers face when they write is their tendency to procrastinate — a trait they share with most other writers, students and professionals alike. Celeste Barrus identifies the problem most succinctly: "There is no one easy thing about writing, except putting it off." Some writers apparently can produce only under great pressure, usually the looming presence of a deadline. John Thatcher, for example, describes his taking "perverse delight in watching the time slip by until it is almost too late to begin writing." For him, getting started is "like a game of literary Russian roulette."

And the stratagems these student writers use to put off writing are often almost as ingenious as the methods they finally discover to write successful essays. Todd Senturia describes his preparation for writing in what may well sound like familiar terms to many students:

> I find that I have a remarkable memory for the unimportant whenever I have to spend any protracted amount of time seated and writing. The papers which I haven't organized in the last five minutes, the bed which has remained unmade for the past week, the letter to Grandma and Grandpa which I forgot to write all become urgent in direct proportion to the time I have been sitting in one place. . . . If I'm writing with a pen, then it runs out of ink, and if with a pencil, then the point is never quite sharp enough. If the refrigerator contains anything edible, then another few minutes can be spent deciding what to eat. When all else fails, I get up and walk around. I walk around a lot during the course of a long paper.

As Senturia notes, the kitchen is the favorite place for student writers to procrastinate. And eating appears to be the most common source of pleasurable distraction for writers intent on postponing the work they need to do. Few descriptions of putting off writing match Allison Rolls's — at least in terms of putting on weight:

> I have come up with many methods to avoid writing, but the primary one is eating. It works like this: I gather up everything I need to start — pens, pencils, paper, references, etc. — and then I arrange them very neatly for maximum efficiency. After brooding about it for some time, I finally decide that writing is very tiring, so I should gather some strength. I go to the kitchen and fix myself a snack and a cup of tea. When I am through eating, I make more tea and go out for an ice cream cone and to ponder my

> subject. When I return, my tea is cold, so I wait for the
> water to boil and eat and think some more. . . . And by
> the time I actually sit down to write, I am exhausted.

Most writers are as finicky about the circumstances of where and when they write as they are about whether they will start writing at all. Laura Morgan summarizes one extreme when she reports that she needs "complete solitude" to write. For Doris Egnor, a working mother of three and a full-time student, writing best takes place at five o'clock in the morning at the dining room table with a cup of coffee in her hand: "My children are still asleep, and I am fairly confident that the phone won't ring and that no one will come to the door this early in the morning!"

At the other extreme, many students need some form of sound in the background to offset the silence and solitude of writing. Chris Gardinier prefers to work in "the living room, in front of the television. . . . I welcome the distraction of the television. I watch television and think, often writing during the commercials." James Seilsopour's sound is the radio. For Cynthia Jane Thompson it is the stereo. Thompson describes herself in her "ideal" environment for writing: "As I lie stretched across my bed, my mind thumps thesis sentences with each beat of my blaring stereo. Wadded balls of paper lie scattered over the floor beneath me, along with Reese's Cup wrappers and a few stray kernels of popcorn—the residue of my trying to keep pace with the beat of my stereo and my mind."

Discarded food and packaging, half-filled coffee cups, jugs of Kool-Aid, crumpled papers, mangled pencils, disgruntled expressions, furrowed brows, and lingering curtains of cigarette smoke are fairly common features of a productive environment for writing. Sanford Boxerman offers a particularly appealing précis of such circumstances: "If the President of the United States were to walk into my room as I was trying to begin writing, the room might qualify for federal disaster funds. Papers are strewn everywhere; books are scattered here and there. In the middle of this mess, I sit, staring blankly at the empty piece of paper before me. 'I'll never get this paper written!' I cry."

Yet student writers do get started on their papers, however perilously close to the deadline they may be and even if it means, as some report, using "favorite" pens or pencils or wearing "lucky" clothes while writing. Annie Glaven, for example, always wears her "work sweater (a battered Brooks Brothers cardigan)" when she is writing. Whatever the quirk, the superstition, or the curious concern, many writers feel that certain circumstances must be present before they can even begin to write. The number of different tactics the student writers use to find their ideas and to get started on exploring them is virtually endless — from deliberate reading and research to peer group discussions and random, casual mental association.

Dianne Emminger notes that writing invariably involves a great deal of patience. Celeste Barrus agrees in the following dramatic, if not anxious, terms: "Writing is waiting — unsettled waiting — for ideas to come." Mel Tennant reminds us that such silent waiting can be strenuous. Like most of the writers in this collection, Tennant spends a great deal of time "staring at a blank piece of paper," but his strategy to expedite the composing process is to tap the paper with a pen repeatedly, "as though to awaken the words lying dormant within." If that should fail, he reports, "I furrow my brows, as if trying to squeeze a drop of inspiration from my forehead that would run down my nose and drop onto the page."

For many writers, ideas come when they least expect them—while taking a shower, driving a car, or reading a newspaper, for example. Dianne Emminger recounts the unexpected origins of her essay "The Exhibition":

> I had a great deal of difficulty choosing my topic for this essay. I had been out of town that week and was, in fact, sitting in a plane in Atlanta, full of frustration at my failure to begin writing, when I made the decision to write about the most insignificant thing I could see there in the plane. It was raining that day, and the most insignificant thing I saw were the raindrops on the window — one looks right through the raindrops. Several days later, while reviewing the notes I had taken on the plane, I began thinking of the prismatic effect raindrops have on light and was reminded of what I had seen while visiting a gallery years earlier.

Many writers find that they can discover ideas about a subject by writing down everything they know about it. Charlotte Russell aptly summarizes this technique as a "violent rush of flurried words and incomplete sentences. The floor is littered with unworkable thoughts. This tempestuous stage in my writing, like a summer shower, is brief. I then organize all of this confusion into a first rough draft so I can more clearly see the words in black and white. Developing my idea is a lot easier when I have all of that material in front of me. And corrections of comma faults, wrong tenses, paragraphs that are too short, and information that belongs someplace else are also easier to fix when I can see them in front of me." Barbara Howell also tries to do her thinking as she writes. To develop ideas, she writes without interruption and without pausing to consider such elements of composition as spelling, grammar, sentence structure, and word choice. She calls this her "most successful method of writing. . . . My mind violently spits out incomplete phrases and sentences. In this way, my first draft may not be coherent, but it does record my thoughts and feelings in black and white." Such an exercise is an excellent confidence builder, especially for a relatively inexperienced writer. Such a writer can produce a greal deal of writing in a very short period of time and can better resist the urge to edit the work prematurely. Such an exercise also enables a writer to see rather quickly just what he or she has to say about a subject.

Other writers prefer to work with a journal, making frequent entries, sometimes several a day, that record their thinking about a variety of subjects. Susan Zurakowski explains the special benefit of writing in a journal: "It keeps me limber, and since I write in it every day, I don't panic when I get a paper assignment in a class." Daniel Dietrich takes this notion one step further: "A journal is an essential tool if you are looking to develop your ideas and improve your writing at the same time. A journal isn't just a diary that contains a general recap of what happened to you that day—no way. Instead, your journal holds ideas and problems that may be pounding on the inside of your head, waiting for you to take them out and examine them, and what better place to do this than in a journal?" Whether you write in a leather-bound journal or on the inside of a matchbook, doing your thinking in writing is perhaps the best way to discover what you want to say. A practiced writer is usually an effective writer.

Once they have settled on a subject, most student writers decide on a purpose for writing about that subject. A purpose in writing consists of the decisions writers make about what to say about a subject and how they plan to say it. The first of these concerns establishes the general contents and the overall goal of the essay. The second focuses on the structure and tone of the essay. Whether an essay is designed to narrate, describe, explain, convince, or persuade, a clearly stated purpose marks most of the essays printed in this book. In most cases, the students' motives for writing include—but are rarely restricted to—the understandable desire to earn an outstanding grade. For some student writers, the pure pleasure of working with words is an added attraction of writing. For others, writing offers the prospect of helping change our nation's attitudes and behavior: to defeat prejudice of all sorts, to underscore the dignity of the oppressed, to change long-standing opinion on public issues, or, as Linnea Saukko hopes, to save our environment. Saukko reports that she wrote her ironic essay "How to Poison the Earth" to draw attention to the increasing threats to our environment, "to shock or inform enough people to make an impact." A better-informed public, she feels, "will make this earth a better place to live." The purpose of Sanford Boxerman's essay is far more narrow, although just as ambitious: to challenge one of our country's leading economists, Milton Friedman, on the issue of the social responsibility of American corporations.

A clear purpose need not be as public or as issue-oriented as that of Linnea Saukko or Sanford Boxerman. For many writers, the principal purpose for writing is as simple as wanting to narrate or describe an experience, to record a personal anecdote, to remember a family story, to recover the pleasure of reading a book, hearing a concert, or seeing a film or play. Just as there is no single, sure-fire way to succeed at writing, there is no single, limited definition of an appropriate subject or purpose in writing.

Having an audience for their writing looms large in the mind of every writer. David Landman speaks for many when he says, "I could not write if I could not imagine that someone were going to read my work." The writer's view of the reader is an important aspect of getting started, and it invariably helps determine the extent of an essay's success. Thinking about the reader before writing helps the writer make decisions about appropriate subjects, the kinds of examples, the type and level of language, as well as the overall organization of the essay. The writer usually asks: "Who is my reader? And what do I have to do to lead that person to understand what I want to say about the subject?" The first question addresses the knowledge, background, and predispositions of the reader toward the subject. The second points to the kinds of information or appeals that the reader is most likely to respond to.

Since all student writers prepare papers to satisfy course requirements, they are mindful of their instructor's presence in their audience. Allison Rolls deals with what many students regard as their instructor's intimidating presence by imagining herself writing for a teacher with whom she feels comfortable. Sanford Boxerman explains that whether he is writing for a teacher, his peers, or an audience beyond the classroom, "the fact that someone is going to read my writing imposes a good deal of discipline on me. In my mind, an essay I write with my name on the cover is an extension of myself." And every writer finally wants, as Virginia Bean notes, to make sure that his or her thoughts "will be clear and coherent to another human being. It's frustrating to be misunderstood."

To minimize the possibility that they will be misunderstood and to maximize the likelihood that they will appreciate the implications of their own ideas, many writers find it particularly useful to outline their ideas before they begin to write a first draft. Sanford Boxerman, for example, reports that he makes "heavy use of outlining":

> I prefer to get a fairly good idea of what I intend to say
> before I actually say it. Outlining for me facilitates orga-
> nization, cuts down on redundancy, and makes, I trust, the
> particular argument more persuasive. I doubt whether
> I could write a decent essay without an outline of some
> sort. . . . I find writing without an outline to be the equiv-
> alent of driving without a road map.

Karen Buchanan, while describing a slightly different procedure, develops a
similar line of reasoning with an equally apt metaphor: "I always develop a
strong thesis, then outline. Outlining is as essential to my finished essay as a
good pencil drawing is under an oil painting. I have so much confidence in
the potential of the finished product that I can relax and enjoy the creative
detailing."

In contrast, Paige Turner finds outlining inhibiting: "Outlines only make
me lazy. I become a slave to five paragraphs, and I find myself calculating how
few thoughts I can get away with."

Susan Zurakowski offers a fairly balanced view of the benefits and liabilities
of outlining. On the one hand, she argues that "some kind of outline is absolutely necessary" in the early phases of writing an essay. "Whether it is formal
or informal, an outline helps overcome problems organizing. On the other
hand, an outline, if emphasized too much, can draw attention away from the
actual writing." John Ross Thompson offers a sensible solution. After outlining
the basic points of what he wants to say, he concentrates on developing each
of the parts separately from the others. "The reason this works," he says, "is
that I am actually writing, and as I write I get ideas. I don't get too many
ideas chewing on my pencil."

WRITING

It would not be practical to enumerate all the different ways writers work
during the second phase of the writing process—completing a full draft of an
essay. Instead, both the brief introduction to each essay printed in Part II and
the Questions for Reading and Revising and Suggestions for Writing that
appear after each essay include detailed information about the specific circumstances in which each essay was written. Here we present just a few general
statements from the student writers on their characteristic styles of composing.

Some writers write to discover what they want to say. In one sense, such
writers must see their ideas on paper in order to explore, develop, and revise
them. They must write in order to discover and shape their own meaning.

Hope Cohen's description of her writing process exemplifies the main features of this style of composing. She reports that "I generally think up topics for writing when I'm doing something else—walking to breakfast, taking a shower, etc. Once I have the idea, I just sit down and write it. I usually don't know the end (or even the second paragraph) as I begin. Each idea comes to me as I write, and I really write the paper as I go along." Such writers usually need to examine their ideas as they are unfolding to clarify, develop, or revise them. John Thatcher creates a provocative metaphor to characterize his method of writing: "I write fast and furiously while chewing all the flavor out of a pencil. . . . I write like I run, until I'm finished and can't go on anymore." Such writing works incrementally: the writer produces a very rough, quick first draft to explore and develop the controlling idea of the essay and then focuses in subsequent drafts on organizing and polishing that idea.

Other writers proceed at a slower pace. They think carefully about what they are going to say before they commit themselves to writing it out. These writers generally are more comfortable composing in their heads than on paper. They usually regard thinking and writing as separate, and in fact sequential, intellectual activities. Joanne Menter describes her style of composing in just such terms: "When there is something I really want to say, I usually have it organized in my mind. This works out many problems ahead of time. Writing is a matter of taking the revised copy out of my head and putting it down on paper." Celeste Barrus expresses a similar point: "It takes me a very long time to write anything, mainly because I mull each sentence over and over in my mind, taking it apart and putting it together again in different ways, changing words, and so on before I even put it on paper." David Landman recounts a similar method: "I generally have everything organized in my mind before I even put fingers to my typewriter. I seldom need to write more than two drafts of anything, and many times my first draft is in most respects my final draft. I don't know why this works. It does, though. In fact, it works so well that sometimes it is a little scary." And as is the case with most accomplished writers, Landman knows not to tamper with what works best for him.

Most of these writers continue to be aware of their audience as they write, and that awareness helps shape the ways in which they write. Bruce Adams puts it this way:

> We always write for an audience of some sort. Knowing
> this drives me to describe events in terms which a reader
> with no knowledge of my subject can understand and en-
> joy. As I write, I try to detach myself . . . and observe
> what I've done from a neutral perspective. I try to ask
> questions that a reader would ask: "What is he trying to

say?" "Do I really understand what he is trying to get across?"
"Do I find this enjoyable and interesting?"

For many writers, such questions help expedite the process of writing an essay.
For an equally large number, such questions prompt them to revise.

REVISING

Many writers appreciate the power and permanence that revision can add
to the act of writing. When writers revise, they reexamine what they have
written with an eye on strengthening their control over their ideas. As they
revise, they expand or delete, substitute or reorder what they have written. In
some cases, they revise to clarify or emphasize. In other instances, they revise
to tone down or reinforce particular points. And, more generally, they revise
either to simplify what they have written or to make it more complex. Revising
gives writers an opportunity to rethink their essays, to make them accomplish
more clearly and fully their intentions. Revising includes larger concerns such
as determining whether the essay is logically consistent, whether the main idea
is supported adequately, whether the organization is clear enough, and whether
the essay addresses its intended audience in engaging and accessible terms,
whether it satisfies their specific needs or demands. Revising includes looking
at the whole essay as well as at each part, at paragraph as well as sentence
structure, at concepts as well as specific word choice. Revising enables writers
to make sure that their essays are as clear, precise, and effective as possible.

Although revising is often the most painstaking phase of the composing
process (James Seilsopour, for example, equates revising with "cutting yourself
with a hot blade"), it is crucial to successful writing. Some writers revise as
they write. Chris Gardinier explains her method of revising:

> I write a whole page or more and then go back and pencil
> around weak areas, maybe adding words or thoughts. . . .
> I rewrite and rewrite and rewrite, sometimes revising a sin-
> gle sentence twenty or more times if it is an idea that I
> really want to use that doesn't quite work. Usually, by the
> time I consider a paper to be finished, I am fairly content
> with it — and also tired of it. Yet if I go back after a month
> or so, I can still find more weaknesses and make more
> changes.

Paige Turner also rereads each sentence and paragraph several times before
she starts a new one. And if her text begins to get "messy," she copies it over,
making additional revisions as she writes. Jackie Scannell follows a somewhat

similar procedure: "I read and reread my writing as it progresses. Doing so helps assure a continuity of thought and a smooth flow of sentences."

Some writers revise after they have written a very quick and usually very rough first draft. Once they have something on paper, they revise for as long as they have time and energy. Teresa Moss underscores this point: "I just write out a rough draft to glue my thoughts down. After I've got it down, I keep rewriting it until it sounds like English." But Doris Egnor's method offers some practical advice as well as a caution: "After I write my first draft, I put it away for a day or so before revising. I do the same after each revision. It seems as though I can look at it in a new light if I don't try to do it all at once."

Many of the student writers mention the value of reading their work aloud as an aid to revision. Chris Gardinier says:

> Writing is still communication — it is speech on paper. I find it helpful to hear what I write when I read it back to myself. The weak parts jar, just as they would in speech. College students have read enough to know how something should sound. The problem is knowing how your own writing sounds. Read it and listen.

Todd Senturia calls this method "writing by instinct": "If I can't read the phrase aloud fluently, then I change it until it sounds 'right.' . . . It is much easier to catch grammatical mistakes and verbal malapropisms with the help of the much-practiced tool of the ear than to try to pick them off the flat page." Other students remind themselves of their audience by asking family or friends to read their essays aloud to them. Charlotte Russell strives for the same effect in revising by "talking to myself a lot when I'm writing. . . . Besides the author, I am the audience, the teacher, and also the critic. I think about what each of these characters might say — any comments, suggestions, or criticisms they might have. Playing these roles helps me revise and edit."

When writers and publishers *edit* a piece of writing, they read it with an eye to preparing it for publication, whether that occurs literally in a newspaper, magazine, or a book or figuratively in the exchange of essays within the community of a classroom, department, college, or university. When writers *proofread*, they reread their final drafts to detect any errors — misspellings, omitted lines, inaccurate information, and the like. Susan Zurakowski offers what she calls a "fail-safe" method for proofreading her essays for spelling mistakes: "I read the work backwards. . . . This shifts the emphasis from structure and form to spelling. I can then see the words clearly and out of context." For Zurakowski, and for many other student writers represented here, revising means, as she notes, "isolating a problem and working with it through a series of drafts." In general, experienced writers concentrate on the larger concerns of writing—their ideas, argument, purpose, and structure—before they are concerned with searching for the "right word."

When asked to offer some final, general advice to first-year college students to help them improve their writing, the thirty-one Bedford Prize winners gave responses as varied as their descriptions of the distinctive ways in which they compose. Among their common responses were such good-natured imperatives as trust your own experience, write about what you know or about what you are interested in learning, "listen to your teachers," read as widely, voraciously, and rigorously as possible, and "write and write and write." Daniel Dietrich speaks for many of his peers when he says that "Every person's thinking is unique. When a person finishes a paper, it contains that person's style and beliefs. It's not simply reiterated facts, but instead a unique, personal piece of work that reflects who the person is and what he or she thinks." For Paige Turner, "the pleasure of writing an essay is that you not only satisfy a course requirement, you also satisfy something in yourself. Writing is just having something to say and caring enough to try and say it."

Most important, these are all students who write because they have something to say. For Rita Hollingsworth, "Writing is fun, and while it is the hardest thing that I do, it is the experience that has given me the most pleasure. I have found writing to be my personal 'sorting tool.' It is a method that I use to organize, finalize, and give permanence to my ideas, feelings, and experiences. Writing is the best way that I have found to share my story with others."

Questions for Thinking and Writing

This exercise gives you an opportunity to examine your own attitudes toward writing in general and, more specifically, toward each stage of the composing process outlined in this chapter. Respond in writing to each of the following questions in as much detail as possible.

1. What are your earliest recollections of writing?
2. Have any members of your family, teachers, or anyone else encouraged you to write? Explain the circumstances.
3. What is the easiest thing for you to do when you write an essay?
4. What is the most difficult aspect of writing for you?
5. What method of getting started is most successful for you? Why do you think that method works for you?
6. If someone walked into your room and observed you trying to get started writing, what would this person see? Write your answer in a paragraph or two.
7. Do you try to avoid writing? If so, what do you do to avoid it?

8. What special habits do you have when you write?

9. What is the ideal environment for you as a writer?

10. How does the fact that your writing has an audience influence the way you write? How do you take an audience into account when you are writing an essay?

11. Describe in detail the specific procedures you follow when writing the first draft of an essay.

12. What does revising mean to you? Describe your methods of revision. How many drafts do you usually write? How do you decide when a paper is finished and there is nothing more that you can do with it?

13. What general advice would you offer other first-year students to help them improve their writing?

14. Add any comments on or clarifications of any aspect of your writing that was not addressed adequately in these questions.

THE ESSAYS

Part II

BRUCE W. ADAMS

University of Colorado at Denver
Denver, Colorado
Anna V. Casey, instructor

Medicine is the center of Bruce Adams's attention both on the job and in the classroom. Born in Baltimore, Maryland, in 1959, Adams worked for three years after high school graduation as an emergency medical technician. In 1980 he was hired by Denver General Hospital as its youngest paramedic. In addition to his full-time work, Adams is majoring in psychology and preparing for medical school.

Bruce Adams's job requires that he write patient charts for every person he treats during his daily tour of duty, and he reports that he has become quite proficient at writing quick and concise "stories" about each of them. When he is working on papers for his college courses, he prefers to seclude himself. "I usually sit at my desk with soft music in the background and just start writing. I try not to make a big deal about writing. I am very lucky. Writing does not take a lot of energy for me."

Asked to write a narrative about an event in his life, Adams drew on his experience working for Denver General Hospital. He notes: "I wanted to show a situation that health care professionals are put into every day. Emergency medicine is not like the portrait that is often painted on television. Everyone does not make it out of the hospital. Death is a reality that we deal with every day."

For an extended discussion of Bruce Adams's essay, see pages 257–270.

Emergency Room

By looking out the window of the ambulance, I can see we are getting close 1 to the hospital. As we speed by the familiar buildings, the flashing emergency lights turn them into hundreds of freeze-frame photographs. The strobe lights turn everything that their light falls on a monotone hue of either red or blue. The siren's only rival is the screaming of my patient, which pierces the air like an explosion in the night. I struggle for balance while crouched on the floor as the vehicle makes a sharp turn into the parking lot. Finally, the ambulance jerks to a stop. I know that we have arrived at our destination, the emergency department.

The pain in my hands grows worse as the time goes by. The amount of 2 pressure I have had to put on the subclavian artery to stop the bleeding is causing my hands to cramp. Suddenly, my mind is diverted from the pain as the rear doors fly open and the cool night air rushes in, chilling the sweat on my face. The doctor looks at me. I shake my head. This patient is probably going to die no matter what we do. Most of his life-sustaining blood lies in the parking lot of an east-side bar where he was shot. With the swiftness of a cobra strike, his assailant struck the fatal blow with a sawed-off shotgun. Where once were an arm and chest wall there are now grotesque fragments of human form.

As I stand up, I feel the warm sensation of liquid running down my pant 3 leg into my shoe. For the first time I realize that I am covered with warm, sticky blood. We wheel the patient from the ambulance onto the ambulance loading dock. The heat lamps overhead radiate a soothing warmth against the cool, humid night air. The calloused police officers look on casually at the action passing before them. They have seen all this too many times to be shocked or even curious.

My adrenaline is peaking as we hit the malfunctioning electric doors with 4 a crash. As the three of us enter the emergency department, we turn sharply into room two: the crisis room. The humming white lights are almost blinding after the darkness of the night. The room is lined with people in statue-like poses in anticipation of our arrival. As we position the patient onto the hard table, I notice that the once screaming man is now silent and motionless.

A crash shatters the silence as an over-eager intern knocks over a mayo 5 stand, scattering the once-sterile surgical instruments onto the floor. The charge nurse just rolls her eyes as she bends over to begin picking up the instruments. The body is quickly enveloped by a group of surgeons. A sterile and gloved surgeon signals to me and simultaneously I withdraw my paralyzed hand as he reapplies pressure to the damaged artery. The once-quiet room is now a flurry of activity with blood pressure cuffs squeezing, electrocardiogram indicators beeping, and oxygen outlets hissing. The attending emergency room physician stands with his arms folded watching the orchestration of activity. He gives his nod of approval to the chief surgeon as he walks toward the head of the table.

The chief resident of thoracic surgery is now standing directly beside the 6 table. He carefully surveys the damage done by the shotgun. He quickly turns toward the mayo stand and grabs a bottle of betadine solution and pours it over the entire chest. The betadine turns the flesh orange as the excess spills onto the floor, staining the surgeon's tennis shoes. The charge nurse adjusts the overhead light which illuminates the surgical field. The surgeon squints as he looks at the skin in the reflection of the overhead light. He turns to the mayo stand and carefully picks up the shining stainless steel scalpel. With his left hand he palpates the chest wall. Precisely but quickly, he cuts the skin between the protruding ribs. As the blade slices through the skin, the skin separates without help. The normally yellow fat globules, turned orange by the betadine, balloon from the incision. With his second pass of the blade, a popping sound is made as he enters the pleura of the inner chest wall. Blood spurts out with a forceful gush, covering the surgeon's gown and gloves as he separates the two sections of the rib cage. The charge nurse hands him the rib spreaders with a slap.

He deftly inserts the apparatus into the separation between the two ribs. 7 He manipulates the spreaders with machine-like precision. The cartilage of the ribs pops like the knuckles of a boastful schoolboy as they are spread to form an unnatural opening into the man's chest. The surgeon reaches his gloved hand into the cavernous opening and works his way past the ribs, clotted blood, and lung tissue to the heart. He carefully palpates the organ. It is flaccid and void of life's blood. He shakes his head as he examines the heart further. He grimaces as he feels the large puncture wound in the posterior aspect of the left ventricle. He instinctively reaches for the cardiac patches and sutures but stops short as he realizes the damage is too extensive for repair. He looks at the emergency room attending physician as if to ask a question. The attending just shrugs his shoulders and sighs. There is a moment of stillness as the surgeon removes his hand from the man's chest and pronounces the time of death.

The feeling is just coming back to my hands as I attempt to write my trip 8 report. My clothes are wet with blood and smell like a slaughter house. My legs are beginning to itch from the combination of dried sweat and blood. My mind drifts as I think of how much we can do for some patients and how little we can do for others. I ask the unanswerable question of why some people die as others live. All we can do as paramedics is give each patient our all.

I look toward the emergency room doors to see my partner coming toward 9 me. He calls my name and motions toward the ambulance. He says we have another call waiting for us. "The natives must be restless tonight," he says. "We have another shooting."

QUESTIONS FOR READING AND REVISING

1. What is the dominant impression of the emergency room that we get from reading Bruce Adams's essay?
2. As gripping and powerful as this incident is, it is business as usual for the people in the emergency room. What is the effect of such an incident on the people in the emergency room? What is the effect on Adams?
3. How does Adams's picture of a hospital emergency room compare with your own experience of one or with the way it is portrayed on television?

4. As readers, we have a sense of being in the emergency room and being involved as we hear, see, and smell exactly what Adams is writing about. Select specific sensory details that you find powerful and explain their effect.

5. Why do you think Adams chose to write his essay in the present tense? What effect does that choice have on your involvement with his experience? What would have been the effect if he had told his story in past tense?

6. Adams uses a lot of operating room terminology. Does this terminology hinder your understanding and interrupt the flow of the piece or does it contribute to the effectiveness of the essay? Cite specific instances to support your answer.

SUGGESTIONS FOR WRITING

1. Although not all jobs present emergencies as frequently as does Adams's work, most of us have faced crises connected to our work experiences. Write an essay describing such a situation and explain your own responses to the event.

2. Adams reports that one of his motives for writing this essay was to show his readers the reality of an emergency room. Write an essay about some aspect of your job or life that most people imagine another way. Describe this aspect to show your readers what it is really like.

3. All the medical personnel in Adams's essay reveal a combination of warmth and distance toward their patient. Consider your own intended career: will you, too, need seemingly paradoxical qualities in order to do the job well? Write an essay, using concrete examples, explaining why one needs those qualities and how one can strive for the proper balance of them. Your end result, perhaps, is to explore not only the external but also the internal aspects of your intended job.

CELESTE L. BARRUS

Boise State University
Boise, Idaho
Karen S. Thomas, instructor

Born in Nampa, Idaho, in 1939, Celeste Barrus, the mother of seven children, decided to enroll in college in 1982 along with her oldest son. In fact, Barrus and her son, Marc, were in the same composition class. Besides school and family, Barrus's major interests are violin, piano, singing, and writing. She taught herself to play an old violin her aunt resurrected from the hay loft of a barn: "Even though nicotine fly spray had been spilt on it, giving it a strong, unforgettably pungent odor, I learned to play it," she recalls.

Celeste Barrus describes writing as "waiting, unsettled waiting. Waiting for ideas to come; staring into space a lot." She has written stories and essays for her church's monthly paper under the name Heppsaba Hepplewhite. "In case my writing was bad I didn't want the church congregation to know who wrote the articles. If they were good the people didn't need to know anyway."

Asked to write a personal essay, Barrus immediately thought of writing about her son Todd. She reports: "Our teacher read some sample essays to the class. All were humorous. I changed my mind, thinking that my original subject wasn't what the teacher wanted. I tried to write something funny about the dating habits of my teenage daughter. It just didn't work. I needed to write about Todd."

Todd

Trauma comes to every life. It can leave us helpless. But finally we realize 1
that the world still turns and life goes on. We keep living and doing, although
many times automatically and without feeling. Then, when the crisis is over,
we find we have more understanding, a greater depth of feeling, and a sparkle
of love that enriches life.

It began in August, the month Bill and I started preparations for our move 2
to Biloxi, Mississippi. Bill was assigned, by the Idaho Air National Guard, to
an eleven-month radio-electronics school at Keesler Air Force Base.

All three of our children were small. Marc was barely three; Todd would 3
turn two in a month; and Kelly had just had her first birthday a few days
before. I loved all three dearly, but even in normal circumstances it was sometimes trying, dealing with three "almost" babies. Their demands were greater
than my energy.

The problem was Todd. I was at my wit's end trying to cope with him. He 4
cried all the time and when he wasn't crying he would toddle into his bedroom,

crawl onto the lower bunk and lie there, listless and apathetic. Then he would get up, cry again while he clung to my leg, demanding that I pick him up. Every week I took him to the doctor and after each visit I came home with a "new" medicine to try for the ear infection that just wouldn't clear up.

I remembered what a good baby he had always been. With an imp-like 5 smile he would gather my cheeks between both tiny hands, grinning widely as he forced a pucker from my lips. As he grew, he looked like a broad-shouldered football player, but in miniature.

I felt despair at the total change in him. Wild thoughts clouded my mind: 6 "Is his personality changing? Why is he so different all of a sudden? Why does he cry constantly? What more can I do for him? How can I be a good mother when I am so tired?"

Night after night I put Todd beside me on the couch, trying not to disturb 7 Bill as he slept in the bedroom. Night after night I sang and talked softly to him, all the while gently brushing his back with the palm of my hand as I tried to quiet the cries and groans that emitted from his thinning frame.

Somehow, though the nightmare continued, the month of August passed. 8 The trailer Bill was building was finally finished. With our furniture loaded and with tearful good-bys from parents, we left, heading for the Mississippi Gulf Coast.

One event stands in my memory of our seven-day car ride. One evening 9 after a day of fussy babies and long miles, we stopped at a motel in Arkansas. We ate our supper, then bathed, diapered and pajamaed the little ones. That night I had such a hard time getting Todd to settle down. He seemed to hurt all over. Even as I held him in my arms he cried out if I moved wrong. His cries turned to screams as he flailed by my side on the bed. As tears of worry and frustration clouded my eyes, a knock sounded at the door. I opened the door to see a balding, paunchy man leaning sleepily against the door frame.

"Hey folks," he drawled, "I'm sorry, but if you can't keep that kid quiet, 10 you're gonna hafta find another place. I got other customers that wanna get some sleep." Murmuring assurances, I closed the door, then folded into a sobbing heap on the bed.

That night we did something purposely that we never had done before or 11 have done since to any of our children. In our anguish, we literally drugged Todd with aspirin, orange flavored, that we dissolved and poured down his throat. I held him for the rest of the night, watching as his body began to limply relax, petting him, listening closely with my ear to his mouth, feeling the pulse in his neck, afraid to sleep for fear he wouldn't wake. That was the first night in over a month that he was quiet.

In the days that followed, everything improved. We moved into a rental 12
house in Biloxi; Bill enjoyed his radio-electronics classes; and little Todd was
smiling, though still not active.

One muggy morning about a month later, as I sat on the front step watching 13
Marc and Kelly play in the sand, I noticed Todd walk slowly from the house,
taking small, plodding steps on the line where the sand of the front yard joined
the pebbly surface of the pavement. Suddenly he tripped, striking the crown
of his head on the hard asphalt. I rushed to him and scooped him up. Holding
him close, I brushed the sand from his face. A knot was beginning to rise on
his forehead. Whimpering, he was limp in my arms as though the plug to his
energy had been pulled, leaving him drained.

I carried him into the backyard where Bill was mowing the lawn. Turning 14
off the motor, he took Todd from me and carried him into the house, questioning me on the way. We began to notice that Todd's head was turning
black and blue, not just around the lump, but continuing down to his neck.

Almost sure he had a skull fracture, we dropped everything and took him 15
to the hospital on base. The only doctor available at the time was a Dr. White.
He was of medium height, in his early thirties, and of an arrogant disposition.
A feeling of distrust came to me, of immediate dislike.

We waited in his 10 × 10 foot cubicle. Without saying one word to us, 16
he strode into the room, took a pocket flashlight and a tongue depressor from
his pocket, and proceeded to examine Todd from the neck up.

"Okay, parents," he challenged indifferently, leaning against the wall with 17
his arms folded and legs crossed. "What's the problem?"

I began. "Well, doctor, about an hour ago Todd tripped on the asphalt in 18
front of our house and fell. He hit his head pretty hard; then he started turning
black and blue. We thought maybe he had a skull fracture."

"I'm sure anyone would turn black and blue if they fell on the asphalt," he 19
returned, looking quite bored.

"But look at him! He's really black and blue," I said, shocked at his indif- 20
ference.

"It must have been a pretty hard fall. Just let him rest and he'll be fine." 21

Enraged at his arrogance and complete lack of compassion, I was at a loss 22
for words. I could feel Bill stiffen with indignation as he stood up from his
chair, facing this "doctor" who militarily out-ranked him.

"Sir, you need to know also that Todd has had a fever lately and seems 23
very tired and listless all the time."

"I noticed, sergeant," clipped the doctor, "that this child has a slight ear 24
infection, his tonsils also being somewhat enlarged, all of which would account
for the fever. This penicillin ought to do the trick."

As he ripped the prescription from the pad, he began again. "We doctors 25
like to follow up on the same patients. The second paper there is for one week
from today. Come any time of the day; first come, first served basis." Then
without a smile he lifted Todd from the table and stood him on the floor.
With that, he started toward the door.

Tears of rage and disgust and smoldering dislike began coursing down my 26
cheeks. Standing quickly, I blocked his path to the door. With my arms locked
stiffly to my sides and my hands clenched tightly into balled fists, I began
spitting the words out slowly, my enunciation perfect.

"Doctor White," I began in a soft hiss, "something is wrong with this child. 27
I watch him day after day and I know from the changes I've seen that something
is wrong. Look at him! Look at his arm!" My voice was rising. "Look at my
hand print on his arm!"

I had taken my hand from around Todd's tiny arm and there was an almost 28
perfect five-fingered print, turning black and blue. Looking up at the doctor
with icy eyes, I continued.

"This child is sick! I want a blood test done and if you won't do it, I'll find 29
someone in this hospital who will!"

"Okay, mother. Okay. Don't get upset," he acquiesced as he jerked a paper 30
from another pad. "Here, just to satisfy you," he said in a condescending tone.
"Take this to the lab. They'll do the rest. Come back in a week." And with
that he strode, steely eyed, from the room.

After the exhaustion of the blood test, Todd slept heavily in my arms as we 31
drove home. Walking into the house, Bill took the appointment slip and stuck
it between the switch plate of the living room light and the wall—an instant
bulletin board. Then after eating an early lunch he left for his six hours of school.

While washing dishes about one and a half hours later, I was startled to see 32
Bill walk in the front door. He took the appointment slip from behind the
switch plate, ripped it in two, and said, "We won't need this anymore."
Noticing an indignant protest rising in my throat, he quickly added, "The
hospital just called me out of school. We are to get Todd there right away."

A knot immediately tied in my stomach. I felt my eyes enlarge with fear 33
and could feel the whine in my ears as the blood rushed to my head. Even so,
I knew my face was chalky white. Without saying anything more, Bill handed
me my purse, picked Todd gently from the couch, and walked to the car,
knowing that even in my stupor I would follow.

Riding in the car with Todd in my arms I felt a consuming love for him, 34
along with overwhelming fear; and I knew. The ugly word of the disease came
to my mind without my consciously ever before thinking about it. I could

never remember reading or hearing the word before — but I knew. It was like someone beyond myself whispering the word in my mind.

Todd was a very independent little spirit even in those months of lethargy. 35 Getting out of the car, Bill reached for him to carry him up the hill to the hospital.

"No Daddy," he said, pushing Bill's hand aside, "I walk."   36

So we walked. Todd began with two steps. Then rest. Another step. Rest. 37 But still he would not be carried.

Looking toward the hospital I saw a man standing outside the door in the 38 same type of tan air force dress pants and white calf-length smock that Dr. White had worn, but this man had a heavier build. He stood there and watched us for the full ten minutes it took to walk the one block from the car to the hospital emergency entrance.

Taking a step forward he said knowingly, "Sergeant Barrus, Mrs. Barrus, 39 I'm Dr. Haney. I'm sorry we had to call you out of school, but we felt a few more tests were needed." And then bending, he ever so gently picked Todd up, cuddled him over his shoulder, reassured him in a quiet voice, and said to the two of us, "Follow me, please," as he walked in the door and down the hall.

Pediatrics was on the third floor. After getting off the elevator, the doctor 40 took us to a room that already had Todd's name on the door.

"Now, Mrs. Barrus," he stated kindly, "if you would get Todd undressed 41 please and slip this hospital gown on him. Sergeant, there's a wheelchair right behind the door there." Handing Bill two pieces of paper he explained, "There are three tests we must do. First he has to be x-rayed totally. Next take him to the lab for more blood tests. While you're gone, I'll set up down the hall for the third test, which I'll do myself. Give those papers to the people in charge. They'll know what to do."

Turning, he started briskly down the hall only to stop in mid-step. "Oh, 42 Sergeant Barrus," he called back, "it is imperative that you hurry." With that he was gone.

Riding the elevator was the first chance we had to look at the papers shaking 43 in my hand. On both, scrawled across the bottom, were those dreaded words, those words I knew already — "possible leukemia." As we rushed from test to test, the words reverberated in my mind, bringing pictures of a tiny pain-racked body and possible death, because death was all I knew of those horrible words.

After the attending orderlies finished each test, they would always say, 44 "Sergeant, it's extremely necessary that you hurry."

I was acutely aware of things going on around me that day, but as if I were 45
watching from outside my body. I could see myself as I felt—staring vacantly,
yet not seeing, knowing what was happening but not participating. And yet
it was me. I was there, clinging to hope as hard as I was clinging to Bill's
hand, all the while tears streaming down my face.

When we got back upstairs Dr. Haney and Captain Shiller, the head nurse, 46
were waiting for us by the elevator. As she hurried off, pushing Todd, the
doctor explained to us what would happen next.

"Mrs. Barrus," he began, "this last test is one we do only when absolutely 47
necessary. It is very painful and hard on the patient but we have no other
choice." Apologetically, he went on. "I cannot give him an anesthetic." He
waited for the statement to sink in.

"We take a syringe with a hollow screw-type bit on the end of it and drill 48
either into the breastbone or in one of the vertebra in the back. We'll probably
do the breastbone. After we are in the marrow of the bone, instead of injecting
into it, I'll suck the marrow into the syringe, then unscrew the drill and it
will be over." He paused, anticipating a question from us. There was none. I
was too numb and hollow to reply. Bill, also, was silent.

Then Dr. Haney looked at me. "Mrs. Barrus, I'd like you to go to the far 49
end of the hall where you can't hear. Mr. Barrus, if you'll follow me please,
you can be one of the four people we need to hold him down."

They left me then, standing solitary, alone in the middle of a crashing 50
world. Crying silently, with my face pressed to the hard comfort of the wall,
I heard Todd scream. Five, ten, fifteen minutes of constant screaming seemed
an eternity. Then, silence. It was over. The door opened. Bill, his usually
dark face now a pallid white, came out first, taking me gently in his arms. Dr.
Haney came next, pushing Todd on an ambulatory stretcher across the hall
to his room. Nurses and orderlies converged through the open door bringing
I.V. stands, glucose and plasma drips, tubing and needles necessary for the
next step.

Bill and I clung together in numb amazement in the corner. This time there 51
were no screams from Todd as they strapped him to the bed, no screams as
the transfusion needles entered his unconscious body.

The rest of the day was a haze to me. Dr. Haney, always so thoughtful, 52
explained everything he was going to do and why. He explained the reason
for the rush; Todd's hemoglobin level was so low that total heart failure could
have occurred at any time; thus the necessity for blood transfusions as quickly
as possible.

Every day for thirty days I left Marc and Kelly with a babysitter and walked 53
up the hospital hill. Little by little I saw a change in Todd. It was very slow

at first: from his unconscious state, to smiling slightly as he lay in bed, then to clapping and laughing as he saw me come down the hall for our daily visit. On the thirtieth day he ran the length of the corridor, waving his discharge papers as he tackled my legs.

In the next nine months as Todd made his daily and then weekly visit to 54 the hospital outpatient clinic, I watched a love develop between him and every nurse, orderly, and doctor that he came in contact with. They gave him candy and gum constantly. Whatever he asked for he got. Dr. Haney even gave Todd his tiny flashlight and an unopened box of tongue depressors. Because of this affection for him, Todd never had to wait in line, always getting preferential "stat" treatment.

The day before our return trip to Idaho they all gathered to give a small 55 tow-headed boy, who sparkled with mischief, a send-off, knowing most likely they would never see him again.

Todd died one year later on September 3, 1964, three days before his fourth 56 birthday.

QUESTIONS FOR READING AND REVISING

1. Did you find this essay powerful and moving? Why?

2. Barrus focuses on the day she found out about Todd's illness rather than trying to cover all of Todd's life, the whole course of his disease, or even the day of his death. What does she gain with this focus? Is her purpose to narrate a traumatic event in her life or to reflect on or examine its effect on her now? How does her focus serve that purpose?

3. In paragraph 4, Barrus writes, "The problem was Todd." The question of what is wrong with Todd is repeated throughout the essay, but it is not until paragraph 43 that we learn what the exact problem was. What effect does this delay have? Did you want to know what was wrong with Todd right away? What other techniques does Barrus use to keep her readers reading?

4. Barrus writes about a difficult subject, the death of her child. This essay could become sentimental or maudlin, but it never does. How does Barrus avoid sentimentality?

5. Part of the power of this essay comes from Barrus's effective images. She describes Todd after his fall, "as though the plug to his energy had been pulled." Identify other specific images and details that you find especially effective.

6. Barrus uses dialogue effectively to catch the nuances of style and the manner of speaking of her characters, such as the Arkansas motel owner in paragraph 10 and the arrogant Dr. White in paragraph 17. Identify specific instances of

dialogue that you find effective and explain what you learn about the character from the dialogue.

7. Barrus added her introductory paragraph in her final draft. Reread the essay without this paragraph. Which version is more effective? Why? Which introduction best suits Barrus's purpose?

SUGGESTIONS FOR WRITING

1. Barrus writes: "Trauma comes to every life. It can leave us helpless. But finally we realize that the world still turns and life goes on." Write a narrative essay about a time when trauma came to your life and about the realizations you made afterward.

2. If a member of your family has had a long or serious illness, write an essay describing the effects of this illness on the rest of the family.

3. Both Celeste Barrus and Doris Egnor describe conflicts with authority figures (doctors, bureaucrats). Using their experiences and your own, analyze the indifferent or arrogant behavior of a few of these figures and suggest possible causes for this behavior. Use specific examples, and concentrate on the verbal and physical evidence of the behavior. What did the person look like? What was his or her posture or telltale gestures? What did he or she say? What was his or her tone of voice?

VIRGINIA MARIE BEAN

Ventura College
Ventura, California
Robert Y. Rithner, instructor

"*If someone were to observe me getting started on a writing project, he would see me getting a glass of diet soda (lots of ice), leafing through a thesaurus, putting papers in piles, and quite possibly staring into space. To avoid writing, I stare a lot, eat, begin a trivial conversation with my mom, play a record, turn on the radio, turn off the radio, read a magazine, brush my hair, change my clothes, run, worry, or sleep. When I finally have exhausted all distractions, or when the deadline can't be avoided any further, I sit down, chomp on my ice cubes, snap my gum, and start writing.*"

Born in Ventura, California, in 1963, Virginia Bean's earliest memories of writing are her scribblings on the underside of her sister's Monopoly game with a green crayon. In high school, she was selected to participate in the Talented Young Writer's Program of the South Coast Writer's Project and also received her school's Creative Arts Scholarship. She is the lead vocalist of a rock band and plays the acoustic guitar and dulcimer.

Bean reports that the most important thing to her as a writer is to limit her topic: "Since I haven't been around long enough to be an authority on the decline of the West, I need to be humble and write from my own experiences." Asked to write an essay based on a personal experience, Bean decided to draw on her years of babysitting experiences with oversophisticated children.

Bitter Sitter

Babysitting isn't what it used to be. Gone are the days of entertaining kids 1 with Tinker Toys, bribing them with junk food or intimidating them into submission by pulling rank. Contemporary kids are obnoxiously sophisticated, and babysitting them, with their twisted views of amusement, is a repugnant chore. Attempting to entertain a third-grader of the nineteen eighties with conventional babysitting methods is like trying to get Friedrich Nietzsche to sing "It's a Beautiful Day in the Neighborhood" with Mr. Rogers.

In a recent babysitting experience, my charge had the abnormal desire to 2 read a book rather than watch television. Appalled, I made it perfectly clear that I would tolerate no flippancy, and sat him firmly down in front of a *Sha Na Na* rerun. To my dismay, the little ingrate yawned loudly at Bowser's appearance and suggested we turn to *Masterpiece Theatre* on the Public Broadcasting station. It seemed there was to be a "brief biography of one of the more obscure British playwrights of the nineteenth century." My ward refused to miss it. Stunned by this young degenerate's request, I calmly ordered him to plug in the home video set and play Space Invaders. Rising to answer the telephone, I returned to find the little exhibitionist punching in answers to a "Learn Chinese at Home" educational cassette.

Openly discouraged, I attempted to distract him from the spidery-looking characters. Sneaking into the kitchen, I began a methodical search for the perfect bribe. After careful surveillance of the pantry and refrigerator, I found the perfect means by which to reestablish my dominance — Hostess Twinkies. Smugly entering the den with a handful of the tooth-rotting bribes, I waved them in front of the T.V. screen. "Now take only two. This is junk food and it's not good for you," I offered, planting the key words sure to make him stuff his face in defiance of my warning. Glancing up with wide eyes, he said reproachfully, "Oh, no! I'd much rather have some yogurt." Straining to keep myself from dropping the bribes on his healthy little head, I sneered, "Would you like granola with that?" "No," replied the little wretch. "I've had sufficient fiber content today."

Handing the imp his plain white yogurt, I sank glumly onto the couch and watched him correctly answer five successive questions on a "Calculus for Kiddies" cartridge. Glancing over his shoulder, he asked as he sucked on his spoon, "Aren't you having some?" "I'm not hungry," I lied, postponing my own attack on the cupboards until after this health fanatic was safely in bed.

I was becoming fidgety. "Why don't we find something we both can do?" I complained as he plugged in a "Fun with T. S. Eliot" video game. "Wait till I'm done," he snapped. "I'm doing Prufrock." That was it. I was fed up. "Come ooooonnn!" I whined, stamping my foot. "I'm bored!" "Okay, okay," he said, reluctantly tossing aside the control unit. "We'll go play with the toys."

Anticipating some action at last, I skipped into his playroom and immediately grabbed a true-to-scale fighter spaceship. "Buzzzzz — I'm gonna vaporize you!" I hummed, sailing the model through the air above him with elaborate turns and dives. Raising a questioning eyebrow, the urchin moved to the corner of the room and began to dismantle a transistor radio.

As I was happily amusing myself with the spaceship, the killjoy suddenly announced, "I'm tired. May I go to bed now?" "Aw c'mon," I pleaded between sounds of laser fire. "We're having so much fun!" His eyes began to well up with tears, so I gave in.

"Okay, pick a bedtime story," I mumbled. He promptly removed an Edgar Allan Poe anthology, turned to "The Tell-Tale Heart," and begged for a narration. "I like the part where he goes insane," the monster murmured, contentedly sinking between the sheets. He corrected my pronunciation as I stumbled over the five- and six-syllable words. In spite of myself, I soon became thoroughly engrossed with the ghastly tale and continued reading aloud for the next twenty minutes. Eyes wide and pulse pounding as I closed the book, I glanced wildly at the shadows in the room, then down at the face of my ward. There he lay, lost in a blissful slumber. "Little brat," I grumbled as I tiptoed into the darkened living room. I spent the rest of the evening on the couch in motionless horror, my ears straining to catch the sound of a phantom heartbeat.

What kind of society encourages the obnoxiously precocious behavior dis- 9 played in this account of that unendurable night? Whatever happened to Bugs Bunny, Sugar Cocoa Puffs, and bogeymen? The child who discards Batman comics for *Forbes* is not a budding genius. He's preschizophrenic.

"Did you enjoy yourselves?" the parents inquired as they escorted me to my 10 car. "Sure," I said as I checked the back seat for a beating heart. "But, I don't know." I shuddered and added gravely, "You may want to have him examined. It *can't* be healthy for a child to find E. A. Poe entertaining."

QUESTIONS FOR READING AND REVISING

1. What does Virginia Bean mean when she claims that "babysitting isn't what it used to be"? How are children different today? What is Bean's attitude toward today's sophisticated children?

2. Bean reports that she "wanted to exaggerate without becoming totally unreal- istic." Does she succeed? How does she maintain a realistic framework? For instance, what is realistic and what is exaggerated in paragraph 3?

3. Of all the experiences Bean might have written about, she selected babysitting. What evidence is there that she has had plenty of babysitting experiences?

4. Bean offers us a wide range of examples to support her observations, such as the child's preference for *Masterpiece Theatre* over *Sha Na Na.* Select details and passages that you find especially effective. What makes them effective?

5. Bean reports that she finds outlining extremely helpful. Outline Bean's essay. How has she organized it? Do you find her organization effective?

6. Many of Bean's sentences begin with participial and prepositional phrases. For example, in paragraph 2 we read: "In a recent babysitting experience," "To my dismay," "Stunned by this young degenerate's request," and "Rising to answer the telephone." Examine Bean's sentence structure, especially in para- graphs 2, 3, 4, and 5. What effect do these frequent sentence openers have? Do you think Bean overuses these constructions? What is the danger of over- using any sentence style? How might some of these sentences be revised?

SUGGESTIONS FOR WRITING

1. Bean shows us that babysitting isn't what it used to be. Can you think of
   something in your experience that isn't what it used to be? Or can you think
   of something that you value because it remains the same? Write an essay in
   which you reflect on one of these questions.

2. Do you feel that you were forced to grow up too fast, pressured to leave your
   childhood behind you and become an adult too soon? Write an essay in which
   you describe your experiences as a sophisticated or unsophisticated child.

3. Part of the energy of Bean's essay comes from taking a familiar experience and
   exaggerating it both to make a point and to make a lively, amusing essay.
   However, Bean does not exaggerate the situation beyond recognition—in fact,
   we understand her point better because of her exaggeration. The situation
   becomes absurd, but its core remains believable. Consider a familiar situation
   that might be exaggerated in a similar fashion to make a point: Christmas
   shopping, preparing Thanksgiving dinner, a first date. Alter the truth and
   exaggerate to make a point.

SANFORD J. BOXERMAN

Washington University School of Business
St. Louis, Missouri
Betty Evans White, instructor

"*If the president of the United States were to walk into my room as I was trying to begin writing, the room might qualify for federal disaster funds. Papers are strewn everywhere; books are scattered here and there. In the middle of this mess, I sit, staring blankly at the empty piece of paper before me. 'Help, I cry. I'll never get this paper written.' *"

Sanford Boxerman was born in St. Louis in 1962 and graduated from Ladue High School, where he was a prominent member of the student government and the varsity track team. Currently a business major, Boxerman plans a career in law and politics. He has held summer jobs in law and accounting firms and has interned for Senator Thomas Eagleton. He has also earned a place on the dean's list and has received Washington University's Honorary Fellowship in Business and Accounting.

Asked to write an essay on any topic, Boxerman chose to respond to what he had been reading in his business management class — Milton Friedman's ideas on corporate social responsibility. Boxerman reports: "My management class was entitled 'Business, Government, and Society.' As I was outlining my responses to Friedman, I noticed that his assumptions fell loosely into each of these categories. I therefore drew up an outline that organized my response around these categories. This helped me by allowing me to knit what had been isolated jabs at Friedman into a coherent, organized rebuttal. I hoped that after reading my essay my readers would recognize the flaws in Friedman's argument and would agree with me that business does have a responsibility to society."

Not So Fast, Milton Friedman!

Businessmen should love Milton Friedman. With one stroke of his Nobel Prize–winning pen, Friedman grants executives and managers free reign to indulge in profit-maximizing activities to their hearts' content. Get all you can while the getting's good — just don't break the law, he exhorts. The suggestion that business has an obligation that goes beyond making money, that it has a basic responsibility to the society in which it operates, evokes indignation and cries of "Socialist!" from Friedman. This doctrine of corporate callousness might appeal to the pot-bellied, cigar-puffing robber baron of the late nineteenth century, but most businessmen today reject it. Contemporary business leaders realize that Friedman's argument is flawed, and a close examination of Friedman's beliefs reveals that the flaws lie in his assumptions. A number of

Friedman's assumptions concerning business, government, and society are simply invalid.

Friedman bases much of his argument upon his perception of the relation-   2
ship between a corporation's stockholders and its managers. Friedman makes the undeniable point that a corporate executive is an employee of the stockholders and as such has the "responsibility . . . to conduct the business in accordance with their desires."[1] When Friedman strays from this generally accepted position, however, and enters the more controversial realm of attempting to define just what stockholders' "desires" are, his argument loses much credibility. Friedman asserts that, in general, stockholders' sole wish is "to make as much money as possible." Furthermore, he claims that "to say that the corporate executive has a 'social responsibility' in his capacity as a businessman . . . must mean that he is to act in some way that is not in the interests of his employers."

What a narrow and uncomplimentary view Friedman takes of stockholders!   3
He rashly assumes that they possess an insatiable lust for profit that is irreconcilable with social responsibility. Friedman completely ignores the possibility that stockholders might actually *want* their managers to exercise some degree of social responsibility. Investors, in fact, have frequently called upon managers to take action consistent with certain social goals. In 1972, for example, stock-owning church groups filed stockholder resolutions in an effort to influence the policies of oil companies in South Africa. In 1975, other church-affiliated investors offered similar resolutions concerning the marketing of infant formula in developing countries. Friedman and his devotees might try to dismiss these examples as having emanated from "untypical" investors. Such an argument disregards the fact that churches require funding for their charitable activities and therefore do invest in order to make money. Their desire for profit, however, does not blind churches to the need for social responsibility. In addition, more traditional investors — the Ford and Carnegie foundations, universities, life insurance companies, pension funds — often supported the churches in these efforts, placing enough pressure on managers and garnering enough votes to prompt one observer to describe the situation as "a minor investor revolt."[2] Thus, contrary to Friedman's assumption, many stockholders do indeed want their corporations to exercise social responsibility.

---

[1]This and all subsequent quotations on Friedman's position come from Milton Friedman, "The Social Responsibility of Business Is to Increase Its Profits," *New York Times Magazine*, 13 Sept. 1970, p. 32.

[2]Tim Smith, "South Africa: The Churches vs. the Corporations," *Business and Society Review* (Fall 1975), 61.

Friedman also overlooks another component of the stockholder-manager relationship. He says that managers who spend corporate funds for socially responsible activities "impose taxes" upon the stockholders, a situation he likens to "taxation without representation." Implicit in this contention is the assumption that stockholders are powerless, that they have no recourse against executives who make such expenditures against the stockholders' wills. Friedman's language in this section of the argument is particularly revealing. He speaks of managers who are able to "get away with" spending stockholders' money. Get away with! As though managers furtively creep behind their employers' backs trying to subvert their interests! Once again, Friedman's assumption fails to stand up to critical examination. In the first place, managers are hardly shy when it comes to publicizing their socially responsible activities. No public television show, for example, has ever been preceded by the announcement that "this program was made possible through a grant by an anonymous oil company." On the contrary, the logo of Exxon (or Mobil or Shell) is prominently displayed. And the notion that stockholders have no recourse against recalcitrant managers is similarly absurd. Should a socially responsible expenditure infuriate stockholders, the options available to them are plentiful. They can file stockholder resolutions outlining their opposition to such actions. They can fire the "guilty" manager. Or they can participate in what Friedman himself lauds as a wonderfully "voluntary" market by selling their shares and investing in a presumably less responsible but more profitable corporation. Whatever course of action the offended stockholders decide to follow, the fact remains that a number of choices are open to them, choices which Friedman entirely neglects.

Friedman does not limit his erroneous suppositions to the business world itself. Invalid assumptions concerning business's relationship to the government also figure prominently in his philosophy. Friedman deplores the "short-sightedness" of businessmen who advocate social responsibility for themselves and their peers. He claims that such espousals of responsibility "strengthen the . . . view that the pursuit of profits is wicked and immoral and must be curbed." That curb, he glibly concludes, "will be the iron fist of Government bureaucrats." Friedman offers no evidence to bolster this conclusion, possibly because no such evidence exists. History is, in fact, replete with examples of government stepping in precisely because business *failed* to be responsible. The Interstate Commerce Act was a consequence of the railroads' failure to exercise responsibility. The Sherman Antitrust Act was a consequence of the trusts' failure to exercise responsibility. The Pure Food and Drug Act was a consequence of those industries' failure to exercise responsibility. As Professor Keith

Davis's Iron Law of Responsibility puts it, "If business fails to evince a higher degree of responsibility today, it will have much less freedom tomorrow." In view of this evidence, Friedman's assumption that business's acceptance of social responsibility invites regulation makes very little sense.

Even more damaging to this assumption is the experience of Cummins 6 Engine Company, a corporation that has actually done what Friedman dreads so much—adopted social responsibility. Cummins takes the position that, in the words of Chairman Henry B. Schacht, "The government is legitimate and . . . ought to regulate."[3] Such a pronouncement has not resulted in, as Friedman would expect, a plethora of unreasonable regulation. On the contrary, this approach has often mitigated the sting of government decrees. In 1975, for example, the federal government proposed a strengthening of the Clean Air Act. Cummins refused to take the traditional but irresponsible approach of bitterly denouncing the government and pleading that the revisions were impossible to meet. Instead, Cummins acknowledged the necessity of modifying the law and for two years worked with government officials in drafting standards that were both effective and attainable. Friedman's abstract, theoretical assumption concerning social responsibility and government thus dissolves in the face of this confutative experience from the real world.

Later in his paper, Friedman considers the situation in which a belief in 7 social responsibility subjects business to pressures not just from government but from society at large. He contrasts the principles of "unanimity" and "conformity," saying that unanimity—voluntary cooperation—underlies the market mechanism, while conformity—the obligation of the individual to submit to society's wishes—underlies the political mechanism. Friedman then asserts that "the doctrine of 'social responsibility' taken seriously would extend the scope of the political mechanism to every human activity." In other words, he hastily assumes that an adherence to the doctrine of social responsibility would obliterate all vestiges of corporate freedom, that corporate executives would lose all control over the operations of their businesses. Perhaps he envisions a scenario in which an angry public storms into the offices of General Motors demanding, in the name of social responsibility, that the price of a car be reduced to $500?

Even Friedman probably doesn't go *that* far, but this fanciful example is no 8 less ridiculous than his assumption. Friedman's outlook indicates a complete misunderstanding of what social responsibility actually entails. Milton Mos-

---

[3]Henry B. Schacht, "Responsibility at Cummins—A Commitment in Search of an Institutional Arrangement," Keynote Remarks, Project on Corporate Responsibility, Spring Hill Center Conference, 15–16 Nov. 1977, p. 5.

kowitz once described what he called "The Ten Best Companies" in terms of demonstrating social responsibility. Each company assumed responsibility in a way unique and appropriate to its own organization and structure. One promoted low-cost auto insurance; another sponsored consumer information programs; a third planted trees. The lesson that emerges from Moskowitz's study is that social responsibility has different meanings to different companies. While the doctrine of social responsibility "taken seriously" would compel business to be responsible, individual corporations would retain wide latitude in determining the most appropriate means by which to meet that responsibility. Business professors S. Prakash Sethi and James E. Post neatly summarize the refutation of Friedman's assumption when they write, "Social responsibility does not require a radical departure from the usual nature of corporate activities or the normal pattern of corporate behavior."[4]

Another misconception upon which Friedman builds his argument concerns 9 the proponents of social responsibility themselves. He claims that those who urge business to demonstrate responsibility — to eliminate pollution, say, or to fight unemployment — turn to the corporations only because they have failed to achieve their aims through the political process. Friedman labels these people a minority attempting to impose their views on the majority, another unsubstantiated and fallacious assumption. Many examples exist in which the political process fails to accommodate the wishes of the majority. Poll after poll, for instance, indicates that a majority of Americans favor gun control laws. Yet, for whatever reason, Congress refuses to enact such legislation. A 1974 magazine article by University of California business lecturer David Vogel provides another blow to Friedman's assumption. Vogel describes a trend originating in the mid-1960s in which "many civil rights activists, antiwar activists, and consumer and environmental groups began to confront big business directly for 'redress of grievances.' "[5] Thus, in many instances, advocates of social responsibility bypass the political process completely, thereby discrediting Friedman's supposition. This tendency of individuals and groups to avoid the political system and deal directly with the corporation does not prove that responsibility's adherents represent a majority. But it clearly demonstrates that Friedman should not be so quick to dismiss these concerned citizens as merely a stubborn minority snubbed by the political process.

Friedman's entire philosophy can be reduced to one sentence: Business's 10

---

[4]S. Prakash Sethi and James E. Post, "Public Consequences of Private Action: The Marketing of Infant Formula in Less Developed Countries," *California Management Review* (Summer 1979), 44.

[5]David Vogel, "The Politicization of the Corporation," *Social Policy* (May–June 1974), 58.

sole social responsibility is "to make as much money as possible while con-
forming to the basic rules of the society, both those embodied in law and
those embodied in ethical custom." Of all Friedman's declarations, this is
the one with which he should have taken the most pains; this is the one he
should have made certain was free of unfounded suppositions. Yet, even this
most crucial of lines contains a groundless and invalid assumption. Friedman
conveniently neglects to define "ethical custom." The remainder of his argument, however, demonstrates quite clearly Friedman's assumption that ethical custom does not include the belief that business should exercise social
responsibility.

Friedman has absolutely no foundation upon which to base this claim. An   11
abundance of speeches and articles illustrates that to a broad cross section of
Americans, social responsibility and ethical custom are inseparable. Cummins
Engine, for example, actually defines "ethical standards" in terms of social
responsibility. The company's "ethical practices memo" declares that "individuals who work in communities in which the company is located are affected
by the company's policies and actions, so the company must have the concern
to act always in a way to be helpful and beneficial and never harmful."[6] In
the words of Cummins' Schacht: "Ethical standards . . . [are] really the whole
idea behind corporate responsibility."[7]

Similarly, leaders from the academic community also emphasize the link   12
between ethical custom and responsibility. Sethi and Post, for instance, brand
as "unethical"[8] the disregard infant formula distributors exhibited for the societies in which they operated. The two professors equate ethics with responsibility even more explicitly when they state that "social responsibility implies
bringing corporate behavior up to a level where it is in congruence with currently prevailing social norms, values and expectations of performance"[9] — in
other words, the society's ethical customs.

Thus, Friedman builds his doctrine of corporate nonresponsibility upon a   13
number of invalid assumptions concerning business, government and society.
Friedman's argument brings to mind the story of the engineer, the chemist,
and the economist shipwrecked upon a desert island. A large supply of canned
food had also washed ashore, but the castaways lacked a device with which to
open the cans. The engineer proposed exerting pressure in strategic locations
upon the cans, thereby forcing open the lids. The chemist suggested building

[6]Schacht, p. 16.
[7]Schacht, p. 16.
[8]Sethi and Post, p. 41.
[9]Sethi and Post, p. 44.

a fire underneath the cans and forcing the lids open that way. They then turned to the economist.

"Assume a can opener," he began.   14

Friedman, like his marooned counterpart, bases his proposal upon a can 15 opener that just doesn't exist.

Bibliography

Friedman, Milton. "The Social Responsibility of Business Is to Increase Its Profits." *New York Times Magazine,* 13 Sept. 1970.

Schacht, Henry B. "Responsibility at Cummins — A Commitment in Search of an Institutional Arrangement." Keynote Remarks, Project on Corporate Responsibility, Spring Hill Center Conference. 15 – 16 Nov. 1977.

Sethi, Prakash, and James E. Post. "Public Consequences of Private Action: The Marketing of Infant Formula in Less Developed Countries." *California Management Review* (Summer 1979).

Smith, Tim. "South Africa: The Churches vs. the Corporations." *Business and Society Review* (Fall 1975).

Vogel, David. "The Politicization of the Corporation." *Social Policy* (May – June 1974).

QUESTIONS FOR READING AND REVISING

1. Boxerman's essay is an example of a research paper that starts from the writer's strong reaction to an idea and then investigates the ramifications of that idea. What evidence is there that Boxerman has a strong reaction to Friedman's ideas? What evidence shows a reader Boxerman's excitement about his topic?

2. Boxerman's strategy is to attack the assumptions inherent in Friedman's argument. What are these assumptions? How does he go about attacking these assumptions? Why is this an effective strategy for arguing? Cite specific instances from Boxerman's essay to support your answer.

3. What is the definition of corporate social responsibility implicit in Boxerman's argument? What responsibilities do corporations have to society? Does Boxerman resolve the importance of these responsibilities with a corporation's need to make a profit? (See paragraph 8, for instance.)

4. Do you find Boxerman convincing? How do you think Friedman would respond to Boxerman's points?

5. What assumptions does Boxerman make about his audience's familiarity with Friedman and his ideas? Does he provide enough background information? Are there any places where an uninformed reader might get lost?

6. Boxerman reports: "Writing without an outline is the equivalent of driving without a road map. Outlining facilitates organization, cuts down on redun-

dancy, and hopefully makes the particular argument more persuasive." Analyze how Boxerman has organized his ideas and information.

7. Describe Boxerman's tone. Do you think he overstates his case? How do you react to such strong phrases as "simply invalid," "completely ignores," and "erroneous suppositions"?

SUGGESTIONS FOR WRITING

1. Think of someone whose ideas you have read and would like to argue against. Write an essay presenting the writer's assumptions and then arguing against them. Use your outside reading as the basis for the essay and integrate the readings into the essay.

2. Define an ethical problem related to being a student, such as the ethics of term paper writing services or plagiarism. Define a position concerning the problem and explain the reasons for your point of view.

3. Boxerman's argument maintains that corporations should, can, and do perform socially responsible deeds. But social responsibility also belongs to individuals. Recall your last socially responsible act, either large or small: giving blood, fighting pollution, buying girl scout cookies, being a little league booster, capturing terrorists. Consider all the reasons you may have had at the time plus reasons that occur to you in retrospect. In a well-argued, persuasive essay, convince your reader to perform a similar act. If you recall no acts of social responsibility, justify yourself.

KAREN R. BUCHANAN

Highline Community College
Midway, Washington
William J. Hofmann, instructor

Karen Buchanan describes herself as a "painfully shy child" whose "fear of the limelight" prompted her to maintain a very low profile throughout her elementary and secondary school years. Born in Bremerton, Washington, in 1955, the second of five children, Karen Buchanan has spent all of her life in the Pacific Northwest. She graduated with honors from Kentridge Senior High School in Kent, Washington, in 1973, where she won several awards for her artwork. "College being an expensive dream, I went to work full time as an office clerk in a tiny loan office three days after graduation."

Since 1975, Buchanan has worked as a secretary and administrative assistant at the Boeing Commercial Airline Company in Seattle. An avid mountaineer, she has climbed four of Washington State's major peaks in the past three years, including Mount Rainier. In 1982, prompted by what she calls her "lifelong motivator, an obsession with self-improvement," she enrolled in Highline Community College as part of Boeing's undergraduate degree program.

Asked to write a biographical sketch, Buchanan focused on her grandmother to pay tribute to a woman she never understood as a child. She reports: "This essay was the second of two biographical sketches assigned in class. I considered Grandma as a subject for my first sketch, then mistakenly put her aside and wrote about another, far less loved character instead. By the time my second chance to write a biographical sketch came, ideas about Grandma were exploding like fireworks in my mind, and I found her essay to be delightfully easy to write. I was thrilled with the finished product and especially thrilled to have finally paid a lasting tribute to a very special lady."

Dancing Grandma

Grandma celebrated her fifty-third birthday just weeks before Grandpa died 1 of cancer in 1965. Although his passing was tremendously difficult for her, I think their shared struggle to prolong his life taught Grandma that good health was not to be taken for granted, and she vowed to live the remainder of her own life as fully and as long as she could. Although we always suspected Grandma had dutifully subdued a zest for living during the long years of Grandpa's illness, we were hardly prepared for the personality that emerged from within her after he died. When she announced her decision to invest part of Grandpa's life insurance benefits in lessons at the Fred Astaire Dance Studio in Portland, Oregon, where she lived, we rolled our eyes in embarrassment and helplessly wished she would just stay home and bake cookies as normal

grandmothers did. Many years filled with countless dance lessons passed before
we learned to appreciate the wonder of having a dancing Grandma.

I suppose Grandma's primary motivation for wanting to learn to dance was   2
social. She had been a shy girl, always very tall and heavy, and had married
into Grandpa's quiet lifestyle before developing any grace or confidence in her
personal appearance. Dancing, on the other hand, filled her life with glittering
lights, wonderful parties, beautiful gowns, dashing young dance instructors,
and the challenge of learning. Although the weekly dance lessons did not
diminish her ample, two-hundred-pound figure, Grandma surprised everyone
with energetic performances on the dance floor that soon gave her as much
poise, grace, and confidence as any Miss America contestant.

Never one to lack confidence in her own decisions, Grandma signed up   3
from the beginning for enough weekly dance lessons to last for years. She
learned the rumba, the cha-cha, and various waltzes easily and was soon participating in dancing contests all over the Northwest. When I was fourteen,
Grandma proudly invited me to watch her compete in one of these contests
to be held in the grand ballroom of Seattle's Red Lion Inn. My attitude was
still unenthusiastic at that point ("Grandmas aren't supposed to dance," I often
grumbled), but to make her happy, my mother and I attended the competition.
As if to prove me wrong, Grandma made a spectacular showing in every event
she entered. The one dance that I particularly remember was a Spanish dance
involving a dizzying amount of spinning, dipping, and fast-paced twirling. Her
timing was perfect, her sparkling smile never wavered, and her lovely hand-
made black and red dress shimmered under the spotlights, swirling in rhythmic
complement to every movement. I thought she was truly the belle of the ball
during that dance, and my thoughts were echoed by the judges a short time
later when she was awarded a glistening gold trophy for her outstanding performance.

Grandma's dance costumes were dazzling, and most were her personal crea-   4
tions. Because she was never conservative in her choice of colors or styles,
designing glittering, eye-catching ballroom dance dresses came as naturally for
Grandma as baking apple pies comes for ordinary grandmothers. Since a costume was rarely repeated from one dancing event to another, she had huge
cardboard boxes of tissue-wrapped dresses in her basement, most of which had
been worn only once. I discovered those boxes while helping her move from
Portland to Seattle in 1975 and was promptly given my own private showing
of the vast collection. As she tenderly unfolded each dress and held it up for
me to admire, her eyes glowingly expressed the well-earned pride she felt
toward each costume and the vividly remembered moment on the dance floor

that it represented. Consequently, I felt warmly honored several months later when Grandma wore one of her favorites to my wedding, although she nearly stole the show when she stepped majestically down the church aisle in the stunning dress of glossy white satin, boldly printed with bright red roses and billowing about her to the floor. Topped with her crown of snow-white hair and wearing her proudest smile, Grandma was an unforgettable picture of dignity and grandeur.

Occasionally, I still long for a grandmother who rocks cozily in a rocking   5
chair next to a warm fireplace, knitting afghans and feeding everyone chocolate chip cookies that she has baked herself. Then I think of my own version of a grandmother and burst with pride for her in spite of myself. Although it took many years for me to appreciate the wonder of having that very unique and talented lady for my grandmother, I will never again begrudge her chosen path in life. In fact, someday I may follow in her dancing footsteps.

QUESTIONS FOR READING AND REVISING

1. Buchanan might have focused on other characteristics of her grandmother, but she chose to focus on the one characteristic that she believed would give her readers the clearest description of the overall person. She says, "To describe Grandma's dancing is to describe Grandma." Besides her love of dancing, what do we learn about Buchanan's grandmother?

2. Buchanan expected her grandmother to rock in a rocking chair, knit afghans, and bake chocolate chip cookies. Why did she feel this way as a child? What is her attitude toward her grandmother as an adult? What lessons has she learned about life from her grandmother's example?

3. Buchanan writes about her introduction: "Working out my introductory paragraph was most difficult because I wanted not only to introduce a very colorful, headstrong, and dynamic character but also to relate some of my own feelings toward that character." Which aspect — a description of her grandmother or her feelings toward her grandmother — is her dominant purpose in the whole essay?

4. Buchanan reports: "Outlining is as essential to my finished essay as a good pencil drawing is under an oil painting." Analyze how Buchanan organized her ideas and information.

5. We see Buchanan's grandmother very clearly in this essay, but sometimes Buchanan uses phrases such as "glittering lights," "dashing young dance instructors," and "sparkling smile," which might be classified as clichés. Does the

overfamiliarity of these phrases make them ineffective? Locate such details and phrases and revise with fresh expressions or images.

6. Compare the portraits of grandmothers in "Dancing Grandma" and "Teapot Whistles." How does the difference in the authors' attitudes affect the picture presented of each woman?

SUGGESTIONS FOR WRITING

1. We all have conventional, stereotyped expectations for different members of our families. Write a portrait of some unconventional member of your family or of someone who refuses to live by the stereotypes imposed by his or her family or friends. Try to focus on one particular characteristic or habit to give readers a clear description of the total person.

2. People often make vows to significantly change their daily patterns — to act more responsibly, to be kinder, to finish all their work on time — but somehow these vows get postponed until "tomorrow." Write an essay describing someone you know who, like Buchanan's grandmother, actually effected some important change in his or her life. How has that change affected the whole person? And, just as important, how has your view of that person changed and how have you come to terms with the new person who has emerged?

HOPE COHEN

Harvard University
Cambridge, Massachusetts
Perri Klass, instructor

"I generally think up topics for papers when I'm doing something else — walking to breakfast, taking a shower, etc.," Hope Cohen explains. "Once I have the idea, I just sit down and write it. I usually don't know the end or even the second paragraph when I begin. Each idea comes to me as I write, and I really write the paper as I go along."

Hope Cohen was born in Alexandria, Virginia, in 1964 and raised in Great Neck, New York. Her principal interests include classical music, crossword puzzles, old movies, and Sherlock Holmes. A former National Merit Finalist and a National Council of Teachers of English Writing Awards Finalist, she is also an IBM Thomas J. Watson Memorial Scholar at Harvard University, where her major is history and science.

Hope Cohen wrote her essay in response to an assignment to describe a piece of scientific research and her sense of its implications. She reports: "I knew I wanted to write about something at least vaguely astronomical since I have always been fascinated with astronomy, but I didn't know what exactly the subject should be. I went to Cabot Science Library and flipped through some magazines. Two articles in The Sciences, "Missing Matter" and "The World According to Hoyle," caught my thoughts and later became the basis for my essay. I knew I liked the articles, but I had a lot of trouble tying them together and getting something out of the combination. I was taking a shower when the solution came to me, and I kept repeating the idea to myself so I wouldn't forget it."
The result is "The Matter of Maids and Mops," which explores the question of whether protons disappear forever or redistribute into new matter.

The Matter of Maids and Mops

The Walrus and the Carpenter
Were walking close at hand.
They wept like anything to see
Such quantities of sand.
"If this were only cleared away,"
They said, "it would be grand."

"If seven maids with seven mops
Swept it for half a year,

47

Do you suppose," the Walrus said,
"That they could get it clear?"
"I doubt it," said the Carpenter,
And shed a bitter tear.
                            — Lewis Carroll,
                            Through the Looking-Glass

Perhaps if Lewis Carroll's two famous oyster-nappers read the January 1982   1
issue of *The Sciences*, they would not be so mournful. In the article "Missing
Matter," Paul Davies, a theoretical physicist at Newcastle-on-Tyne, discusses
a cosmic currycomb far more effective than maids with mops: this electric
broom sucks up not only stray rubbish but also the very cleaning apparatus
itself. "Missing Matter" is about protons disappearing, disintegrating into quarks
and positrons.

Particle decay is, of course, nothing new to nuclear physics, but protons   2
have always been considered infinitely stable. It now appears, however, that
protons are only *almost* infinitely stable, lasting billions of years but eventually
decaying into other particles (and doing so particularly rapidly in very hot
surroundings). Protons are the basis for all atoms and thus for all matter: vanish
protons and vanish all the universe. Thus, if the Walrus and the Carpenter
had been willing to wait longer than six months, they eventually would have
seen the tideland tidied (except, of course, that they would have been flushed
away with the rest of the dirty business).

Davies's article goes on to tie all of this together with the Big Bang theory   3
of the beginning of the universe. The unimaginable temperatures of that epoch
would have caused extraordinary particle behavior — including proton breakdown at phenomenal rates. The Grand Bang, a kind of echo of the Big Bang,
would then have taken place. This is the conventional — "standard model" —
depiction of How the Universe Came to Be.

Eleven months after Davies's piece appeared, the same journal carried an   4
article entitled "The World According to Hoyle," by Sir Fred Hoyle, Royal
Society astronomer and Steady State theorist par excellence. The Steady State
theory was the major rival of the Big Bang cosmology through many years and
scientific battles, until 1965 when Arno Penzias and Robert W. Wilson discovered cosmic background radiation. This microwave radiation is considered
the echo of the Big Bang itself — the cooled-down evidence (reduced to 3K
from unimaginable) of a very violent beginning.

Both the Steady State and Big Bang theories acknowledge the expansion   5
of the universe. The concept of a specific moment of creation is central to the
Big Bang model. Since the explosion in the initial instant, the fate of the
universe has depended on the critical density. If the density of matter in the
universe is less than (or equal to) the critical quantity, cosmological expansion

will be eternal; if not, the universe will expand for a while and then collapse back on itself. The Steady State theory, on the other hand, eliminates the notions of critical density and a critical moment and instead presents a universe infinitely extended in both time and space. Yet if the universe has been expanding forever, everything in it should now be infinitely distant from everything else, and we should see nothing at all when we look at the sky; obviously this is not the case. The Steady State model is steady only in appearance; the universe looks isotropic through space and time, but only because it is experiencing basic and constant change. The Steady State theory calls for "continuous creation" of matter to fill in the gaps left by expansion. In order to maintain the isotropism as the universe expands, matter is created spontaneously. Thus, although the Steady State theory was long the philosophical favorite of physicists because it avoids a Genesis scenario, it most certainly has its aesthetic (as well as scientific) drawbacks.

This much Hoyle himself discusses in the article. Nowhere does he mention 6 the mystery of the disappearing protons. This omission is hardly surprising; after all, such a discovery seems to put the final nails into the proverbial coffin of the Steady State model. Steady State calls for "continuous creation [integration]" of matter, and the proton problem provides a situation of "continuous disintegration." Surely if matter must be manufactured to offset the macrocosmic expansion, more matter still must be produced to make up for the effect of proton decay. This makes Hoyle's hypothesis even harder to accept than it already is. All these "if's" and "thus's" warn of smothering surmises, and, as Macbeth noted (Act I, Scene iii), smothering surmises always remind us that "nothing is but what is not."

Let us then take Shakespeare as our linguistic guide to truth and say that 7 Steady State *is* since it seems so likely not to be. Instead of pointing away from the Steady State model, proton disintegration points toward Hoyle's theory because of the conservation of mass-energy. (Mass and energy are interchangeable by Einstein's equation, so we can hyphenate and speak of one entity.) When an old proton dies, it doesn't just fade away: it breaks up into several reusable quarks and a positron. The positron is the antimatter equivalent of the electron, and when the two meet, their mutual annihilation causes a tremendous release of energy (Einstein again) in the form of gamma rays. But energy can be reconverted into mass. (Einstein for the third time.) True, it takes a lot of energy to make a little particle; nonetheless, the re-formation is possible, and even probable when scads of energy are available — as would have been the case during and immediately after the postulated Big Bang.

Thus, a proton could decay into a positron in one part of the universe; that 8 positron and the first electron it encountered would then go to glory in a great gush of gamma rays. Radiation so created could then go merrily through the universe and at any random spot be converted back into matter. The antiparticle would be left to undergo mutual annihilation with some electron and thus repeat the process, while the newly formed particle could combine with other stray particles.* Those particles could acquire more and more matter (through the various forces of the universe — strong nuclear, electromagnetic, weak nuclear, and gravity) until they formed flecks of gas and dust. The gas and dust would then condense into stars in the manner described by currently accepted models.

Thus the distasteful concept of "continuous creation" of matter becomes much more palatable as the idea of "continuous redistribution" of matter. This is all very well for Hoyle, Shakespeare, and Einstein, of course, but it doesn't help our poor beachcombers, the Walrus and the Carpenter, at all. Perhaps if they want the seashore swept spotless, they should use a black hole.   9

*Theoretically, the antiparticle could join up with other antiparticles to form antimatter, while the stray electron could be wiped away by a wandering positron. This is extremely unlikely, however, because there is lots of matter around and very, very little antimatter.

Bibliography

Carroll, Lewis. *Through the Looking-Glass.* New York: Collier Books, 1962, pp. 215 – 16.
Davies, Paul. "Missing Matter." *The Sciences,* 22 (January 1982), 15 – 19.
Hoyle, Fred. "The World According to Hoyle." *The Sciences,* 22 (November 1982), 9 – 13.
Shakespeare, William. *Macbeth.* Ed. John Dover Wilson. London: Octopus Books Limited, 1980.

QUESTIONS FOR READING AND REVISING

1. Hope Cohen has tackled an ambitious subject. What evidence is there in the essay that she is enjoying writing about her topic? What evidence is there that Cohen is quite knowledgeable about her subject?

2. What is the frightening implication of the breakdown and disappearance of protons? What does Davies say is the probable cause of this breakdown?

3. How do the Big Bang and Steady State theorists differ in their views of how matter is formed?

4. How does Cohen use proton disintegration to support rather than invalidate Steady State theory? What is her argument? Is it convincing?

5. How would you define Cohen's purpose? Is it to summarize the two articles, contrast them, or offer a synthesis of them? How does Cohen move beyond summary to her own ideas?

6. Cohen uses a quotation to begin her essay. Why is her introduction effective?

What is the effect of Cohen's reference to the same quotation in the conclusion of her essay?

7. Does Cohen provide enough background information for someone who is unfamiliar with scientific theory? How much does Cohen assume her audience knows about scientific theory? Should she have provided more background information? Should she, for example, have explained in more detail the Big Bang and Steady State theories or 3K (paragraph 4), critical density (paragraph 5), and isotropic (paragraph 5)? Does she need to define proton? Can she assume her readers are all familiar with it?

8. Study paragraphs six and seven. What is the main idea of each paragraph? Does the Shakespeare quotation help to connect the two paragraphs or to obscure the connection? Why?

SUGGESTIONS FOR WRITING

1. Choose a scientific controversy with which you are familiar (the disappearing ozone layer; acid rain; the existence of the Loch Ness Monster, for example). Read the views of at least two authorities with differing opinions on the topic. In an essay, compare the two views, evaluating which seems more likely to be valid.

2. Find two conflicting reviews of a recent movie you have seen or of a book you have read. Write an essay in which you contrast the two reviews and offer your own synthesis.

3. In an essay, explain the Big Bang theory to an audience hostile to the theory. Or choose any theory and try to explain it to an audience that would be hostile to it.

DANIEL SCOTT DIETRICH

University of Wisconsin, Stevens Point
Stevens Point, Wisconsin
Isabelle Stelmahoske, instructor

The second of three children, Daniel Dietrich was born in Red Wing, Minnesota, in 1964. He graduated from Central High School there and enrolled at the University of Wisconsin at Stevens Point with a double major in English and communication. Dietrich serves on his college's English Advisory Council, volunteers in the local Big Brother program, and writes an "opposing opinion column" for his dormitory newspaper. His work experience includes service as an instructor at an environmental learning center and as a naturalist at a state park. He plans to combine his interest in the environment with his career goal, to write for a magazine.

Daniel Dietrich includes writing on his list of "unique personal highs" — along with such activities as white-water kayaking, parachuting, and mountain climbing. He says, "A perfect night of writing starts with a long hot shower to relax, then some Phil Collins or Bread (music) to get the ideas forming. After this, I sit at my desk and try to get my ideas flowing. After an hour or so of writing, I have a cup of coffee, which makes me feel like a writer. It's funny, but when I feel like a writer, I think I write better."

Asked to write an essay about an experience that had "a formative or profound influence" on his life, Dietrich worked through nine drafts of "The Teapot Whistles." "Even now," he reports, "I can pick up the essay and find ideas that should be added and others that need revision."

The Teapot Whistles

Violet Dietrich lay awkwardly on her bed; her bones beneath the sheets resembled jointed metal pipes. Her eyes were a soft, transparent blue that I've seen only in a few teenage girls, glistening as if a light from somewhere inside had been turned on. She looked at my brothers and me and mustered a smile from her worn, gray face, the rugged skin sagging from her cheekbones to her jaw as a canvas tent does after a storm.

I looked at her and saw death's subduing force, and I thought of her life here on earth that was slowly fading away and about that hazy, mystic road that lay before her. As my mind played with time, I remembered my childhood days at Grandma's house: the one week every summer spent with our bikes and Monopoly game; our wake-a-thons (42 hours was the winning time); and tree fortresses that soon gave way to fishing in Copper Creek with willow branches and worms that we caught by lifting up the baseboards of the sidewalk. I remember the inevitable game of "guns" that took us through an

African jungle and to the upstairs of the house until Mother started yelling that we were too noisy and reminded us that we weren't kids, but young adults. I remember the hot, sweaty game of "witch" that was played with a broom in the basement and could have more simply been called "tag"; the numerous times of laughing at the table during dinner for no real reason; and of kicking small depressions behind the wheels of the car when Dad came to bring us home so that maybe the car would get stuck and we would have to spend another week at Grandma's. I also remember the kitchen, where Grandma spent most of her time: the smiling, yellow ceramic flowers on the wall, whose inscribed words said, "Make a smile, spread some cheer, let's be happy while we're here"; and the sound of the water pump in the basement that went on if someone took more than a thirty-second shower or mixed up a pitcher of Kool-Aid. I remember the teapot and how it would whistle as the water became hot enough, the steam shooting out; and times when we were little kids and had to eat in the kitchen because there wasn't enough room for us at the table in the dining room. Finally we would leave, honking and waving at the end of the driveway, only to scratch all the way home because growing in our African jungle was that disgusting weed, poison ivy.

This reverie created a need to see again some of her special characteristics. 3 She wasn't that nursing-home type (why, she didn't even knit or crochet). The only similarity I could find in her to that type was that she, too, watched Lawrence Welk and his timpani bubbles at 6:30 on Saturday nights. As she worked in the kitchen, an airy, monotone whistle could be heard accompanying the music on the radio. The music wasn't from any particular era, at least that I could tell, but it was just old. If someone walked into the kitchen, she would stop whistling, smile, and continue working. She and Grandpa used to go grocery shopping every Thursday morning in the brown Ford LTD, Grandpa with his hat that Grandpas are supposed to wear (the tweed ones with the two-tone feather on the side) and Grandma with her shopping list in one hand and coupons in the other. She started a garden in the spot where the outhouse used to be, and boy did those tomatoes grow. In all the years that I knew her, never once do I remember her yelling at me; I seldom saw her depressed; and never, from my perspective, did any shadow of selfishness appear close to her.

I can still see Grandma in her chair at the kitchen table, crossing her legs 4 comfortably as women often do. Her left hand rested on her upper knee and the first two fingers on her right hand held a Winston 100. They came in a gray and green carton that sat crouched on top of the refrigerator.

I remember, God do I remember, Christmas shopping at Gibson's. I was 5 passing the jewelry department that displayed the gaudy plastic grapefruit earrings, when I saw something that demanded my attention. I was in seventh grade and my English teacher, a scholarly smoker, said how fantastic this product was that had helped him stop smoking. The product had five or six plastic butts that the smoker attached to the end of the cigarette and, as the smoker went from one filter to the next, each one gradually reduced the amount of smoke inhaled. What a perfect present for Grandma! But what if she took the present as an insult? I wish I hadn't asked myself that question, because the pause gave me a chance to stop and consider. I checked the price and then burrowed into my front pocket to see how much money I had. The more I glanced at the sticker and then back at the prestige of holding the wrinkled Christmas money, the greedier I became. Now I wonder what would have happened if I had bought that present for her.

She died of cancer the second day of school when I was a junior in high   6
school. As her health worsened, I could see her weighing herself with the scale that was in the closet by the stairway, the same scale upon which we had watched ourselves grow when we were young. I feel that the last few weeks she knew that her life was coming to a close, but I sensed that she always retained some form of hope. As she lay on her bed, I can remember her saying to my brothers and me, "After this medicine starts working I'll be O.K. You've just got to give these things time." That was the weekend before school started. Now only the teapot whistles.

QUESTIONS FOR READING AND REVISING

1. How many of the reminiscences in this essay are actually focused on Daniel Dietrich's grandmother? How many on his relation to her? What is Dietrich's purpose in this essay? Is it to describe his grandmother, his feelings about her, or both? What does paragraph 5 tell us about his purpose?

2. What is Dietrich's attitude toward his grandmother? her house? Where do you detect traces of sentimentality or guilt in this essay? How appropriate are they to his purpose?

3. Sketch out the organization of Daniel Dietrich's essay. What is the order of his reminiscences?

4. The strength of Dietrich's description depends largely on his ability to summon apt details and images, especially at the beginning of his essay. (In the first sentence, for example, he notes that his grandmother's "bones beneath the sheets resembled metal pipes.") Locate well-chosen details and images and explain what each detail or image contributes to the essay.

5. The first sentence in the first draft of Dietrich's essay reads, "The sun is setting on Grandma's world. Violet Dietrich lay awkwardly on her bed in the simply

furnished bedroom, her bones beneath the sheets resembling aged metal pipes." Consider the final draft of this sentence: "Violet Dietrich lay awkwardly on her bed; her bones beneath the sheets resembled jointed metal pipes." Identify the specific strengths and weaknesses of each version. What particular features, if any, of the first draft would improve the final draft? Explain.

6. Consider Dietrich's final paragraph and note especially how his use of specific details (his grandmother's weighing herself, her insistence on the recuperative powers of medicine) makes the effect so moving. What would be the effect of shifting the first sentence in the paragraph ("She died of cancer the second day of school when I was a junior in high school") to follow " 'You've just got to give these things time' "? Explain how this reordering would weaken or strengthen the final paragraph.

7. Compare and contrast Dietrich's depiction of his grandmother to Karen Buchanan's description in her essay "Dancing Grandma" (pp. 43 – 45). In what specific ways does each essay succeed? How could the strengths of one essay be applied to the other?

8. Daniel Dietrich's "The Teapot Whistles," Celeste Barrus's "Todd" (pp. 23 – 29), and Doris Egnor's "A Life of Quiet Desperation" (pp. 56 – 57) address the death of a close relative. Which writer treats the subject most objectively? Most emotionally? Explain how the readers of each essay are encouraged to take different views of death and grief.

SUGGESTIONS FOR WRITING

1. In paragraphs 4 and 5, Dietrich recounts his strong feelings of guilt from having failed to buy his grandmother a "stop smoking" kit. Write an essay describing a similar situation in your life and explain the consequences of your failure to act or advise.

2. Dietrich uses the image of a teapot and a bathroom scale to express some of his feelings about his grandmother. David Landmann's depiction of the frailty of a family living in a cardboard shack helps to focus his point in his essay "The House" (pp. 97 – 101). Think about some object that represents a person or a personal value that is important to you. Using that object as the controlling image, write an essay expressing your feelings about the subject.

DORIS EGNOR

Mesa Community College
Mesa, Arizona
Chris Crowe, instructor

The youngest of seven children, Doris Egnor was born in Pine Knob, West Virginia, in 1945. She married soon after graduating from high school and was forced to put off her "dream" of going to college: "I had always intended to, but there never seemed to be enough time or money." Now the mother of three children and a resident of Arizona, she decided in 1982 to enroll at Mesa Community College along with her oldest child. She has worked for the past sixteen years as a secretary and recently received her company's Western Regional Secretarial Award.

Encouraged to write by her family and friends, Egnor has written poems for numerous personal special occasions for the past ten years. She reports that she likes to write at five o'clock in the morning, before the phone starts ringing and when her children are still asleep. "I sit at the kitchen table with a cup of coffee, lots of blank paper, and an appreciation of the early morning quiet," she says.

About her essay, Doris Egnor reports: "I think my subject selected me. We were asked to write an essay about the angriest we had ever been. I discarded numerous possibilities because I kept involuntarily returning to the idea of writing about my sister's death. I didn't want to, though. Yet every time I tried to write about another topic, my thoughts would drift back to my sister. I think it was something I had to write."

A Life of Quiet
Desperation

I was much more naive and trusting ten years ago than I am today. I believed 1
that all policemen were good, all doctors were caring, and all people shared
my concern for their fellow man. I realized with anguish the folly of making
such generalizations when my sister, Laura, committed suicide. I was not only
angered about my own naiveté but also outraged by the uncaring attitude of
the people I encountered following the tragedy.

My own lack of understanding left me unprepared for Laura's death. I often 2
visited her at the Veterans Administration Hospital where she was a patient
of a halfway house for mentally ill veterans. Whenever I was with her, she
appeared to be relatively happy. I realized, after her death, the tremendous
effort she had made to appear that way for my benefit. I knew she had been
diagnosed as a chronic depressive; I did not understand the extent of her

depression. Although Laura had made previous attempts to end her life, I was still shocked by her ultimate success. I should have realized how desperate she was because, in her usual protective way, she tried to prepare me. I received a letter shortly before she died in which Laura had written, "The panic and desperation are overwhelming." I did not heed her cry.

When we first learned of Laura's intentions, my family received no assistance 3 in trying to determine whether she was dead or alive. My sister Carol received a letter from Laura which began, "Please forgive me. I just can't stand to live anymore." We immediately called the hospital and learned that Laura had already been missing for twenty-six hours. But despite our plea, no one at the Veterans Administration Hospital or the police department would agree to search for her. Mr. Thompson of the VA Hospital stated that Laura was no longer their responsibility since she had voluntarily left the hospital grounds. Donna Edwards of the police department's Missing Persons Bureau callously remarked that they could do nothing because Laura was "government property." After driving to the hospital, a four-hour drive from our home, we began a systematic and nerve-racking verbal investigation of Laura's friends, cab companies, and hotels. We found Laura, but our worst fears were confirmed. We were too late.

What really infuriates me is that no one tried to stop her. According to 4 Kathy, a friend of Laura's who was also a patient at the VA center, something particularly upsetting and humiliating happened to Laura that day. After being assured by her doctor's secretary that the doctor would see her, Laura went to his office. Her psychiatrist rudely told her she would have to make an appointment for the following week. When Laura protested, he yelled, "Get the hell out, or I'll call the guards!" Laura got the hell out, determinedly went to her room where she wrote her last letter, then left the center. A short while later, Kathy saw Laura waiting at a bus stop. She asked Laura where she was going, and Laura replied, "I'm on my way to the executioner!" Kathy, aware of Laura's desperation, pleaded with the hospital personnel to do something to stop her or, at least, to call us. They refused. It took us only two hours to find Laura once we arrived in town; her death might have been avoided if we had been notified immediately or if the hospital personnel had taken appropriate action themselves. Despite what might have been, the cruel reality was that Laura's retreat from a life she found intolerable was finally complete.

Laura's life was one of quiet desperation. She mutely screamed out the agony 5 of her existence, but no one listened. She silently pleaded for help, but no one heard. Or cared. At least not enough. The anger I felt at this "don't give a damn" attitude has not significantly lessened after all this time.

QUESTIONS FOR READING AND REVISING

1. Doris Egnor tells us that she was "much more naive and trusting ten years ago" than she is today. What did she learn about life from the tragic death of her sister?

2. Why do you think Egnor titled her essay "A Life of Quiet Desperation"?

3. Although Egnor is writing about her anger, her tone is not hostile or overly emotional. How does Egnor manage to tell her solemn tale with restraint? What effect does her restraint have on readers? Cite specific passages to support your answers.

4. Egnor organizes her essay not with a chronology of the actual events but with a chronology of the way she found out about them. Is this organization effective? Why or why not?

5. One of Egnor's rough drafts began this way:

> On June 2, 1972, at 10:57 A.M., the driver of Checker Cab #43 picked up a thirty-four-year-old, neatly dressed, pretty woman from a Veterans Hospital and dropped her off a short time later in the downtown section of the city. The woman walked to a nearby hotel, checked in, and paid for her room in advance. The woman was my sister Laura, and the hotel clerk was the last person to see her alive. Sometime between the time she checked into the hotel and 11:57 P.M. the following evening, Laura committed suicide. The profound sorrow I felt after Laura's tragic death has gradually subsided. The indignant anger that consumed me following her death, however, has not. I was not only angry at my own naiveté and senselessness of her death, but at the uncaring attitude of the people I encountered following the tragedy.

   Compare this introduction with the introduction in the final draft. What is the effect of the narrative about Laura's death in the first version? What other differences do the two introductions have? Given Egnor's purpose, which is a more effective beginning for her essay?

6. As a reader, do you feel you have enough information to understand the actions and decisions of the individuals involved in this event? Would you like more information about what could and could not have been done by the family, friends, or staff? What would have been the effect if Egnor had provided more information?

SUGGESTIONS FOR WRITING

1. One of the remarkable qualities of this essay, aside from the story itself, is Egnor's restraint and control of her anger. This control invokes the readers' anger more powerfully than any excessive vituperation possibly could. Consider an injustice you have encountered and write an essay describing the details. Also include any change you might have undergone and analyze your present feelings. Your aim is to be detached and controlled so the injustice can speak for itself.

2. We have all been bound up in red tape at some point, though maybe not so tragically as Doris Egnor was. Set out specifically on a mission to get some information that is not easy to get. Give yourself a specific amount of time, depending on what you seek, and then write an essay describing all the details of the process, including whether you got the information in the allotted time. Try to describe vividly the people, your treatment, phone calls, and so on, so that your reader goes through exactly what you went through. Discuss what lessons might be learned from such an experience.

3. Have you ever been in a situation in which a member of your family or a close friend was hurt or threatened by another person? How did you respond? In an essay, describe the experience in detail and include your own reactions.

DIANNE EMMINGER

Point Park College
Pittsburgh, Pennsylvania
James Rosenberg, instructor

"The most important thing to me as a writer is to encourage criticism of my work and to accept it gracefully," Dianne Emminger reports. "I have done my best work when my children have shown me that my writing lacks clarity and I have revised the work until I got it right. Thinking of someone reading and understanding my writing makes me enthusiastic about my subject. It doesn't make much sense to write if my readers don't understand my ideas."

Born in Pittsburgh, Pennsylvania, in 1948, Dianne Emminger enrolled in Point Park College when her children entered elementary school. Currently a part-time computer science major and a full-time data processing supervisor, she has learned "to juggle job, family, and college." Her long-range career goal is executive management.

Asked to write an essay about something insignificant that at one time caught her attention, Emminger reports that she was sitting on a plane in Atlanta "full of frustration at my failure to begin writing" when she decided to write about the most insignificant thing she could see — the raindrops on the plane window. Several days later, while reviewing the notes she had written on the plane, she began thinking of the prismatic effect of raindrops on light and was reminded of something she had seen a few years earlier while visiting a local art gallery.

The Exhibition

It was on a dismal, rainy Sunday afternoon in a local art gallery that I   1
learned how a conscious attempt at art appreciation can, at times, render one
unaware of simple, gentle things. A large exhibition was being presented, and
the gallery was crowded. Some rather good local artists exhibited their works
there, and this was a particularly fine collection, one of the most diverse
exhibitions the gallery had ever hosted. It also drew a very diverse crowd, and
as I strolled through the spacious halls, I alternately focused my attention on
patrons and paintings.

Pearl-draped elderly women, reeking of perfume, promenaded the halls, at   2
times speaking of art, at times of their bridge games. On the wall, an extrav-
agant ballroom scene hung, displaying aristocratic beauties in flowing silk gowns.
Unkempt, long-haired men and sandal-footed women, with toddlers clinging
to their hips, nodded appreciatively at the contemporary selections. Above
them, bold brush strokes and shapeless forms brought an artist's thunderstorm

to life. A few middle-aged men in golf attire slumped dejectedly on marble benches, while their scooting children made a game out of sliding on polished floors. On a pillar hung a solitary painting of stern-faced Dutchmen, staring down from their austere meeting room, as if distracted by the commotion below.

Now, I don't profess to know anything about painting, so I like to follow 3 close behind those who do. Thus, I followed that day, hoping to learn something about art appreciation. I studied each canvas intently, trying hard to comprehend what genius there was behind the bold, blue streak transecting the yellow circle and to understand why my favorite ocean scene was unimaginative. By the time I reached the end of the fourth hall, I no longer knew what I liked and disliked, and, perhaps, I didn't care.

But as I turned the corner, there appeared a small child, a girl of about six, 4 crouched near one of the walls, playing quietly. The rain had decreased to a drizzle, and the sun had come out. The window opposite her was dotted with tiny raindrops, and each prismatic one refracted the sunlight and sent dancing, rainbow-colored lights bouncing on the gallery wall. Each clinging drop shimmied when struck by falling drizzle, and the light on the wall darted out, then back. Some droplets sent out tiny armlike appendages that touched others, and the rainbow colors kissed and parted. The heavier drops crept down the window pane, pulling others within, until their combined weight became so great that they would race, helter-skelter, down the glass. On the wall, small rainbows scurried and darted, changing speeds, changing shapes.

The group I had been following moved farther down the hall, praising a 5 nearby painting — "Such color! Such form! Such movement!" They didn't notice the child or the lights, nor did the child notice them. She was holding out a small hand watching the speckles of color scurry down a finger, up a thumb, across her palm. She removed her hat and tried to catch a rainbow inside. She twisted her head sideways and upside down to see the colors from another angle. Her eyes gleamed like the lights. Such innocence was in this child. She didn't know how the brush danced in the hand of the artist, only how the colors danced on the wall.

The crowd of connoisseurs could still be heard. "Look at this one! The 6 colors seem alive! The artist has such imagination!" The entranced child didn't look; her fingers merely traced circles around the tiny specks of color on the wall. And so she remained until, having been located by her mother, she was quickly rushed away to look at paintings, the reason for which she had been brought to the gallery.

If I could paint, I would have painted those rainbow lights, that child, the 7 wall. I would have permanently preserved the lively exhibition of colored lights that dwarfed great works of art in one young mind. And I would hang that canvas in that very same gallery for the art connoisseurs, for the sandal-footed mothers, for the perfumed bridge players, and especially for the little girl, that she might never let sophistication in art appreciation prevent her from seeing unsophisticated beauty.

QUESTIONS FOR READING AND REVISING

1. Dianne Emminger came to the art gallery to see one exhibition but saw something very different from what she expected. What does the child teach Emminger about art and beauty? How would Emminger answer the question "What is art?" Describe how Emminger learns her lesson.

2. What is Emminger's purpose? Is it to describe the exhibition, the child, or both? Or is it to tell us about her own insights from her experience? How do the introduction and the conclusion reinforce her purpose?

3. What strategies does Emminger use to bring the reader closer to her experience? For instance, how does she show the child, the art, and the gallery patrons as competing possibilities, competing exhibitions?

4. Part of the power of this essay is in its effective descriptions, its ability to put the reader in the art gallery. Select details and passages that you find especially effective.

5. Emminger reports: "This was not a difficult essay to write, but I had a great deal of difficulty with the second paragraph in which I describe the people and the paintings in the gallery. It was awkward taking the readers from one subject to another without confusing them." Do you feel that Emminger was successful? How might the paragraph be revised to be more effective?

6. Both Dianne Emminger and Paige Turner comment on works of art. How do the approaches of the two writers differ? What can a reader gain from each approach? Which do you prefer? Why?

SUGGESTIONS FOR WRITING

1. Emminger describes a perfect moment that becomes, for her, a work of art. Try to recall such a moment in your own experience. What was it that captured your attention? Write an essay describing the details of such a moment and explain its significance.

2. We all have had experiences that have changed our perceptions so that we

develop a new way of understanding something. Describe such an experience by showing not only what changed your perception but also what this change meant for you.

3. Emminger forces us to ask ourselves What is art? What is beauty? Reflect on the meaning of these questions, then write an essay in which you answer one of the questions by giving examples from your own experiences.

CHRIS GARDINIER

Brescia College
Owensboro, Kentucky
Debra L. Hussey Dixon, instructor

Chris Gardinier classifies herself as a nontraditional college freshman. After working for twelve years as a waitress, a real estate broker, and a horse breeder, she entered college in 1982 and is pursuing a degree with a double major in psychology and English. "As a child, I was alone a great deal and I turned to books for companionship," Gardinier recalls. "I was, and I am, a fast and constant reader. I still read several books a week, often beginning and ending one at a single sitting. As a child, I also developed an interest in horses and dreamed of growing up and being a breeder. I now have twenty-one Arabian horses in my barn. Besides reading books and breeding horses, I love to write. I am currently writing a book about the two things that I know best—being poor and wanting a horse."

Born in Stockton, California, in 1951, the daughter of migrant workers, Chris Gardinier knew immediately what she wanted to write about when she was asked to write an essay about a personal experience. She reports: "My early childhood as the daughter of migrant workers has been the subject of many debates with my friends on the issue of poverty versus affluence as a means of character building. I wanted to project the warmth of my childhood and the depth of my feeling for my parents. My mother still feels guilty about the circumstances of my early childhood; perhaps this essay will absolve those feelings."

The Advantage of Disadvantage

1 Our society, accustomed to affluence, looks upon financial comfort as the norm and views poverty as an unacceptable option. A child of monied parents is said to be "advantaged." Conversely, a child of poor parents is labeled "deprived." Understandably, a great amount of well-meaning pity and concern is directed at the poor souls who "follow the crops"—the migrant workers. The children of migrant workers are uneducated, underprivileged, and disadvantaged.

2 My parents followed the crops, living in the car or in a tent unless housing was provided by the grower. It was unthinkable to them that I should be "farmed out" with more stable friends or relatives and so, from infancy through my seventh year, I was a part of the migrant tide.

Those seven years are a kaleidoscope of memories. I haven't erased all of ₃ the bad. I remember my mother wrapping adhesive tape around each of her fingers after the sharp stems of thousands of cherries had cut her flesh almost to the bone. I remember evenings when my father, stiff from an old back injury, could not get off his ladder without help. I remember a Christmas when there were no presents, just a tiny, forlorn tree. But mostly, I remember the good times.

Although we lived a life devoid of material "extras," I don't remember ever ₄ being hungry. I do remember endless pots of ham hocks and beans and thick potato soup with onions and homemade bread. I remember nights in dingy kitchens in fruit camps watching Mother can endless mason jars full of peaches. In the winters, even in the really bad times, we had juicy, golden peaches, their taste no less sweet for the cut-out sections that made them unfit for fancy pack sales.

Rather than being insulated from the differences in people by invisible ₅ boundaries, I was in the midst of a child's United Nations. When Maria Lopez fed her family tacos, she fed me as well. I saw her working in the fields for several seasons and still think of her when I hear about "shiftless Mexicans." I loved my Uncle Pete. Pete rode with us sometimes from orchard to orchard. He was a big man, broad and tall, who used to swing me up above his head and call me his "baby girl child." He was the first man up the ladder in the morning and the last one out of the row in the evening. Pete was Black.

Seven years of driving up and down the West Coast, following the cycle of ₆ apples to pears, peaches to apricots, winter apples to cherries, made me feel that the whole area was mine. My childhood territory, rather than being six blocks square, encompassed six states. My neighborhood parks were Yellowstone and Sequoia and the Grand Canyon.

Yellowstone was as familiar to me as a backyard. I felt the sulphur spray of ₇ geysers and knew Old Faithful when he still performed on schedule. I laughed at playful grizzly bears and never thought to fear them. I played in meadows strewn with wildflowers, lovelier than any planned suburban garden.

At Sequoia, I marveled at the oldest living things in the world. I ran on ₈ the stumps of giant redwoods that had once served as dance floors for lumber camp residents. I galloped along shaded trails and pretended that I was a forest-dwelling sprite.

The Grand Canyon was awesome in its size and frightening in its depth. I ₉ was, however, most impressed with the sturdy donkeys and horses used to ferry visitors down the steep trails.

I didn't know why we spent so much time in the parks. What concern was ₁₀ it of mine that annual camping fees were only ten dollars?

Away from the parks and their wonders, life was still full of riches. I played 11
in the ocean, falling into waves and tasting their salt. I tormented hermit crabs
and was amazed at the pelicans. I still remember the rhyme—my introduction
to "poetry"—"A wonderful bird is a pelican; his beak can hold more than his
belly can."

Bridges had a special sound, a melody of tires on steel. We would cross the 12
Golden Gate at night, and I was always convinced that we were entering a
fairyland. Even the very name Golden Gate invoked a magical picture of an
enchanted land.

One of my favorite places was the San Diego Zoo. We spent countless days 13
wandering its pathways, leisurely, with no pressure to see everything in one
day. There was time to linger by the bears; time to wait for the lion to roar;
always "one more minute" to feed a demanding duck.

Life was for learning too—no fruit picking for my parents' child. I learned 14
to read from road signs, with an assist from Burma Shave. Highway markers
and speed limit signs taught me my numbers. My parents encouraged my
learning and bought an endless stream of workbooks.

I developed an imagination while I listened to *Gunsmoke* and *Suspense* on 15
the radio. I didn't need to see James Arness to know what Matt Dillon looked
like.

I learned about pride and honor when we reached a state of desperation. A 16
poor harvest had left us stranded in a strange town. My father, hat in hand
and shoulders slumped, borrowed ten dollars from the Red Cross. They made
it plain that it was considered a handout. I remember the jar that my mother
saved dimes and quarters and dollars in until there was ten dollars to pay back
the debt. I wish I could have seen the prune-faced do-gooder when she opened
the envelope.

That part of my life ended when I started second grade. I lived in a real 17
apartment and had a real bed, instead of the back seat of our old Studebaker.
I had permanent friends instead of orchard encounters. I had stability, security,
a place. For the first time in my young life, I felt deprived. The first seven
years were the best. I was not underprivileged nor uneducated nor disadvantaged. I was rich, in the truest sense.

QUESTIONS FOR READING AND REVISING

1. Describe Gardinier's attitude toward her childhood. What is her attitude toward
   children who grow up "advantaged" and "privileged?" What point does Gardinier make about what it means to be advantaged and privileged?

2. Gardinier creates a detailed picture of her childhood by showing us how she followed "the cycle of apples to pears, peaches to apricots, winter apples to cherries" (paragraph 6). Select details and passages in which you find especially effective description. How do Gardinier's examples support her purpose?

3. Does Gardinier balance the good and the bad memories? What is the effect of her describing most of the bad memories at the beginning of the essay? Why does she return to some bad memories in paragraph 16? What assumptions does she make about her audience?

4. Gardinier began her rough draft this way:

> I was a deprived child. I know because I have been told and because I have read it in books. All children should be deprived. None should grow up insulated and narrow, with natural curiosity unaroused and exploration limited. My parents were poor crop followers before migrant workers became a socially accepted title. It was before the days of battles and boycotts.

How would you characterize the differences between the first-draft and the final-draft introductions? How does the revised introduction more effectively prepare a reader for what follows?

5. In Gardinier's rough draft, paragraph 13 was written this way:

> Countless summer days were spent at the San Diego Zoo. I would watch the animals for hours, and wish that they were free.

Gardinier revised this paragraph to read:

> One of my favorite places was the San Diego Zoo. We spent countless days wandering its pathways, leisurely, with no pressure to see everything in one day. There was time to linger by the bears; time to wait for the lion to roar; always one more minute to feed a demanding duck.

What point does her final version make that the rough-draft paragraph did not? How does the revised paragraph better suit Gardinier's purpose?

6. Gardinier reports: "The hardest part about writing this essay was connecting all of the different thoughts and avoiding the feeling of choppiness." Review paragraphs 6–15. Was Gardinier successful at avoiding choppiness? Could these paragraphs be revised to be more effective? Try to group the details in these paragraphs into larger paragraphs by adding new topic sentences. What is the effect of your proposed revisions?

SUGGESTIONS FOR WRITING

1. Gardinier shows us how we make a mistake when we classify people according to their backgrounds. Consider the many possible ways in which you might be classified. Write an essay in which you show that although most people believe that you must be a particular type, you are really something else.

2. What central fact of your life — your background, religion, race, ethnic heritage, special talent — has influenced you most? Write an essay focusing on this influence in your life.

3. What does it mean to be educated, advantaged, and privileged? What does it mean to be uneducated, disadvantaged, and unprivileged? Write an essay exploring the meaning of any one of these terms or comparing and contrasting two of the terms.

ANNIE GLAVEN

Lasell Junior College
Newton, Massachusetts
Kenneth C. Matheson, instructor

"*I write at a cluttered desk, wearing my battered cardigan sweater, speaking aloud, and testing my thoughts,*" Annie Glaven reports. "*After writing vigorously for what seems like hours, I slump into my chair from the relief of completing one paragraph. A few more rounds of vigorous writing and I have completed my first draft. Writing is hard work. I probably average about ten drafts per paper.*"

The oldest of three children, Annie Glaven was born in Bellingham, Massachusetts, in 1963 and graduated from the local high school in 1980. She has worked as a ski instructor, as a mental health assistant at Cushing Hospital, and as an assistant in the Financial Aid Office at Lasell Junior College. Her hobbies include painting, gardening, and calligraphy. Glaven is working on an associate degree in nursing and is planning to attend medical school. At Lasell she serves as president of the student government and as the student representative on the college's Board of Trustees.

Asked to write an essay using examples, Annie Glaven chose to work with a series of examples most familiar to her from the special circumstances of her own life. As she explains: "*I wanted to clarify some of the misconceptions people have about what it is like to be handicapped and to reaffirm my own ability to do anything. Being handicapped has not excluded me from being an active participant in the mainstream of society.*"

For further questions about Annie Glaven's essay and the drafts that led to it, see pages 200–214.

What Can You Do?

I am approached quite often by people who are curious about my handicap. 1 Because the questions are so common, I should carry a tape recorder that will play, "Beep! This is a recording," and continue with, "I had my right leg amputated when I was five due to osteogenic sarcoma." However, there have been times when the tape recorder would have been of little value since the questions asked were extraordinary.

The primary motive behind children's questions is simply the need for 2 knowledge. It is imperative to offer factual information regarding my handicap. The following two examples characterize a child's need for such knowledge. A serious young girl once wanted to know, "Do they really make your legs out of trees?" After successfully masking my amusement I answered, "They only use parts of trees."

One day while completing a ski run down the Needle, at Haystack Moun-   3
tain in Vermont, I decided to break for lunch. I glided over to the ski rack at
the base of the lodge and bent over to release the binding of my ski and replace
my outriggers (adaptive poles with crutches) when I felt a tug on my ski pants.
There stood a pint-sized boy muffled to the ears who asked, "What happened
to your leg? Are you all right?" Smiling, I said that my leg had been sick and
it had to be removed so I could continue to live. At this point, his father
spotted him and yelled, "Come eat your lunch." As he waddled away, the
child murmured, "I'm glad you're O.K." The child's unsophisticated question
and his genuine concern touched me.

Unlike children, many adults are unable to see that people mislabeled   4
handicapped do accomplish everyday events as well as more significant tasks.
Once when a woman asked me about my leg and I mechanically reiterated the
story, she went on to tell me about her brother's son who was retarded. The
not so subtle comparisons between her nephew's handicap and my own caused
me to fidget and want to scream, "They amputated my leg, not my brains!"

One day, as a junior in high school, I walked into homeroom and reflected   5
back to the previous night at the harvest dance when I was crowned homecoming queen. A good friend came over to offer her congratulations. In a
hushed tone she then asked if I felt I was selected because of my leg. Initially,
I wanted to scream, "No!" But then, recalling my own first thought, I replied
that yes, I had considered the same idea when first nominated but had resolved
that whether I won or lost, the deciding vote wouldn't be dependent upon my
leg. She quickly reacted with, "Well, I'm glad you feel like this; I'm sure you're
right." From her tone and expression, I knew my friend questioned the fairness
of the decision. Feeling robbed of my chance to feel proud, I wondered how
many others felt similarly.

In my senior year of high school when I was president of the Ski Club,   6
thirty members, two chaperones, and I took a ski trip to Mt. Sunapee in New
Hampshire. We arrived at the rental shop with ample time for everyone to be
fitted with the necessary ski equipment and still be on the slopes when the
chair lifts opened. After helping everyone learn to step into their bindings and
snap on their safety straps, I guided the braver skiers over to the bunny hill
and the less brave over to the instructor's lineup. Because I have an above-
the-knee amputation, in order to avoid injury I don't wear my prosthesis when
I ski; instead, I ski with one ski and outriggers—Canadian crutches with ski
tips welded to the ends. After I stepped into my own binding and grabbed my
outriggers, a group of my closest friends and I traversed over to the chair lift
that leads to the mountain's summit. A woman stopped in front of us and,
looking at me, yelled, "Jesus Christ! Now I've seen everything! What the hell

are you trying to prove?" My friends were quicker than I to defend me. One challenged her to join me in a run down the Wild Goose, the racing trail, if she thought she could handle it. Embarrassed, the woman snowplowed over to another chair lift. I heartily thanked my friends, who continued to stew over the incident. A few minutes later on the chair lift, alone in my thoughts, I was saddened that once again I had been looked at as limited.

Since my amputation I have answered a grab bag of questions. The question that pained and provoked me the most was from a woman who asked, "What can you *do?*" I was unable to respond to this question well at that time. It was as if the countless times that I picked myself up from the pavement while learning to ride a bike, the relay races in second grade on crutches, still trying to win, the times I tried to be as confident as the girl with the smooth gait and nice wiggle when approaching a boy were rendered meaningless. The question compelled me to make a pact with myself never to retreat from any experience or challenge because of my handicap or to be influenced by the prejudice of others. Today, the integrity of the contract I made with myself remains intact, and if I were asked the same question now I would answer, "What can't I do!"

QUESTIONS FOR READING AND REVISING

1. What was Glaven's specific purpose in writing this essay? What messages does she intend to leave with a reader not only about herself but also about other people with handicaps?

2. Although Glaven writes out of her own deeply felt experiences and understandings, how does she avoid slipping into self-pity? Describe her tone in this essay. How does Glaven's "contract" with herself influence her tone?

3. Glaven categorizes people's responses to her handicap by the type of question they ask. Why is this an effective organizational strategy? Is there a logic behind the order in which she presents people's questions?

4. Glaven relies on the use of dialogue to illustrate many of her ideas. Find specific instances of dialogue and explain why they are effective. What would have been the effect if she had tried to make her point without dialogue?

5. Glaven reports that she wanted to convey the intent of strangers and friends as well as her own thoughts. Does she give a balanced view? If not, does she need to? How does she account for her audience's biases?

6. How do you react to handicapped people? Do you feel guilty about your reaction? How does your reaction change as you get to know such people better? What kind of questions might you ask Glaven?

7. Paragraphs 2 and 3 deal with children's questions. Do you think paragraph 2 ends too abruptly? Can you suggest a way in which the two paragraphs could be linked with a smoother introduction to the examples and a parallel treatment of the examples?

SUGGESTIONS FOR WRITING

1. Glaven shows us the reactions and questions people have had about her handicap. Consider some aspect of your life — your ethnic background, religion, looks, hobbies, and so on — that has raised questions. Using a series of examples to illustrate the types of questions you have been asked, write an essay showing the effect of these questions on you.

2. Think of a personal accomplishment that required great determination. Recount in detail the steps or stages in your struggle and describe your feelings and your sense of self after you achieved your goal. Use concrete details and examples in your essay.

3. It has been said that a civilization (or a city) can be judged by how well its buildings accommodate people with handicaps. On this basis, judge your college campus or city and write an essay setting forth your judgment and giving concrete examples as evidence.

WILLIAM G. HILL

Northwest Mississippi Junior College, DeSoto Center
Senatobia, Mississippi
Sally A. Askew, instructor

"I believe that a writer needs to write from his own experiences and know what he is writing about," William Hill says. Asked to write a description of a place, Hill chose a place he knows well—the pool hall in his hometown, Ripley, Mississippi. Although the pool hall no longer exists, Hill didn't want the place to be forgotten, and he wanted his readers to understand something about the culture of rural Mississippi. Born in 1948, Hill has worked as a factory laborer, a printer, an insurance agent, and a security guard at an Internal Revenue Service Center. He has two sons, is a Little League coach, and intends to write and teach school after he graduates from college. About the conditions necessary for writing, Hill reports: "Some people find quiet necessary to be able to write; I don't. I have two children and live almost directly in the landing pattern of the Memphis International Airport, so noises do not bother me. What I need is time, periods from two to three hours where I don't have to be bothered with anything else. Of course, with work, school, and raising a family, time is sometimes difficult to find."

Returning Home

The front door was always propped open in the summertime with a doorstop 1 made from a split two-by-four. Thus it was always difficult to say for sure whether the loafers congregated around the checkerboard were inside or out on the seventy-five-year-old sidewalk that circled the town square.

The windows were washed every year or two, but they were usually tinted 2 with a residue of nicotine from too much smoke in a closed room. They were painted with a sign that read, "RECREATIONAL CLUB ROOM." We all figured that the sign painter was paid by the letter and made more from that sign than if he had painted "Pool Hall."

Whenever I walked in the door, I usually first saw old man Hall and Mr. 3 Monroe playing checkers. Sometimes other people played, but if they did, they usually played one of them. Mr. Hall never took his hat off, and he always had a filter-tipped Kool in one side of his mouth and a toothpick in the other. Mr. Monroe was a little man who wore thick glasses. He usually beat most of the people he played checkers with, but no one really ever kept count.

On the other side of the room was a counter with a glass case on top. From 4

73

behind the counter, J.M. Holly, the man who owned the place, sold candy and cold drinks. He had the widest selection of cigarettes in town. It was the only place I knew of that sold Picayunes. It was also a handy place to stop if one needed a can of lighter fluid, a fishing reel, razor blades, or a hunting license.

The pool tables were in a line side by side from the front to the back of 5 the long, narrow building. The first one was the biggest, and the best snooker players used it. Beyond it were the other tables used by lesser players, except for the last one. This was the bank's pool table, used only by the best players in the county.

The place had an atmosphere of its own. The smell was a mixture of stale 6 smoke, oil from the floor, and, in the winter, fumes from the heater. It didn't smell bad exactly, but it was as unique as the sound. On Friday and Saturday nights the jukebox blasted out Buck Owens, Credence Clearwater Revival, and Ace Cannon. It was beer-drinking music played in a place that sold no beer.

The people were always friendly except for an occasional drunk who got 7 mean. They were an odd lot of folks. Some college students home for the weekend from Ole Miss were there, and also a few rednecks with their blue jeans tucked in the tops of their boots — cowboy boots with gold and white eagles. Old men came in in the early afternoon to cuss the Republicans and stain the walls behind the spittoons with tobacco juice.

There were never many fights. Every time one got started, J.M. would call 8 Possum. When Possum got there, J.M. would say, "Possum, pick up that pool table." Possum would lift one end of the table off the floor with one arm. J.M. would then tell the boys who were about to fight that Possum did not like violence. As a rule, the boys found a more peaceable way to settle their differences.

The last time I was back in Ripley, the place was closed down. Some 9 carpenters were working in the building. I was told that it was being remodeled into a restaurant, one of those fancy places where people wear ties. I couldn't get very sad about my old hangout not being there anymore; I had left first. I did wonder what happened to Possum. And I wondered where high school boys went to warm up after a snowball fight when school was out because of snow. I would like to know where people go now to listen to Cardinals' baseball games on hot summer afternoons and where people who want them get Picayune cigarettes.

I had heard the expression "You can't go home again" all my life. I didn't 10 understand it until the last time I tried.

QUESTIONS FOR READING AND REVISING

1. William Hill creates a picture of his hometown by focusing on the pool hall. He reports: "The original intent of this essay was to describe a place, a building and what was in it. In the course of writing, however, it changed to a description of not only a place but also a time." What did the pool hall represent to Hill as a teenage boy growing up in Ripley, Mississippi? What does the pool hall represent to him now as an adult returning to his hometown?

2. From Hill's description we learn a lot about the pool hall. "It was the kind of handy place to stop if one needed a can of lighter fluid, a fishing reel, razor blades, or a hunting license." Find specific details and explain what they tell us about the place and the people who inhabit the room. To what senses do the details appeal?

3. It is very easy to be sentimental and romantic about places and people from our childhood. What is Hill's attitude toward the place and people he writes about? How does he avoid sentimentality?

4. This essay begins with a description of the front door and "the loafers congregated around the checkerboard." Study the structure of this essay. Why do you think Hill structured the piece as he did?

5. Hill begins his description immediately, without any introductory comments or thesis statement. What is the effect of beginning this way? Is there a thesis sentence anywhere in the essay?

6. In a rough draft, Hill's conclusion was written this way:

   > I had heard the expression "You can't go home again" all
   > my life. I didn't understand it until the last time I tried. If
   > it has been torn down and replaced with a restaurant, then
   > it is true that you can never go home again.

   Hill revised the conclusion by dropping the last sentence. Did Hill improve his conclusion by cutting the last sentence? What effect does the revised conclusion have on you as a reader?

SUGGESTIONS FOR WRITING

1. What does the expression "You can't go home again" mean to you? Write an essay in which you reflect on the meaning of the expression for you. You might want to think about Hill's statement "I couldn't get very sad about my hangout not being there anymore; I had left first" (paragraph 9). What are the implications of "leaving first?"

2. Select a place in your hometown that represents the color and texture of the town. Write an essay focusing on this place and show how it represents what the town is.

3. Observe a place — a street corner, bar, park, pool hall, and the like — where people "hang out." What is it about the place that encourages people to congregate there? What special meaning does the place have? Write a description of the place.

RITA HOLLINGSWORTH

North Idaho College
Coeur D'Alene, Idaho
M. Fay Wright, instructor

"*After an uneventful childhood, I married at twenty and divorced at thirty-nine,*" Rita Hollingsworth reports. "*During those eighteen years my husband and I chased the American dream. I put him through college by working at a bank. We had three daughters and together we bore the burden of a mortgage on the house of our dreams. I gardened, sewed, cleaned, and danced. Then we sold our house and paid our bills. He took the security that we had accumulated and I took the kids that we had spoiled. Now I am working again to put someone through college, but this time it is me. My career goals remain somewhat unclear. With good health, mild winters, and appliances that keep chugging along, someday I hope to earn a degree in journalism and chase my own personal dream.*"

Born in Modesto, California, in 1943, Rita Hollingsworth first recognized the writer within her when she wrote an essay persuading her sixth-grade teacher to make her the school crossing guard and her teacher selected her to be the guard. Since her early school years, Hollingsworth has nurtured her interest in writing primarily through letters to family and friends. "*Writing is fun, and while it is the hardest thing that I do, it is also the thing that has given me the most pleasure,*" Hollingsworth explains. "*I have found writing to be my personal sorting tool. I write to organize, finalize, and give permanence to my ideas, feelings, and experiences. Writing is the best way I have found to share my story with others.*" Hollingsworth's essay concerns a subject she feels quite strongly about: her garden.

Zero Planting

Tucked away in the corner of my cellar, dimly illuminated by a naked, 1 swaying bulb, sit row upon row of dust-laden mason jars. These once filled but long unused jars are befriended in their dejection by two huge blue enameled kettles and one nearly new gleaming stainless steel pressure canner. These dusty relics are mementos of my gardening years. Seeing them, I am reminded that after hours of planting, nurturing, and harvesting, a gardener's reward is a bountiful array of fresh, succulent produce that for taste and color cannot be equaled by any that is purchased at an uptown supermarket. But while it is true that Home-Grown-Picked-at-the-Peak vegetables are unbeatable, it has been my unfortunate experience to find that an overabundant supply of table-ready vegetables can be frustrating, exhausting, and costly.

The first year that I gardened I found that the prospect of munching an 2
assortment of crispy, colorful greens tempted me to select four varieties of
lettuce seed at my local farm and garden store. I began to plant seeds from
packets of sturdy Romaine, classy Red Leaf, hardy Black Seeded Simpson, and
the true epicurean delight, Buttercrunch. My planting continued until each
of the empty seed packets stood guard at the head of a straight, tidy row. I
was proudly surveying my handiwork when my neighbor Louise happened by.
Louise smiled and her eyes sparkled when she said, "It's clear that you don't
know how much lettuce there is in a bunch." Undaunted by her smugness, I
set about the business of my garden. I tended, weeded, thinned, and watered
my red, green, yellow, and variegated crop. Suddenly, on the twentieth of
June, one hundred and ninety-seven tufts of lettuce were ready for my too-
small salad bowl. My family ate salad oiled, wilted, tossed, and chilled. I
decorated plates, platters, and bowls with it. The kids took it to the park and
fed it to the ducks. Louise and all the neighbors accepted a dazzling variety of
my crunchy lettuce leaves. My husband took bags of it to the office. I carted
it off to our local nursing home. On the thirtieth of June when the remaining
thirty-two plants formed stunning seed pods, turned bitter, and died, I was
thrilled. Smarter and thinner, I relegated the unusable fruit of my labor to the
compost pile.

With the experience of all that lettuce behind me, I began to keep a nervous 3
eye on my fifteen robust tomato plants. In mid-July, after picking my first sun-
ripened tomato, I began to relax. The acidy tang of slices cut from that firm,
juicy tomato made our hamburgers a gourmet's delight. Daily the children and
I wandered through our viny backyard jungle and selected one or two of the
fruits that the summer heat had fired red. Soon, though, the stifling stillness
of the August sun accelerated the ripening process. We ate tomatoes whole,
sliced, diced, and chopped. I sprinkled thick slices with Parmesan and broiled
them until the cheese was crusted; I stuffed them with tuna; Louise and all
the neighbors got some; I took them to the office and to the nursing home.
Then one afternoon, while returning from my most recent delivery, I bought
a copy of *It's Sooooo EZ to Preserve Tomatoes*. In my overheated, steamy kitchen
I sauced, juiced, souped, relished, and canned twenty bushel baskets of my
precious vine-ripened tomatoes. The cost of the experience, not including
McDonald's Quarter Pounders on canning days, was eighty-eight crisp, hard-
earned dollars.

Even after I spent a fortune on the necessary canning paraphernalia, dealing 4
with an overabundant supply of tomatoes was as easy as slipping a slug off a
wet vine compared to unloading zucchini. I visited Louise, the neighbors, the
nursing home, the office, and the ducks, but I could not get rid of even the

moistest, firmest, tenderest fingerettes of this summer squash. The very people who had willingly accepted my offerings of lettuce and tomatoes eyed me coldly as they explained, "A little of that stuff goes a long way." One lady, after refusing my offering of a bag of squash, gave me two tins of canned zucchini to sample. She told me that she had bought them on impulse at "three for a dollar" and that I was very welcome to them. After I ate the squash from those cans I learned that God intended people to eat zucchini fresh. What I still haven't learned is, if such a little bit of squash can satisfy so many, why on earth did God make zucchini plants so darned prolific? I considered myself very lucky when I came across a book that was written by a lady who must have pondered the same question. She named her book *101 Ways to Camouflage Zucchini,* and it became my bible. I baked, fried, stuffed, pickled, ground, and chopped zucchini. I buried it in cookies, cakes, muffins, relish, and casseroles. I even pretended that it was pineapple from Hawaii, and I layered it in jars and canned it. The madness ended when the children refused to taste anything that I served them unless I knelt at the table and swore on my rumpled cookbook that it was not laced with zucchini.

After that first summer of frustrating, exhausting, and costly gardening I 5 knew that I was forever hooked on homegrown vegetables, but I also realized that I had to come up with a gardening plan that yielded less surplus and more profit. Each successive year that I gardened brought me closer to the perfect ratio of the required number of plants to the existing number of people in my family. Then, finally, I developed a truly delightful gardening plan that I named "Zero Planting." I threw away my shovel and my hoe. I stopped buying seeds, manure, and bug spray. I gave up gardening and I became a friendly patio-mint-julep sipper who never got tired or frustrated. And since "Zero Planting" freed me to accept offerings of delectable produce from my grateful neighbors who still indulged in zealous overplanting, I operated from a position of pure profit. Today when my tired neighbors lug over their surplus homegrown vegetables, I always reward them with my thanks and one of my famous mint juleps.

QUESTIONS FOR READING AND REVISING

1. Rita Hollingsworth learned that "an overabundant supply of table-ready vegetables can be frustrating, exhausting, and costly." Define the phases of Hollingsworth's changing attitude toward her garden. Give examples from the essay to explain each step of Hollingsworth's progress from committed gardener to committed julep drinker.

2. It is easy to be smug and self-satisfied when we learn something we feel our neighbors haven't learned. Does Hollingsworth avoid being smug? What is her attitude toward herself, her garden, her neighbors, and her mint juleps? Cite specific passages to support your answers.

3. Hollingsworth takes a routine topic and offers us an unusual, entertaining picture of her world as a gardener. What makes her essay fresh? How do her repeated references to Louise, her neighbors, the children, the office, and the nursing home help create her world for readers?

4. In her rough draft, Hollingsworth's introduction was written this way:

> After hours of nurturing and harvesting, a gardener's reward is a bountiful array of fresh, succulent produce. For taste and color these "picked-at-the-peak" vegetables cannot be equaled by those purchased at the local Safeway. It has been my unfortunate experience, however, that an overabundant supply of table-ready vegetables can be frustrating, exhausting, and costly.

What are the differences between the rough-draft introduction and the final-draft introduction? Hollingsworth reports: "I wanted my readers to laugh at my hard work, but I also wanted them to feel the enjoyment that I had known." Is Hollingsworth's revised introduction more successful in accomplishing that purpose? Why or why not?

5. In her rough draft, Hollingsworth wrote her conclusion this way:

> It has taken me several years to come up with the correct ratio of plants to people for profitable planting. I call this method "Zero Planting." Since utilizing this plan, I never get tired or frustrated. Zero planting has provided me with pure profit and has freed me to accept offerings of produce from my grateful neighbors who still indulge in zealous overplanting.

How does the revised conclusion more successfully tie together the various ideas in the essay?

SUGGESTIONS FOR WRITING

1. Think about a project (in your lessons, a hobby, or a club) into which you put the same kind of energy Hollingsworth invested in her garden. Write an essay explaining your experience, including your present attitude toward the project

as well as an evaluation of how you have changed (or not changed) as a result of the experience.

2. Hollingsworth describes how her experience with gardening didn't turn out as she expected. Think of an experience that didn't turn out as you expected it would. What were your expectations? What was the reality? Write an essay in which you show the significance of your experience by contrasting how you planned for the experience and how it actually turned out.

BARBARA D. HOWELL

Yuba College
Marysville, California
Timothy May, instructor

At the time she wrote "Survival and the Pig," Barbara Howell was a sergeant in the United States Air Force, stationed at Beale Air Force Base in California. At the same time, she managed the apartment complex she lived in, jogged "religiously" during her lunch hour, and in her "spare" time rode horses and motorcycles, prepared for her private pilot's license, and studied at nearby Yuba Community College. With six months to go before her discharge, Barbara Howell planned to stay in California to complete her degree before returning home to rural Blackshear, Georgia, where she was born in 1958, to pursue a law degree.

Asked to write an essay detailing a process, Howell wrote the first draft of "Survival and the Pig" in "one sitting of about nine hours on a cold, rainy Saturday." But then she reread and rewrote the essay several more times. "Revision is everything to me," she explains. "That's when I beat my brain for more logical, coherent sentences and when I trample the dictionary. I always feel that there is something else that I can do to revise my work."

For further questions on Barbara Howell's essay, see page 243.

Survival and the Pig

The pig jumped up! He tried to run away as blood squirted everywhere. 1
Tackling the pig, I sat upon him with knife in hand. Soon I had control and could make the slit at the throat bigger, letting the blood gush out more freely. The blood ran out steadily with every last heartbeat.

The scene described above was a typical beginning for a pig-killing ritual 2
that I watched every winter until I was old enough to take part in the process myself. Being a farm girl from a rural community in Blackshear, Georgia, I witnessed and participated in this annual ritual until I left my family's small farm four years ago. The process of the pig killing was very important for the whole family. The pig is a symbol of wealth and security; and rightly so, for there is nothing, I mean nothing, wasted from the slaughter of a pig. Every part is eaten or used in some manner or fashion. Also, a pig can be sold for ready cash if hard times hit, and since the winter always seems the worst for family finances, the animal can be like money in the bank.

The pig killings were always done in the cold months: November, Decem- 3
ber, January, and February. So November and December were the best months

for my family; these months insured fresh pork on Thanksgiving and Christmas. Since the pigs were killed, cleaned, and cut up outside, the temperature had to be at least forty degrees; fresh pork spoils very fast. Another problem the cold abated was the blowflies that are so populous in the summer months. Only a few flies would be left by November; these you could destroy before they deposited their eggs or maggots on the meat. Cold weather, then, had many values as well as faults.

The cold weather signified something else besides the season for the butch- 4
ering of animals and for the celebration of the holidays. The crops that we had struggled over all spring, summer, and fall had been harvested and stored away or sold. The fields where the tobacco, corn, and sweet potatoes had grown were burnt to the ground. Then the beautiful black, sandy soil was plowed under. The dirt would lie idle, neither giving up any of her stature nor taking away any of ours. She was left alone to replenish her fertility. The winter had come.

Yet the idealism of farming would slip out of my mind when the first squeal 5
of a harassed pig would reach my ears. Then I would know it was time for my part in the process. My first job was to clean out the boilerhouse. The eighty-gallon cast-iron boiler had to be washed out with lye soap, then rinsed out thoroughly. Dipping the water out with a lard can took an awfully long time. The boiler had been built off the ground with fire bricks as its base. It looked like a built-in barbecue stand that is frequently seen at beaches and national parks, but with a big kettle built in the middle. I constructed a fire under the boiler, then poured forty gallons of water in. As soon as the water started to boil, I pulled the fire out of the boiler's furnace. The water would boil for a long time then. I ran to the house to tell everyone that we were ready. We would all go to the pen to kill the pig and drag him back to the boilerhouse.

We would arrive at the pigpen just minutes after the water started to boil. 6
My daddy and Uncle Rass would catch the pig and tie his legs up. Daddy would grab his ears and hold his head slightly off the ground, so that my Uncle Rass could shove a tub under the pig's neck. I always made the incision into the pig's throat. We would then wait five or ten minutes until all the blood dripped out and the heart stopped beating. My mamma would then take the blood-filled tub back to the house to make blood pudding and sausage.

After we made sure that Mamma got into the house with her heavy load, 7
we would begin. Dragging the 150-pound pig to the boilerhouse was not easy. Daylight would be just peeking out when we would string the pig up by his hind legs. The rope would be attached to a movable pulley at the top of the boilerhouse. Then we would place a two-by-four across the boiler and position the pig in the middle of the board. Slowly we would let his upper body slide

into the simmering water. But this was only for a few minutes to loosen the hair. The stench from the freshly killed pig was stifling. The air was so cold, clean, and brisk that it would tingle my nose as ginger ale does, but now neither I nor the dogs would want any part of this dead animal.

Then the pig would be ready. We would lift him out of the water and steady 8 his body on the board. With dull butter knives and cold, naked hands we would scrape and pluck the hairy bristles off the pig, paying close attention to the head.

Soon Mamma would come out and inspect our work. "The pig is clean 9 enough to cut up," she would yell. On getting approval, we would move the pig from the boilerhouse to the open shed. A big number-ten galvanized wash-tub (used by the children to take baths) would be placed under his head. With a knife, my daddy cut the pig from his tail down the middle of his stomach, laying open the wound. The innards would fall out neatly; next Daddy would cut the head off and place it in the tub also.

It was now my mamma's job to go through the tub and pick out what would 10 be needed. It seemed nothing was wasted. The brain was taken from the head to be scrambled with eggs and pickled. Then the head was cooked until tender to make hog's head cheese. Mamma would make a stew with dumplings out of the liver, heart, and lung. The intestines were cleaned and readied to fill with sausage. Nothing was wasted.

As Mamma would work feverishly on her task, Daddy would finish cutting 11 up the carcass. All of the meat but one shoulder and the feet would be taken to the abattoir to be cured.

Throughout all these procedures I cannot think of any one thing that was 12 thrown away, except maybe the bristles, which sometimes were saved for the making of brooms. Nothing at the time of the slaughter seemed more important than the pig. He was our security for the long winter months when the fields yielded no crops.

Now as I look back on the pig-killing process, it conjures up vivid memories 13 of a more simplistic lifestyle, a lifestyle that I seem to have lost either to the fast pace of modern society or to time itself. The past sense of security I felt then can never be retrieved in this life, at least not as I am leading it now. For age has brought complexity that will not allow me to return to the golden days of my memories.

QUESTIONS FOR READING AND REVISING

1. What significance does Barbara Howell attribute to the ritual of killing a pig? When and how does she signal that significance to her readers? What is the purpose of her essay?

2. Howell presents a detailed picture of a ritualized process. What is her vantage point for describing this process? Where and how is her point of view established?

3. What is Howell's attitude toward killing the pig? Is she disgusted by it? Does she treat it sentimentally? If not, how does she avoid these attitudes? Does her attitude remain consistent throughout the essay? If not, when and how does it change and with what effect?

4. What specifically does Howell assume about her readers' knowledge of the process of killing a pig? In paragraphs 3 and 4 how does she account for her sense of her readers' familiarity with her subject? Why are these two paragraphs not simply digressions from the forward movement of the essay?

5. Which part of Howell's description of the process of killing a pig is most detailed and vivid? Does she always give her readers adequate information to understand the process she describes? Point to specific passages that might be strengthened with more information.

6. What makes Howell's first two paragraphs effective? How do they successfully introduce her purpose in writing the essay? What devices does she use that successfully create a transition between the two paragraphs? Find other transitions that could be strengthened.

7. Howell notes that in preparing this essay, "the ending gave me the most trouble. The endings in all my essays seem to have the same affliction. I have a tendency to leave the reader hanging; either that or the ending violates the unity." Howell's previous drafts ended with paragraph 12, but in the final draft she added paragraph 13 in which she returns to the present to comment on the overall importance of the process of killing the pig. Analyze the advantages and disadvantages of this addition and decide, based on her purpose, point of view, and tone in the previous paragraphs, whether Howell should or should not have made it.

8. In preparing the final draft, Howell changed the word *champagne* to *ginger ale* in the last sentence in paragraph 7. What do you think motivated her to make this change?

SUGGESTIONS FOR WRITING

1. In your childhood, what rituals did you and your family participate in each year? Write an essay describing with as much detail as possible the specific occasion for one of your family's rituals as well as narrating the sequence of steps in the process. Explain both why that ritual was important to you as a child and how you view the ritual today. What did you learn—either positively or negatively—from having participated in the ritual?

2. In an essay, describe in detail the process of preparing and eating a meal in

which every member of the family participates (such as Thanksgiving dinner). Describe as accurately as possible the precise nature of the process as well as the exact sensual and emotional experience involved.

3. Howell's essay equates survival with killing, an act which in this instance most of us accept without much reflection. Write an essay examining the total "cost" of the food we eat, including the killing of animals as well as the living and working conditions of workers at every stage of the food-production process. Chris Gardinier's essay "The Advantage of Disadvantage" might provide some special insights into this issue.

PATRICIA KLEIN

Gustavus Adolphus College
St. Peter, Minnesota
Luke M. Reinsma, instructor

"I love to write, but I seem to spend a lot of time avoiding writing," Patricia Klein reveals. "I think of all kinds of things that I just have to do. I clean, do laundry, call my friends, or bake something. But usually even when I am trying to avoid writing, I end up thinking about my topic the whole time I am doing something else. By the time I finally sit down to write, I usually have some good ideas of what I want to say."

Born in Marshall, Minnesota, in 1962, Patricia Klein is majoring in psychology, enjoys working with children, and plans to become a school psychologist.

Klein was asked to write a research paper and reports: "I chose the subject of sex-role stereotyping in children's literature and television shows because I wanted to write about a current topic that dealt with children. I had been reading a lot about how sex roles have changed and I wanted to see if in fact this change was visible in children's literature and television shows. My goal was to write a clear, readable, and interesting paper that included some new observations of my own instead of just putting together what other people have found out." Indeed, in reading Klein's essay we have a sense of a writer who is independent, eager, and inquisitive. She isn't satisfied with the information she has found in the library, and she combines her library research with original observations to investigate and confirm her thesis.

Saturday Morning Sexism

Several Saturday mornings ago, at 6:30 A.M. on NBC, the Smurfs—Brainy, Hefty, Handy, and Smurfette—climbed into the mountains to find a magic snow flower. Unfortunately, the Abominable Snowbeast spotted them, captured Smurfette, and made her his princess. Frightened, of course, Smurfette cried. Speaking sweetly and gently, every sentence beginning with "ooh," she begged the Snowbeast to let her go. At last, the rest of the Smurfs were able to rescue Smurfette by throwing snowballs at the Snowbeast.[1]

After the suffragists' active campaigns, the passage of the Nineteenth Amendment, the temporary equality brought about by the world wars, and the current fight for the ERA, it is unbelievable that such sex-role stereotyping still continues in our society. But it does. Beginning with Abigail Adams, who pressed her husband to represent women's rights at the Continental Congress in 1777, women have been fighting for equality for over two hundred years. But still, despite the passage of the Equal Employment Opportunity Act of

---

[1] NBC *The Smurfs*, 4 Apr. 1982.

1972 and the Equal Credit Opportunity Act of 1974, the Equal Rights Amendment has failed in its latest attempt at ratification.[2] The struggle for equality
continues.

And it will continue even longer, until adults begin to realize the long-   3
lasting effects of sex stereotyping on children. At an early age, children con-
struct a picture of sex roles by learning from the most powerful mediators of
our society — parents, teachers, books, and television.[3] The sex roles later
"affect personality characteristics, such as compliance, cognitive development,
and spatial and verbal skills."[4] Once children have grown up believing that
girls have one set of characteristics and boys another, it becomes difficult for
them, as adults, to accept — much less fight for — equality.

It is the primary purpose of this paper to focus not on the effects of sex-role   4
stereotyping but on the causes: on ways in which literature and television
programs create sex-role stereotypes. In order to fully appreciate the impact
literature and television have on sex-role stereotypes, we will first look briefly
at some of the other causes of sex-role stereotyping. Then we will examine
how literature and television programs present sex roles and what children
learn from this presentation. Finally, we will discuss how this stereotyping of
children can be eliminated.

As soon as a baby is born, the news — not just that a baby has been born   5
but that a baby girl or baby boy has been born — travels from obstetrician and
nurse to parents and then on to family members and friends. And almost
immediately, the parents' sexist beliefs begin to separate the young child's
world into pink and blue, female and male. Yet at birth, there seem to be very
few differences between boys and girls. In fact, boys are typically more different
from each other in their behavior than they are different from girls, and the
same is true for girls.[5] Nevertheless, boys and girls are perceived and treated
differently from the beginning of life. By the close of infancy, differential
treatment, play materials, sex-typed clothing, and observations of the role of
gender in society together teach children to identify themselves, too, as stereotyped girls and boys.

Thus, as early as three years old, children begin to choose toys and future   6

[2]Matilda Butler and William Paisley, *Women and the Mass Media* (New York: Human Sciences
Press, 1980), pp. 23–24.
[3]Jeanne Brooks-Gunn and Wendy Schenupp Mathews, *He and She: How Children Develop
Their Sex-Role Identity* (Englewood Cliffs, N.J.: Prentice-Hall, 1979), p. 297.
[4]Dianne N. Ruble, Terry Balahan, and Joel Cooper, "Gender Constancy and the Effects of
Sex-Typed Televised Toy Commercials," *Child Development*, 52 (June 1981), 672.
[5]Butler and Paisley, p. 281.

occupations that reflect stereotypes: boys like trucks, girls like dolls; boys want to be doctors, girls want to be nurses.[6] Four-year-old boys and girls at play reveal their stereotypes: mothers stay at home taking care of babies, cooking, cleaning, and being somewhat helpless and inept; fathers work in offices where they talk on telephones, bring home ice cream, help mommy when asked, and take control in emergency situations.[7] By age six, children believe that sex-typed activities are inflexible and inevitable. Even if their own mothers might be doctors or their own doctors female, children will insist that men are doctors and women nurses.[8] Because children with many different family backgrounds accept these stereotypes, there must be outside mediators influencing how they think. And for most children, these outside influences include television and literature, which, despite our best intentions and despite some changes in sex-role stereotyping during the past decade, continue to confuse myth and reality.

As children grow, so do their worlds. Soon a child is influenced not only   7
by parents but also by schools, teachers, peers, television, and literature. During the past few years, schools have been reducing sex-role stereotyping. Instead of having boys take shop courses and play football and girls take home economics and gymnastics, the schools allow and even encourage both boys and girls to try all kinds of classes.[9] Outwardly, therefore, schools do not seem to promote sex-role stereotypes.

But they still do. Part of the problem is simply that the majority of school   8
principals and administrators are men, while most of the teachers are women. Men work at high-level professions while women are stationed in low-level professions. Another hidden problem is teachers' attitudes toward pupils. Because most teachers were brought up with sex-role stereotypes, they often — whether consciously or unconsciously — reflect these stereotypes onto their pupils. And the pupils themselves also encourage sex-role stereotypes. Most childhood peer groups are either all-boy or all-girl. By limiting their groups to their own sex, children tend to reinforce the sex role they have already adopted.[10] Still, although families, schools, teachers, and peers are all important in establishing sex-role stereotypes, the influence of television and literature is even more pervasive.

Much of the knowledge children gain comes through the use of literature.   9
As babies, children hear a variety of stories — often including such classic

[6]Butler and Paisley, p. 281.
[7]Brooks-Gunn and Mathews, pp. 165–66.
[8]Suzanne J. Kessler and Wendy McKenna, *Gender: An Ethromethodological Approach* (New York: Wiley, 1978), p. 102.
[9]Kessler and McKenna, p. 192.
[10]Kessler and McKenna, p. 202.

favorites as *Grimm's Fairy Tales*. Fairy tales such as "Cinderella," "Snow White and the Seven Dwarfs," and "Little Red Riding Hood" may have enchanted children for many years, but they have cheated them for just as long. Although men play some wicked roles, eighty percent of the evil characters in *Grimm's Fairy Tales*, like Cinderella's stepmother, are female. And even the heroines —weak, helpless, suffering, childlike—are portrayed unfavorably. Inevitably, we find women in these tales as trusting and innocent as Snow White and Little Red Riding Hood; as domestically industrious as Cinderella; or as helpless as any of these three heroines.[11]

Nursery rhymes are no better. They vary from Peter the Pumpkin Eater, keeping his wife in a pumpkin shell; to little boys, made out of snips and snails and puppy dogs' tails (while little girls are made of sugar and spice and everything nice); to Little Miss Muffet, frightened by a spider. The girls tend sheep, care for children, raise flowers, and wear dainty clothes; the boys go fishing, eat pies with their thumbs, jump nimbly and quickly, and take their animals to market.[12]

And when children grow older, they go to school and begin to read of new storybook friends—of boys who engage in sports, play with the dog, and build birdhouses; of girls who play with dolls and help mother cook and clean.[13] True, some publishers have now begun to recognize this problem of sex-role stereotyping and have begun to change their texts. One such text, *Helicopters and Gingerbread*, shows both men and women in the traditional male roles of police, pilots, business executives, and fire fighters. And both men and women are shown asking for help in dangerous situations.[14] But other publishers have not yet begun to change. Father is still solving the problems he solved thirty years ago while mother is still grocery shopping. Men still become policemen and manage the money, and women still stay home.[15]

Once children have learned to read, they go beyond their textbooks and explore the popular books written just for them. In order to see how these books portray men and women, I decided to visit the St. Peter Public Library. One book I found, *The Very Worst Thing*, tells of the adventures of a little boy on his first day in a new school. He arrives at school wearing the new sweater his mother has knit for him and is greeted by his teacher, Miss Pruce, and his male principal. At recess, the girls jump rope and toss a ball back and

10

11

12

[11]Kessler and McKenna, p. 201.

[12]Eulalie Osgood Grover, ed., *Mother Goose* (Northbrook, Ill.: Hubbard Press, 1971).

[13]Women on Words and Images, *Dick and Jane as Victims* (Princeton, N.J.: Carolingian Press, 1972); Helen M. Robinson, Marion Monroe, and A. Sterl Artley, *Fun with Our Friends* (Chicago: Scott, Foresman, 1962).

[14]Theodore Clymer et al., *Helicopters and Gingerbread* (Lexington, Mass.: Ginn, 1976).

[15]Carl B. Smith and Ronald Wardhaugh, *Magic Times* (New York: Macmillan, 1980).

forth while the boys choose football teams and establish a tree house club. For show-and-tell that day, Henry, his new friend, brings a snake and some mice. But Alice shows her foreign dolls, and Elizabeth demonstrates how to make fudge with Rice Krispies. In another book, *Come Back, Amelia Bedelia,* Amelia is fired from her job of baking for Mrs. Rogers, so she tries to find work as a beautician, a seamstress, a file clerk, and an office girl for a doctor. After trying all of these jobs unsuccessfully, she goes back to Mrs. Rogers and gets back her old job by making cream puffs. The rest of the books I looked at contained similar sex stereotypes—boys wear jeans and T-shirts, set up lemonade stands, and play broomball, while girls wear dresses, play dress-up, and jump rope. Men are businessmen, soldiers, veterinarians, and truck drivers. Women are housewives, teachers, and witches who make love potions for girls wanting husbands.[16]

More and more authors may modify their habits, though, as they learn of   13 the studies that have recently linked sex-role stereotypes with the models presented in children's literature. In one such study, only egalitarian stories were read to four- and five-year-olds for one week. Afterward, the children were less likely to say that one type of behavior was more acceptable for men or women.[17] And in another study, nursery school children heard stories about a boy and girl in which (1) the girl achieved while the boy stood around and watched or needed help; (2) the boy achieved while the girl stood around or needed help; and (3) no achievement-related behavior appeared. Afterward, girls were more persistent in solving a difficult puzzle after a story about a girl achieving, and boys were more persistent after hearing about a boy achieving.[18] From these studies, it does seem as though a character's sex and behavior do influence the way children develop their own sex-role stereotypes.

But because children spend so much time watching television, these models   14 have even more influence on the sex-role stereotyping than literary characters. By the time the average American child graduates from high school, she or he has spent more time watching television than attending school, playing, eating, or reading. The only activity that has consumed more time than tele-

---

[16]These books were randomly selected from the St. Peter Public Library in St. Peter, Minnesota: Berthe Amoss, *The Very Worst Thing* (New York: Parents' Magazine Press, 1972); Craig Bertiger, *Follow Me, Everybody* (Garden City, N.Y.: Doubleday, 1968); A. Delaney, *The Butterfly* (New York: Delacorte, 1977); John Feilen, *Winter Sports* (n.p.: Crestwood House, 1976); Joe Mathieu, *Big Joe's Trailer Truck* (New York: Random House, 1974); Peggy Parish, *Come Back, Amelia Bedelia* (New York: Harper & Row, 1971); Tomie de Paola, *Strega Nona* (Englewood Cliffs, N.J.: Prentice-Hall, 1975); Marjorie Weinman Sharmat, *A Hot Thirsty Day* (New York: Macmillan, 1971); G. C. Skipper, *World at War* (Chicago: Children's Press, 1981).

[17]Butler and Paisley, p. 296.

[18]Butler and Paisley, p. 294.

vision is sleep, and the difference is not that large.[19] Because television is so important to children during their most vulnerable and formative years, they are made "either an audience of special risk to be protected or an audience of special opportunity to be exploited," depending on one's point of view. Television managers see children as consumers; social reformers hope to divert them away from sex-role stereotypes.[20] At the present, the television managers seem to be winning.

In an effort to test my assumptions about sexism on television against the   15
facts, I spent a couple of days watching the kinds of television shows that I thought children would watch. I started with children's favorite programs — cartoons, all of which invariably and unceasingly promote sex-role stereotypes. Cartoons can take place thousands of years in the past, like *The Flintstones*, or far into the future, like *The Jetsons*. But it doesn't really seem to matter whether the husband goes to work on a dinosaur or in a spaceship. In both of these cartoons, the men act aggressively, go to work every day, and venture out into the world; their wives, on the other hand, stay home to cook and clean, worry about looking beautiful, spend all of the money their husbands earn, and constantly discuss their problems with each other. Another sort of cartoon involves amazing superheroes — Spiderman, Iceman, and Shazam, for instance — who manage to rescue the world from disaster at least once every five minutes. The male superheroes far outnumber the female and often end up having to rescue them. At one point, for example, Iceman tried to keep the delicate and pretty heroine, Firestar, from a dangerous situation by insisting that "this is no place for a woman." In response, Firestar said, "But I'm no ordinary woman," implying that ordinary women should stay out of dangerous situations and let the men do the work. Almost all cartoons still reflect these sex-role stereotypes; few changes have occurred during the past few years.[21]

Unfortunately, even the educational shows made especially for children   16
contain sex-role stereotypes. During one hour of *Sesame Street* I watched, only two adult females were shown: one worked in the back of a dry cleaner's, washing and ironing shirts, while the other tried unsuccessfully to fix a car. Meanwhile, men managed the shops, learned to play the flute, helped puppets find the letter "O," played the guitar, and narrated the entire program. A male puppet, Kermit the Frog, did a news break in which a mailman, a salesman, and a woodsman all came to rescue Little Red Riding Hood. When asked what a square could be used for, a man said, "Building things," while a girl

[19]Butler and Paisley, p. 289.
[20]Butler and Paisley, p. 280.
[21]NBC, *The Flintstones*; NBC, *The Jetsons*; NBC, *Shazam*; NBC, *The Smurfs*; NBC, *Spiderman and His Amazing Friends*.

said, "It would make a nice picture frame." While the show may have taught children about the letters "O" and "R" and how to count to five, it also reinforced many sex-role stereotypes.[22]

Advertising, of course, is another important aspect of sex-role stereotyping [17] found on television. Almost all of the advertisements for the Saturday morning cartoons showed children with the product being endorsed. The girls danced in cute little costumes, played tennis, played with dolls, performed gymnastics, helped their mothers, and cheered for the boys. The boys, on the other hand, played cowboys, football, soccer, baseball, and basketball and rode bicycles. All of the announcers were men; and no adult women were shown or heard at all. Women did, however, play a more important role in the afternoon and evening commercials—preparing food for their families, shopping for groceries, washing dishes, cleaning up messes, doing the laundry, and learning how to make a burger at a restaurant. Men narrated all of these advertisements, too, and were shown in their traditional roles.[23]

Studies support my firsthand observations of sex-role stereotyping on tele- [18] vision, and they also show how these stereotypes affect the children who watch television. Suzanne Pingree, for example, found that commercials are so influential that they change children's attitudes about women. Half of the children in the study saw five minutes of commercials with women in traditional roles (cooking, cleaning, being beautiful); the other half saw commercials with women in nontraditional roles (golfing, practicing medicine, working as accountants). The children who saw the nontraditional women were themselves less traditional in response to a number of statements about men and women than those who saw women as housewives and mothers.[24]

In another study, Ann Beut asked sixty-three boys and girls, all of whom [19] watched television regularly, what they wanted to be when they grew up. Seventy percent of the children picked a career stereotypically appropriate for their sex; fifty percent of the children who had been classified as moderate viewers chose sex-stereotyped careers for themselves, while seventy-six percent of the heavy viewers did. This is consistent with the widely accepted idea that watching television seems to show a high correlation with strong sex typing.[25]

The cycle of sex-role stereotyping continues in our society today. At an [20] early age, individuals learn sex-role stereotypes from their society and then become a part of that society and pass their stereotypes on to the next gen-

[22]PBS, *Sesame Street*, 20 Apr. 1982.
[23]Information based on commercials on NBC, 17 Apr. 1982 and 20 Apr. 1982.
[24]Butler and Paisley, pp. 295–96.
[25]Butler and Paisley, pp. 292–93.

eration. Research, statistics, and various studies can all be used to prove that children's literature and television programs strongly influence children's views of themselves. In an effort to fit into society, children use these sex roles to plan their future jobs and goals.[26] Unless we want the majority of our women to continue to be passive, dependent homemakers, secretaries, and school-teachers and our men to be strong, masculine professionals, scientists, and presidents, we must be able to change this sex-role stereotyping where it first begins — in children. But as long as nothing is done to change this situation, these stereotypes will continue to be passed on from one generation to the next.

Publishers, producers, and authors should be encouraged to make their ma- 21 terial reflect a sensitivity to the needs and rights of girls and boys without preference or bias. Male and female characters should show emotion as well as courage and ambition. Both of the sexes should be able to solve problems independently, earn money, receive recognition, pursue the same occupations, and play at the same games. This is not to say that all of the characters should act just the same, but that the positive and negative characteristics should be distributed randomly — with as many passive or aggressive boys as girls. Both males and females should be shown practicing medicine, working in a business office, cooking, and cleaning the house. If books and television shows were rewritten in a nonsexist manner, children would learn those nonsexist roles and would be better able to fit into our changing society in which more women are returning to work and demanding equality. Such changes will come slowly and gradually, but they will come about if only we give the children a chance to abandon the sex roles that saturate television and books — if we give them a chance to be free.

[26]Brooks-Gunn and Mathews, p. 208.

Bibliography

Amoss, Bertha. *The Very Worst Thing.* New York: Parents' Magazine Press, 1972.

Beltinger, Craig. *Follow Me, Everybody.* Garden City, N.Y.: Doubleday, 1968.

Brooks-Gunn, Jeanne, and Wendy Schenupp Mathews. *He and She: How Children Develop Their Sex-Role Identity.* Englewood Cliffs, N.J.: Prentice-Hall, 1979.

Butler, Matilda, and William Paisley. *Women and the Mass Media.* New York: Human Sciences Press, 1980.

Clymer, Theodore, et al. *Helicopters and Gingerbread.* Lexington, Mass.: Ginn, 1976.

Delaney, A. *The Butterfly.* New York: Delacorte, 1977.

de Paola, Tomie. *Strega Nona.* Englewood Cliffs, N.J.: Prentice-Hall, 1975.

Feilen, John. *Winter Sports.* N.p.: Crestwood House, 1976.

Grover, Eulalic Osgood, ed. *Mother Goose.* Northbrook, Ill.: Hubbard Press, 1971.

Kessler, Suzanne J., and Wendy McKenna. *Gender: An Ethromethodological Approach.* New York: Wiley, 1978.

Mathieu, Joe. *Big Joe's Trailer Truck.* New York: Random House, 1974.

NBC, *The Flintstones.*

NBC, *The Jetsons.*

NBC, *Shazam.*

NBC, *The Smurfs.*

NBC, various commercials.

Parish, Peggy. *Come Back, Amelia Bedelia.* New York: Harper & Row, 1971.

PBS, *Sesame Street.*

Robinson, Helen M., Marion Monroe, and A. Sterl Artley. *Fun with Our Friends.* Chicago: Scott, Foresman, 1962.

Ruble, Diane J., Terry Balaban, and Joel Cooper. "Gender Constancy and the Effects of Sex-Typed Televised Toy Commercials." *Child Development,* 52 (June 1981), 667 – 73.

Sharmat, Marjorie Weinman. *A Hot Thirsty Day.* New York: Macmillan, 1971.

Skipper, B. D. *World at War.* Chicago: Children's Press, 1981.

Smith, Carl B., and Ronald Wardhaugh. *Magic Times.* New York: Macmillan, 1980.

Women on Words and Images. *Dick and Jane as Victims.* Princeton, N.J.: Carolingian Press, 1972.

QUESTIONS FOR READING AND REVISING

1. What is Klein's thesis? Where does she state it?

2. What are the causes of sex-role stereotyping that Klein lists? Why does each exert such a powerful influence on children? What are the dangers of sex-role stereotyping?

3. What type of evidence does Klein use to support her thesis? How does she organize her evidence?

4. How do Klein's own observations help strengthen her essay? Do you find, for instance, the information on *Sesame Street* surprising? Find specific passages from Klein's original research that you find especially effective.

5. Analyze how Klein is able to seem so reasonable and believable while still taking such a strong position. How does her use of outside sources contribute to her effect?

6. What point of view does Klein assume her audience has on the topic? Does her evidence convince you? What objection does she answer in paragraphs 2 and 3? Why is the opening example also effective in answering this objection?

7. In her rough draft, Klein wrote the following paragraph after paragraph 15:

> But stereotypes do not stop here. They continue on into the afternoon and evening shows that are commonly watched by children — *Here's Lucy, Happy Days, The Waltons, Gilligan's Island,* and *Little House on the Prairie,* for instance. Many of these are either old reruns or shows that take place

in the past, and most of them also contain sex-role stereotypes. True, some of the prime-time television shows
have begun to change, picturing fewer of the traditional
sex roles, but even in those shows that have a woman as
the main character, sex typing does occur.

Why do you think Klein deleted this paragraph from her final draft? How is it
constructed differently from the others in her essay?

SUGGESTIONS FOR WRITING

1. Observe a sampling of Saturday morning television programs. Write an essay
   refuting or agreeing with Klein's argument using the evidence you gather.
2. What sex stereotypes did you grow up with? Write an essay exploring the causes
   of those stereotypes as well as their effect on your life.
3. Klein's essay focuses on the image television and literature portray of women.
   Select another group (men, elderly, teenagers, children, athletes) and analyze
   how that segment of the population is represented on television and in literature.

DAVID G. LANDMANN

East Texas State University
Commerce, Texas
Richard Fulkerson, instructor

"If someone walked in the room as I was starting to write," David Landmann
explains, *"he or she would see me with a coffee cup in one hand and a cigarette in the
other. I would either be sitting back in my chair, staring at a spot just below the space
bar of my 1928 Royal Standard, or I would be standing in the middle of the floor, looking
at my feet."*

*Born in Washington, D.C., in 1946, David Landmann reports that he has always
been encouraged to write. His earliest recollections of writing go back to third grade when
he sat in class and wrote ghost stories when he was supposed to be doing other things.
He also recalls writing picture stories about an imaginary alter ego named Jim who was
the athlete and adventurer he thought he could never be. Landmann dropped out of college
in 1966 because he was a "kid who enjoyed skiing more than studying." At the age of
thirty-six, with the urging of his wife, he sold his house and car, returned to school, and
began what he considered his last chance at formal education.*

*Asked to write a description, Landmann remembered an experience ten years ago in
which he was the photographer half of a reporter-photographer team covering a family he
had discovered living in a cardboard shack. Landmann had always wanted to write
something about the family, and this assignment gave him the opportunity.*

The House

The House, if you could call it that, stood in shambles just fifty feet from   1
a major intersection. Hundreds of people passed it daily on their morning and
afternoon trips between their comfortable middle-class homes two miles to the
south and their comfortable white-collar jobs in the high-tech glass and steel
industrial complex two miles to the north. Hundreds of times each day, The
House, the cardboard and scrap wood structure that was home for Isiah Lewis
and his wife and three children, was virtually not seen. If it was, its images
were not allowed to register. Water-warped, refrigerator-carton walls; the single, crate-frame window; the door, made of two discarded coffee-table tops
wired to a rusted iron bed frame; the cluttered yard; the ancient, one-eyed
man; the odd-looking, stoop-shouldered young woman, holding an infant whose
clothing was stained with its own excrement; the older children, whose hungry,
haunting eyes scanned the big cars on the street: If those things weren't seen,

they didn't unsettle. They didn't distress. Avoidance of The House and its images became a simple matter of passersby preserving the sanctity of their to-and-from-work drives. Out of sight, out of mind.

Isiah Lewis never thought himself invisible. When he held his hand up to   2
the light, it was there, solid, black-skinned, yellow-nailed, leathery, arthritic. That hand and its twin had served him for the better part of his (as near as he could figure) seventy-three or seventy-four years. Those hands had built The House. They had fashioned the window and the door. They had kept Isiah Lewis and his wife and "babies" alive in the nearly six years since he had found "the woman" hiding in the city dump, pregnant and half-dead from malnutrition. Mute, probably retarded, "the woman," whom no one else seemed to want, stayed with the old man, who nursed her back to health, delivered her first baby, and fathered two more. The House had sheltered the oddly conceived family since the shack, in which Isiah had lived since middle age, had burned five years earlier. "Good Lawd willin'," The House would continue to keep them alive.

In summer, keeping alive meant scrounging bits of wire screen from the   3
dump — screen to cover the window and the door — to keep the "babies" from "gittin' too bad skeeta-bit."

"Dat ol' watcherman at the dump, he be blin' or sumpin'. I be walkin' in   4
there big as day, an' carryin' stuff out wid dem no trespassin' signs all 'roun', an' he don't even bat a eye. He don't be sayin' nothin'. It's jus' like I ain't there."

Summer also meant keeping the paint can that served as his family's toilet   5
outside and emptied. Lewis said he tried at the beginning of the last summer to rig a lean-to privacy screen, but his arthritis kept his hands from doing the job. Consequently, the Lewis paint can and its patrons were visible at any time to everyone driving by.

"Dey jus' look 'way," Lewis recalled. "One time dey was dis white man in   6
a big white car. He be yellin' he gonna bring the health bo'd down on me. But dey never come. I seen dat big white car. But dey never come."

Food and water were year-round problems.   7

"We usta git our water from the man who be livin' down the road. But he   8
up an' die. So we gits our wash water from the bar ditch, an' we got us a rain barrel for drinkin'. Some of the church ladies up yonder usta bring us hot foods. But the church done moved, an' we ain't got us no cookstove. Can't put no cookstove in no cardbo'd house. Den the welfare usta git us some dat commode [commodity] food. But dey done los' our card an' dey don't know we here no mo'," Lewis said.

When the church ladies stopped coming, Lewis began to send his two oldest   9 "babies" to fetch what food they could find in the trash bins behind the supermarket that stood a half-mile south of The House.

"Ain't never nobody 'roun' back there. If dey is, dey don't never pay no 10 mind to the babies. The babies climb right inside them big ol' hoppers and carries lots of good stuff back here. If the white folks sees them babies, dey jus' don't say nothin' nohow."

But now it was winter, and winter in The House was what Isiah Lewis called 11 "the wustest time."

There were never enough rags in the dump to stuff in the holes in the 12 makeshift walls of The House — never enough to keep the north wind out. The cold outside meant the paint can had to be brought into the comparative warmth inside, where the can sat steaming next to the pile of newspapers and rags under which the Lewis family huddled at night. The only heat came from their own bodies (because you "can't put no cookstove in no cardbo'd house").

It was winter now, and Isiah Lewis was telling the story of The House to a 13 white folks' newspaper reporter, who two days earlier had had a flat tire while driving through the intersection The House overlooked. He had overlooked The House every day for the past year, never seeing the ramshackle collection of cardboard and weathered wood until his right front tire blew and a broken jack handle forced him to go looking for a telephone. What he found was Isiah Lewis, who offered him all he had to offer — a tin can of cold rainwater and a place to sit out of the wind.

The story and pictures of Isiah Lewis, "the woman," "the babies," and The 14 House hit the streets on the day before Christmas. The following letter was published two days later:

> Dear Editor:
>
> This is to inform your readers that Isiah Lewis and his family are now being taken care of by our department. It is with regret we must admit that we were neither aware of the Lewises nor the conditions in which they lived. We didn't know they existed simply because no one ever reported their existence to us. How hundreds of people could drive past the Lewis' helplessness each day and never see there was a problem is a question for which there are only unpleasant answers. The answer, however, remains. We simply chose not to see the Lewises. Unfortunately the old saying is still true. Out of sight, out of mind. Now . . . the Lewises are in our minds. Let us not forget them.
>
> > Sincerely,
> > County Department of Public Welfare

QUESTIONS FOR READING AND REVISING

1. One purpose of this essay is to describe the house and its occupants, but Landmann has a larger purpose. What statement does Landmann make about society's attitude toward poverty? How does he use his description to achieve this purpose?

2. How would you characterize Landmann's attitude toward Lewis and his family? What effect does Landmann's attitude have on his readers?

3. Landmann uses dialogue to give us a clear picture of Lewis and his condition. In effect, he allows Lewis to tell his own story in his own words. What does the dialogue reveal about Lewis?

4. Do some of Landmann's details shock you? Does Landmann intend that his readers have this reaction? Why?

5. Why does Landmann wait until almost the end of the essay to tell us about the reporter's discovery of the house? How does this organization further the effect of his description?

6. Landmann reports: "The hardest thing for me to do is to stop writing, to cut myself off, to keep my writing brief and to the point." Has Landmann been successful at being brief and to the point? Do all his details support his purpose? Does he include any irrelevant details?

7. The essay ends with a letter to the editor from the county department of public welfare. What effect does this letter have in the essay? Is it a more effective conclusion than a summary of his main points would be?

8. In his rough draft, Landmann wrote his introduction this way:

> The house, if you could call it that, stood in shambles just fifty feet from a major intersection. Hundreds of people passed it daily on their morning and afternoon trips between their comfortable middle-class homes two miles to the south and their comfortable white-collar jobs in the high-tech glass and steel industrial complex two miles to the north. But they never saw the cardboard and scrapwood House that was shelter of Isiah Lewis and his wife and three children. Or if they saw it they didn't let it register. If they didn't see it, they didn't have to think about it. Out of sight, out of mind.

Compare this rough-draft introduction with that of the final draft. Why do the added details in the revised version make it more effective?

SUGGESTIONS FOR WRITING

1. Landmann describes a house and its inhabitants who were "out of sight, out of mind." What does the expression "out of sight, out of mind" mean to you?

Write an essay describing something that illustrates the meaning of this expression.

2. Landmann discovered the cardboard shack that hundreds of people passed every day without noticing. Spend a day walking around your community, looking for something you have never noticed. Write an essay describing what you find and try to explain why you never noticed it before.

3. Landmann contends that most people ignore the misfortune of others unless they are absolutely forced to confront it. Do you agree or disagree? Develop one or two examples to explain your opinion in an essay.

JOANNE L. MENTER

University of Nebraska at Lincoln
Lincoln, Nebraska
Jacquelynn Sorensen, instructor

Joanne Menter describes herself as a "twenty-six-year-old nontraditional student" who identifies "one of the great challenges of life to be to see how many things can be done well at one time." Born in Omaha, Nebraska, in 1956, Menter is a teacher at her church's Sunday school and vacation Bible school, an aide in the Bellevue, Nebraska, public schools, an avid seamstress, and a "meticulous organizer." She left college in 1975 to pursue a career as a graphic artist. In 1982, after considerable success in graphic arts, she returned to the University of Nebraska at Lincoln "to learn to write" and to study journalism.

"Write only about what you intimately know," she says. "The reader can't be fooled. You should have respect for the reader and gain the reader's trust by writing what you know best." In her essay, Menter takes her own advice to heart and draws a portrait of her father, his illness, and its impact on her family's relationships.

Home Is
Where the Heart Is

The cold half-light of a November afternoon filters through the bare branches, making a dark network in the window of our home. It filters its way thinly across the room and the heavy figure of my father slumped in his chair. There is a stillness in the room during which I always look up to check his stomach. But I see it softly heaving; the motor still works. He sits in a worn peach-velvet occasional chair, smeared with printer's ink and surrounded by newspapers and other periodicals. There is an end table hidden to his right with a lamp and several weeks' issues of the *Omaha World Herald* on it. A magazine rack on his left is stuffed with a year's supply of *National Geographic*, piled over with *Time*, *Nebraska Farmer*, and more *World Herald*. All this and a thin layer of dust. Sometimes when I vacuum, I threateningly aim the suction tube at him and his papers or start to vacuum his arm, and this makes him laugh. I like that. I like to think he is still in there somewhere, that he can still be reached.

Something unheard or unseen by me suddenly startles him, and his head and hands jerk up in unison, pulling the rumpled newspaper with them. Then the characteristic rustling starts again, as his palsied hands try to hold the paper up so that he can read. This is a pattern he goes through. The motor starts; the paper comes up; the head starts to bob forward, sinking lower and lower in unison with the hands. Eyelids reflex until the paper rests in his lap again; then the motor stops. Sometimes he spends days on one page. But, as he says, "Life is always new to me."

He does not look the way he used to look five, ten, or even fifteen years 3 ago, before Parkinson's was diagnosed: a tall, dark, broad-shouldered, blue-eyed German now permanently bent forward at the shoulders with bulging eyes that peer up over the top of glasses that forever slide down his nose. The left foot drags and the gait is shuffling. He has lost control of facial movement within the last three years and makes involuntary noises but still gets around under his own power. The springs in his reading chair are broken, and he's broken the bed frame too, with his habit of just letting his two hundred pounds go once he's gotten to his destination. Thirteen years have passed this way in our family as we watch the degenerative process take over this man. It has been six years since the confusion set in, which my mother and I mark as a blessing because he seems unaware of the passage of time and with it what is happening to him. As he sometimes says, "I'm just putting my time in here."

But there are those of us who are left to watch. Most notable is my mother, 4 who silently fulfills the vow of November 22, 1940 — for better or worse, till death us do part. They met while working in the Office of Price Control in Minneapolis, Minnesota. And when government spending was cut by a Republican administration in the fourth year of their marriage, the OPC was closed. She followed him back to his native Nebraska, where they raised their five children. She has often told me what a happy life they had together. How proud she was of him! He was all the things she had looked for in a husband: smart, kind, religious, someone on whom she could depend in so many ways.

The relationship is changed now. He has become a demanding total de- 5 pendent, and much of the former joy in their life together is gone. She has the stress of the added family responsibilities that he once took care of, plus the additional care of him — which is very time-consuming — plus her full-time job — all this and more at age fifty-nine. And my two younger brothers have the extreme ignorance to accuse her of a lack of compassion for him and to suggest that she spend more time with him. All I will say is, it's not easy to look death in the face, you know. People love to hold babies and be near to youth, which is the regenerative side of life, but which of us wants to watch the process of death take hold of someone we love? She did and does love him, but her love is not the simple love which would be obvious enough for these two young ones to see. She holds it in her memory and it motivates her to care well for a house left vacant, a mind without a spirit. And she shares with him what she can, in the context of their new relationship. Like a parent who watches a child die an untimely death, she loves from a distance.

QUESTIONS FOR READING AND REVISING

1. Joanne Menter's skillful use of precise details evokes a powerful image of the effect of her father's illness on her family. What impression of her father do the details in the first two paragraphs create? How do the details of the room and the weather reinforce this impression?

2. Menter writes with great control about an emotionally charged situation. What words or phrases in her essay summarize her attitude toward her father's illness and its effects on her? On her mother? On her younger brothers?

3. Compare and contrast Menter's attitude toward her father and his illness with her mother's attitude. Discuss the effects of the change in Menter's focus in paragraphs 4 and 5? What additional details does she give her readers in these paragraphs? Explain how these details add to or detract from the overall impact of the essay. What point does Menter make here?

4. In the first draft of the essay, the last sentence in paragraph 4 read: "He was all the things she had looked for in a husband: smart, kind, religious." Menter revised the sentence by adding the phrase "someone on whom she could depend in so many ways" and by starting a new paragraph with "The relationship is now changed." In what specific ways does each change improve the essay?

5. What is your reaction to Menter's comments about her two younger brothers in paragraph 5? What function do her comments serve? Why couldn't she simply omit them?

6. Now that you have worked through the essay, consider its title. Where have you heard this phrase before? With what do you associate it? What does it call to mind? In what ways does it prepare Menter's readers for her essay? How could it be improved?

SUGGESTIONS FOR WRITING

1. As an exercise in observation and inference, reread the first paragraph of Joanne Menter's essay, in which she describes the "stillness" of the room in which "the heavy figure of my father" sits "slumped" in a "worn peach velvet occasional

chair smeared with printer's ink and surrounded by newspapers and other periodicals." Choose a room in which a relative or friend regularly reads or knits, or simply sits and thinks. Observe the room carefully and note its details and the specific reading material that can be found there. Write an essay in which you describe the person, the room, and the reading material and draw reasonable inferences about the likes and dislikes, the hopes and fears of that person.

2. Write an essay describing the changes in someone you know well who has had to contend with a serious illness, the death of a family member, the loss of a job, or some other serious problem. How have these changes affected that person and those who care about him or her? Recalling what Joanne Menter did so successfully in her essay, include as many evocative details as possible in your essay.

LAURA A. MORGAN

Williams College
Williamstown, Massachusetts
David L. Smith, instructor

Born in 1953, Laura Morgan has lived in the Albany, New York, area all of her life. Since her graduation from Shaker High School in 1971, she has worked primarily in newspaper distribution, first for several local dailies and most recently for the Wall Street Journal. *In 1982, she reports, "discouraged by the lack of intellectually stimulating experiences connected with my job and inspired by my interests in literature, I decided to enter college." She attended the State University of New York at Albany for a semester and then transferred to Williams College.*

Morgan describes herself as a writer who is "continually revising, so as to eliminate all ambiguous phrasing for my readers." In the following essay, which is her third draft, she demonstrates just how effectively paraphrase, quotation, and literary analysis can be combined to create a lucid and convincing essay. Asked to write about some aspect of the symbolic use of darkness in Joseph Conrad's "Heart of Darkness," Morgan responded with a reading of the novella that maps out and explores both the implications of darkness throughout the story and the significance of Conrad's moral tone.

Widely recognized as a masterwork of short fiction, "Heart of Darkness" tells the story of the journey of the narrator, Marlow, up the Congo River to find Kurtz, a brilliant young idealist transformed by greed and power into a degenerate colonialist who exploits the natives. Kurtz dies in conscience-stricken horror, but when Marlow leaves the jungle, he feels compelled to tell another version of what he saw there. Most readers find in Conrad's tale an attack on imperialism and an indictment of the loss of moral responsibility by a society preoccupied with materialism.

Man's Moral Bankruptcy

In Joseph Conrad's story "Heart of Darkness," the darkness is apparent in 1
the hearts of men as well as in the unknown and mysterious jungle where nature runs riot. But the evil that is associated with the darkness is entirely man-made; it exists not only in the jungle but outside in the Belgian city and, indeed, on the Thames. Yet in the darkness of the jungle, "moral" man's immorality is made more explicit. This is why Marlow, the story's chief narrator, declares that the darkness, paradoxically, illuminates.

The story begins with the narrator conjuring up images of the glorious past, 2
which break through the foreboding gloom of the sunset. Instead of viewing the scene as Marlow does—as a place of darkness—the narrator speaks of the

"unceasing service" of the "tidal current" (p. 252, *Norton Anthology of Short Fiction*). The waters become a fountain of memories, overflowing with majesty — jewels, gold, kings, knights, memories of men and ships, the pride of a nation. But there is another side, the dark side of conquests past, which is all but forgotten, except perhaps by those like Marlow who have been initiated into the degradation accompanying "progress." The gloom of the setting sun reminds Marlow that the site was also once a place of darkness. The town where the threatening darkness lingers overhead was at one time an unknown landmass, a wilderness, with all the savagery of the Dark Continent. The waters of the Thames that saw the likes of Drake and Sir John Franklin were also the waters that carried the invasion of the Romans. Marlow envisions the difficulty the Romans would have had in meeting with the demands of an uncivilized land — the hostile climate, unfriendly natives, the unnavigable terrain, and death. He paints a picture of all the evil lurking in the darkness of the unknown. Thus, a reverse is made in the narrative from the brilliance of history to the dark, gloomy atmosphere of a pre-Drake era.

Marlow has prepared his audience for his own modern-day descent into 3 darkness. He explains that his experience with darkness has somehow illuminated his thoughts. Hence, not only does the darkness become an instrument whereby one learns, but also Marlow implicitly suggests that the darkness exists in the mind. To learn, one must shed light on the mind by seeking truths, or absolutes, via conflicts with evil. Charmed by the memories of childhood and a seemingly self-imposed heavenly mission, Marlow seeks the ideals that remain immutable in a lawless land. As he transports his audience from their "sleepless" port through the nightmares of his voyage, the darkness — and evil — become more and more pronounced. The darkness he so vividly described as an occasion in the past — the Roman invasion — is reenacted in the narrative of his expedition into the Congo.

As he foreshadowed his tale with the example of the Roman conquest of 4 Britain, he foreshadows his own experience with the tale of his predecessor Fresleven. In it there exist all the elements of evil seen previously in the Roman example. Out there, in the center of the jungle, Fresleven is slain by a stab through the heart. The brute savagery, the "robbery and violence" (p. 255) that made the Romans "men enough to face the darkness" (p. 254) is supplemented in the conquest by Fresleven and his company with the introduction of an alleged "noble cause" (p. 257). Thus, the symbolic death: something is wrong at the heart of things here. The gentle, quiet creature Fresleven beats an old man "mercilessly" (p. 257). The darkness that dwells in the interior of Africa is augmented by imported elements. The close conditions of survival and the apparent failure of ideals transform the gentle man Fresleven into a beastly creature, wild to recapture "his self-respect in some way" (p. 257), behaving in the same wanton manner as a Roman two thousand years before.

The first indications that the darkness is in the heart appropriately adum- 5 brate Marlow's next step: his visit to the company headquarters. He describes the city as a "whited sepulchre," an image which suggests evil disguised by falsehoods. And guarding the door of hell are the two knitters of black — dispassionate, heartless creatures who knowingly introduce men into a perdi- tion from whence they are never expected to return. There, Marlow signs a contract—the archetypal contract—with the faceless man, who in retrospect appears more clearly as the devil's disciple. The doors to the devil's house stand invitingly ajar for men like Marlow to slip through the cracks. There is no need for the angel of death to *guard* such structures. The contract is a seemingly meaningless document, since dead men tell no tales, nor do they give away company secrets. The conflicting ceremonies raise the issue of the corruption and evil, the meaninglessness and uselessness, the heartlessness and moral insensibility of the men who constitute the bureaucratic regime. The company doctor exemplifies the same paradox. The man who by the very nature of his profession should exhibit a concern for the physical well-being of his patients examines Marlow while contemplating other things. The "other things" that take precedence over the health of his charges are his enigmatic scientific experiments, which will never reach maturity since the participants all vanish. Like the contract, there is no substance to them; they are as hollow as the men who conduct such ceremonies.

From the heart of darkness—this bureaucratic network of moral dissolution 6 —flows the agent of its conspiracy. All along the coast of Africa, Marlow witnesses inexplicable destruction and waste. The baffling scenes of tax col- lectors and soldiers disembarking only to drown or to be swallowed up by an unfathomable wilderness, or of the man-of-war stoically shelling the bush while its crew is dying, show the relentless force behind heartless bureaucracy. Prior- ities seem to be all mixed up, for at every nightmare the people encounter, they simply glide on by as though nothing out of the ordinary had occurred. The facade of moral ideology is gone by the time Marlow reaches the company's station. There, in the middle of the jungle, a white bureaucrat sits in white starched collar and cuffs ruminating over his figures, while outside the ill-clad shadows of natives pass out of existence from starvation and exhaustion. The absolute horror of such a scene no words can possibly paint, and yet they move on with their "objectless blasting" and tireless unconcern (p. 263).

Marlow's only hope for salvation is the work for which he was hired, and 7 as he passes through the jungle toward his steamship at the central station, he encounters the same wanton waste he has seen with growing intensity since he passed through the doors of hell: paths lead nowhere, and men keep up roads that don't exist. Finally, he reaches the central station, the apotheosis of degradation. Faithless pilgrims with long staves wander about praying for ivory. There exists an air of sterility, with men absorbed in the production of nothing. Like the contract and the scientific experiments, everything lacks substance. Even the men appear to Marlow as hollow devils, things without substance. The darkness, now, inhabits the hollowness of men. As Marlow sits in useless occupation, waiting for rivets to repair the steamer, he envisions the elusive Kurtz as being the redeeming man of moral rectitude in the mire of bureaucracy. In the interim, before the arrival of the repair materials, he contemplates how the man of moral ideals — Kurtz — might work once *he* reaches the top of the administration. Will he backslide into the darkness of bureaucracy, or will he resurrect the ideologies of "civilized" man?

The white man went to Africa expecting to find immorality — darkness —   8 in the natives, from which in his ignorance he expected to reclaim them; but what he brought them was worse. The evil side of darkness existed not only in the minds and the hollowness of the white man but in his ideologies as well. The whole moral justification for the white man's actions lay in his conviction that the black man needed improvement, and his moral bankruptcy was exhibited when instead of improving the natives he degraded them. Throughout the story the image of the jungle is one of teeming, burgeoning, riotous, brutal life, which asserts itself implacably against all contrary forces and embodies the power of nature which knows no rules beyond self-preservation and boundless growth. The life of the jungle even invades man's preserves before he is quite done with them; grass grows up through the city streets in Belgium. In the extremity of their suffering, the workers hide in the grove of death, and after the killing of Fresleven the grass grows up through his bones; the irony is that the jungle has reclaimed the white man.

QUESTIONS FOR READING AND REVISING

1. What, in Laura Morgan's judgment, does the darkness in "Heart of Darkness" illuminate? What significance does she attribute to the darkness in the jungle? Summarize her thesis about the relationship between the darkness and the immorality of civilized people.

2. Outline the major points of Morgan's analysis. Show how each paragraph supports her main idea. What is the difference between the evidence used to support the points in paragraph 4 and the evidence used in other paragraphs?

3. What are the specific strengths of Morgan's literary analysis? For example, where in her essay does she draw on details from Conrad's story most effectively? What other strategies does she use to strengthen her analysis? Point to specific passages to support your answers.

4. How does Morgan organize her ideas: from simple to complex? From the beginning to the end of "Heart of Darkness"? Or according to some other principle of organization? Explain with specific examples.

5. What assumptions does Morgan make about her readers' familiarity with Conrad's story? In her opening paragraph, for example, how does she introduce the story and what does she tell her audience about it? Approximately what percentage of her essay is devoted to plot summary? To literary analysis?

6. In what specific ways does Morgan make clear her own attitude toward "man's moral bankruptcy"? How directly does she state her own feelings on the subject? Which part of speech does she rely on to express her attitude? In the final paragraph, for example, is it the verbs or the adverbs or the adjectives that express her attitude most forcefully?

7. How is paragraph 5 different from the others in terms of purpose, content, and structure? What would you suggest that Morgan do to make this paragraph more consistent with the rest of her essay?

SUGGESTIONS FOR WRITING

1. Morgan observes that Marlow, the narrator of "Heart of Darkness," believes that "to learn, one must shed light on the mind by seeking truths, or absolutes, via conflicts with evil." What is your reaction to Marlow's idea of how moral knowledge is acquired? Write an essay focusing on a specific incident or on another work of literature to support or refute the proposition that only through "experience with darkness" can one's moral spirit be illuminated. Develop each of your points with as many details and examples as possible.

2. Reread Morgan's essay and summarize her argument about the "bureaucratic network of moral dissolution." Write an essay applying her point to the actions of a supposedly humanitarian organization. Be sure to support each of your points with specific examples. You might find it helpful to read Doris Egnor's essay "A Life of Quiet Desperation" (pp. 56–57), for some insight into one institution's inhumane practices.

TERESA L. MOSS

University of Nevada at Reno
Reno, Nevada
Kathleen A. Boardman, instructor

"*I hate being caught not doing something,*" *Teresa Moss confesses. But given the nature and scope of her daily activities, Teresa Moss's anxiety hardly seems justified. A wife, mother, part-time horse trainer, and full-time student of agriculture at the University of Nevada at Reno, Moss was born in Rome, New York, in 1956, graduated from nearby Camden Central High School, and spent several years in the Navy before settling in Nevada. Her career goal is "to own and operate a horse-breeding stable and breeding farm."*

Asked to write an essay comparing the way something used to be done with the way it is done now, Moss decided to draw on her professional interest in horses and drafted "Bronc Busting vs. Equine Education." She has combined an insightful comparison of old and new methods of horse training with an analysis of a complicated process in an essay that, as she notes, commanded a great deal of time and hard work: "I find I have to do a lot of daydreaming about my topic before I even grab a pen; then I just write out a rough draft to glue my thoughts down. After I've got it down, I keep rewriting until it sounds like English."

Bronc Busting
vs. Equine Education

Everyone has seen an old western in which the local ranch hands rope a   1
five-year-old mustang and put a burlap sack over his head to keep him quiet
while forcing him to submit to the saddle. With the horse's eyes still covered,
the bronc buster leaps into the saddle and prepares himself. As soon as the
blind is removed, the mustang hunches his back and explodes—barely allowing the ranch hands enough time to jump out of the way. The horse, lathering
and dripping with sweat, fights for his life as if a mountain lion were on his
back. All hell breaks loose during the next thirty minutes, with the wrangler
spurring the horse to frenzied terror. Finally, standing exhausted, the horse
realizes he'll never be free. He has been broken.

This method of training developed out of the Old West, when wild horses   2
were abundant and easily exploited. Today, bronc busting is still somewhat
popular as a training method. It's exciting and always attracts a crowd; however, it's not very efficient. The reason for its lingering appeal seems to have
more to do with padding a cowboy's ego than with making the horse useful.

Under this method, the most a wrangler can hope for is a bad-mannered mount. More often, crude manhandling either breaks a horse down into a useless nag or rouses him into a dangerous outlaw. With an endless supply of wild horses, an owner could afford to discard mistakes. Now, because the numbers of mustangs are limited and the old days of the "forty-dollar saddle on a ten-dollar hoss" have been obscured by the current high costs of domesticated horses, horsemen have been forced to develop a more proficient training program.

To accomplish this, researchers have conducted extensive observations of   3 wild herds. One of their most important discoveries was that horses aren't the fierce animals bronc busters assumed them to be. Through time, horses have evolved into basically timid running machines for whom life and freedom are synonymous. Even lead stallions attempt to avoid dominance battles; through the use of threat rituals they elude the slow, torturous death that a shattered jawbone or a broken leg would bring. However, their timidity is not to be confused with cowardice: when a fight is unavoidable, a horse will use every available weapon and trick to save his life. Another important discovery is that horses always sustain a clear-cut hierarchy. Each herd has only one lead stallion, whose position is frequently challenged by roving bachelor stallions. The mares bicker among themselves to determine their status; once their pecking order is established, it's not questioned until a newcomer enters the herd.

Knowledge of these facts gives the horseman distinct advantages over the   4 bronc buster. The trainer, by providing feed and protection, steps into a dominant position in his student's hierarchy and avoids that confrontation which the bronc buster relies on so desperately. Once a trainer's dominance is established, the horse will accept any challenge he is offered. The trainer can now utilize a general plan for training — individualized for each horse.

Most trainers prefer that their programs start while the horse is still a foal.   5 Because a foal learns to distrust new things as he grows older, it is essential that he be haltered as soon as possible after birth. Since he naturally follows his dam, teaching him to lead is fairly simple: an assistant leads the dam, while the trainer leads the foal behind them. In learning to trailer, the foal is again following his dam's example. Gentling — the most important lesson — is accomplished through daily grooming, from which the foal learns to trust his handler.

As a yearling, the young horse is ready for longeing. With a hackamore, a   6 longe line, and a training whip, he learns the basic gaits and associated verbal commands expected of him. If he's working well, the colt can be saddled. At two, he is accustomed to the mouthing bit, usually a smooth, jointed snaffle. Next, the trainer ground drives his pupil. He attaches twenty-foot reins to either side of his student's headstall and works the horse without mounting him. In this manner, the horse learns to be responsive to the bit. The colt receives his final basic lesson at around three years of age, when his trainer steps into the saddle and draws all of his previous lessons into perspective. The horse can now graduate either to a life as a family's pleasure horse or, with more advanced training, to a career as a cowboy's cutting horse.

The bronc buster of old accomplished a job of training in thirty minutes   7
and ruined at least half the horses he dealt with. The modern horseman's job takes a minimum of three years packed full of repetitive and tedious work. He is careful to be patient and to remain gentle while maintaining firm control over his student; and because a good trainer adjusts the training program to meet the individual needs of each horse, he doesn't get dropouts from his school.

QUESTIONS FOR READING AND REVISING

1. Why is bronc busting no longer a viable way to train horses? What are the advantages of an equine education?

2. Teresa Moss combines a sophisticated process analysis with an effective contrast. List the steps she discusses in both the old and the modern methods of training horses.

3. Outline the major points of contrast Moss establishes between bronc busting and an equine education. At which point in the essay does she most successfully blend a process analysis with an informative contrast? How does she manage to do both at once?

4. Moss explains that her biggest problem in writing this essay was the introduction: "I knew the scene I wanted, but I didn't know how to write it. After I got that done, the rest flew into place." Reread her opening paragraph. What makes it successful? How does it announce and support her principal purpose in writing the essay?

5. Consider Moss's word choices. Why is the word *padding* in paragraph 2 an especially appropriate choice? Point to other words that you consider to be particularly effective. Identify word choices that you think could be strengthened. How might they be revised?

6. Moss reports that "if I don't keep an audience in mind when I write, my essays become confused." How would you describe the audience Moss seems to have in mind in this essay? How much technical knowledge of horse training does she expect her audience to have to understand and appreciate her points? In paragraphs 6 and 7, what language would you suggest she clarify or delete? Why?

7. Compare and contrast Moss's essay with Charlotte Russell's "Logging: Then and Now" (pp. 120–23). How does each author express her feelings about differences between doing something in the past and doing it in the present? How do the details presented in each essay justify the thesis of each?

SUGGESTIONS FOR WRITING

1. Comparing the old and the new is an effective way to analyze and understand the advantages and disadvantages of a particular process or subject. Write an essay in which you compare and contrast an early-twentieth-century magazine advertisement with a current-day advertisement for similar products. Examine each ad carefully, noting the nature and placement of the pictures and the text as well as the relation of all the parts of the ad to the product being sold. Explain which advertisement is more effective. What do the changes you have noticed indicate about advertising?

2. Write an essay contrasting old and new methods of doing something — for example, doing computations with a slide ruler and with a pocket calculator or writing papers with a pen and paper or typewriter and with a word processor. Include in your essay the process involved in each method and show the superiority of one.

3. Consider the way we use animals for entertainment — in bullfighting, horse racing, dog racing, bronco busting — or to further our individual or collective interests — as police dogs and laboratory animals. Write an essay explaining why we feel free to use animals for our own ends rather than to protect or nuture them as creatures who share our world.

ALLISON ROLLS

San Francisco State University
San Francisco, California
Nancy A. Sours, instructor

Allison Rolls describes herself in elementary school as "an average unmotivated student plastered with the label 'mentally gifted minor.' I considered myself completely and irrevocably ordinary. I never won anything and gave no one any reason to suspect I would." Born in San Francisco in 1960, Rolls was raised in Richmond, California, where she graduated from John F. Kennedy High School. Her interest in forensics and drama sustained her during her high school years, and she helped write and produce a number of highly acclaimed skits and historical dramas. She started working "at the tender age of sixteen" and has since earned a living at "renting tuxedos, designing bridal bouquets, making sandwiches, acting at California's Renaissance Faire, running a personnel office in Beverly Hills, selling office machines, and currently answering the telephone at the Exploratorium, a marvelous science museum in San Francisco." She is also a student at San Francisco State University.

Rolls reports that the origins of her satiric essay on Britain's royal couple can be found in both "the absolutely ridiculous amount of coverage the American and British news media give the British royal family — each sneeze and chuckle is reported" — and the "touch of jealousy" that surfaced when Prince Charles finally chose his bride: "I couldn't help but think to myself, 'What's Diana got that I ain't got?' . . . and so an essay was born."

Lady Diana: He Married the Wrong Woman

In light of the recent publicity involving the British Royal Family — the celebration of the Wedding of the Century; the birth of little Prince Willie; the Falklands war; a scandal involving Prince Andrew, Duke of Marlborough (or Randy Andy, as he is also known), and a young porn starlet; and the royal tiffs and spats (heaven knows, it's hard to keep track!) — I think that one very important point has been overlooked. After all the time and deliberation that went into getting Prince Charles, future King of England, hitched, he seems to have wound up marrying the wrong girl. Lady Diana Spencer, now Princess Diana, while outwardly possessing suitable credentials (looks, youth, money, lineage, virginity, etc.), was, in my opinion, the totally wrong choice to fill the position. While youth, looks, money, and family ties do have their advantages, the perfect mate for Charles should transcend all these petty details and rise above all this superficial nonsense. Rather than marrying a member of the idle aristocracy, Charles would have done much better with a sensible, perhaps more experienced, diamond in the rough. The logical choice, when one really examines the issue closely (as I will do here), would have been, of course, me. Along with sharing Diana's youth, beauty, charm, and sparkling personality, I have other down-to-earth qualities which neither vast amounts of money nor centuries of breeding can instill in a person. Unfortunately, Charles lacks the presence of mind to see this fact staring him in the face, so he missed his chance. Instead of choosing a girl whom many would consider the catch of the year, he ended up with the delicate and decorative Lady Diana.

To begin my comparison, I would like to point out that I have known 2
Prince Charles much longer than Diana has. I pasted his picture on my bed-room mirror long before she could even pronounce his name, and, of course, he has all my school photographs, even the one where my hair is sticking out all over. He also received invitations to every party I ever threw, starting with my Sweet Sixteen; although, doubtlessly due to state matters of great importance, he was never able to attend, I know he was there in spirit.

I also think that he displayed rather poor form in marrying one of his own 3
subjects. I feel that a marriage such as this imparts a certain lack of dignity and implies something of a slave-master relationship, which looks bad when a couple are co-ruling a country. Apart from the important international relations breakthrough which would have been accomplished in marrying an American, such as me, Charles could have been assured of a wife who wasn't overly awed by his exalted royal stature.

Another factor in my favor, when compared to the current Princess of 4
Wales, is the large amount of money that I could have saved the British treasury. First of all, I *hate* big weddings and could have done away with all the silly and expensive conceits that I'm sure Lady Diana considered necessary, such as her $10,000 wedding gown with a train longer than the Chattanooga Choo-Choo (complete with three copies should she muss the original), a dozen carriages, hundreds of bagpipers, zillions of guests, and a choir comparable in size to the Mormon Tabernacle, not to mention her honeymoon wardrobe. I hate to think of the cost! Why, her weekly hat budget alone would more than likely feed a dozen Irish coal-mining families for a year! I, on the other hand, prefer to dress unostentatiously and usually make my own clothes. Furthermore, I do not have hordes of hungry relatives flocking to Balmoral Castle for a weekend visit. On the contrary, I am on speaking terms with few, if any, of my relatives, whereas Diana has a family tree whose branches grow for miles in all directions, including her step-aunt, the illustrious Barbara Cartland, of

great literary fame. (Anyone who has read one of Miss Cartland's lush, romantic novels knows exactly where Diana got her idea of how to throw a wedding.) Doubtless Diana also has many relatives (especially the imaginative Miss Cartland, who was snubbed at the wedding) who must be bribed with spectacular sums of money to keep them from circulating photos of Diana in braces as a child or unflattering family anecdotes.

It also appears to me that the Princess, to put it delicately, is not possessed 5 of a superior intellect; however, we have little evidence of this since the only time she has ever been allowed to speak out loud in public was while taking her wedding vows. (Unfortunately, the Lady Diana just couldn't seem to remember exactly the order of all Charles's names.) But certainly her batting eyelashes and vacuous expression speak for themselves, while on the other hand all Charles had to do was take a peek at my SAT scores and the doe-eyed Di would have been out of the running. Obviously to anyone who pays attention, she is naught but a silly fluff-head with nothing better to think about than making babies.

Which brings me to my next point—babies. Certainly the British subjects 6 have a right to expect an heir eventually, but for heaven's sake, did it have to be so soon—a scant ten months after the wedding? I suppose that Diana felt that it was important to stay in the international limelight and immediately sought to set the fashion world aflame by introducing her royal maternity wardrobe. However, to simply "lie still and think of England," as Diana certainly did on her wedding night, displays to me a certain lack of character, and to feel that one's role in life (besides that of a worldwide trend-setter) should be as a baby factory seems a sadly outmoded outlook. A reasonable princess, such as I would have made, would have held out for at least five years. Keep the subjects guessing; why rush it all? Imagine Charles proudly looking on as his wife goes out to work for worthy causes, such as dedicating libraries and handing out royal largesse, instead of changing diapers and suffering morning sickness. In addition, my child would have certainly been born perfect, never crying or fussing. And I never could have settled for such an ordinary name as William Charles Phillip for my child, who would be called Balthazar Sidney Caleb or maybe Maud Eliza Shrub.

Another cause for concern for Prince Charles is the behavior of his younger 7 brother, the amorous Andrew, who recently embarrassed and outraged his family by cavorting around in the company of Miss Koo Stark, a budding nude actress. Had I been princess, this scandal would have been completely avoided by keeping Andy (by far the best-looking and most fun of all Queen Elizabeth's sons) otherwise occupied in the proper and respectable company of his sister-in-law.

The sad conclusion to all my observation in this matter is that instead of 8 choosing a stimulating, practical, articulate, and independent wife, Charles (who must have been deliriously desperate when he proposed) decided upon the first runner-up in a Barbie-doll look-alike contest to be the next Queen of England, and I am quite positive that he, his country, and the future history books will be all the more bored for it.

QUESTIONS FOR READING AND REVISING

1. Allison Rolls pokes fun at British royalty by comparing and contrasting herself and Princess Diana. List each point in her comparison and contrast. What order or sequence does she use? Does she organize her essay point by point or subject by subject or with some combination?

2. Consider the way Rolls presents herself. What do we learn about her in the essay? What impression does she create of herself in paragraph 2? Does this image remain consistent throughout the essay? If so, how does she sustain it? If not, when and how does it change?

3. What is Rolls's attitude toward Lady Diana? When is it first expressed? What are Rolls's specific objections to Lady Diana and to her marriage to Prince Charles? What, for example, are the implications of the phrases "to fill the position" in paragraph 1 and "to simply lie still and think of England" in paragraph 6?

4. Rolls explains that she is fascinated with words: "I love the way you can string them together and mold them and sculpt with them. Words are a very powerful tool and that is why it's very important to have a good rapport with them. I usually try to figure out the tone of the paper before I start writing. The tone — whether formal, conversational, or just plain off-the-wall — determines which words I use and how I shape them around the skeleton of my idea." Characterize Allison Rolls's tone in this essay. Point to specific phrases she uses to sustain that tone.

5. How familiar does Rolls assume her audience is with her subject? Why does she make this assumption? How much background information does she provide?

6. Rolls reports that "the hardest part of this essay was finding things wrong with Princess Diana, who is so secretive about her faults that I had to take some liberties with the truth and act on intuition alone." Identify instances of Rolls's taking "liberties with the truth." Do those instances strengthen or weaken the impact of her essay? Explain.

7. How effective is Rolls's use of parentheses to comment on her subject? Where

could she have eliminated parentheses and incorporated her points directly into the essay?

8. Reread the opening sentence of paragraph five: "It also appears to me that the Princess, to put it delicately, is not possessed of a superior intellect; however, we have little evidence of this since the only time she has ever been allowed to speak out loud in public was while taking her wedding vows." Rolls's previous draft of the first sentence in paragraph 5 read, "It also seems to me that the Princess, to put it delicately, is somewhat lacking in the brains department; however, there is not much evidence of this fact due to the fact that the only time she has ever been allowed to speak in public was when taking her marriage vows." Which draft is more effective? Why? How could the final draft be improved?

SUGGESTIONS FOR WRITING

1. Select a major political or social event that the media have treated solemnly during the past year and write an essay poking fun at it.

2. Have you ever admired or been infatuated with a public figure? Write an essay explaining the origin of your admiration or infatuation, the lengths to which you went to cultivate it, and, if appropriate, the means you used to extricate yourself from it.

3. Rolls notes "all the silly and expensive conceits that I'm sure Lady Diana considered necessary" for her wedding. In many respects, the United States displayed similar extravagance during the last presidential inauguration. Write an essay justifying occasions of state for which the expense could "more than likely feed a dozen Irish coal-mining families for a year." Depending on your point of view, your essay could be either ironic or straightforward.

CHARLOTTE M. RUSSELL

Umpqua Community College
Roseburg, Oregon
Greg Jacob, instructor

Charlotte Russell lives in Days Creek, a small logging town in northwest Oregon. With her husband and two children she cultivates what she describes as a "back-to-the-land lifestyle" on ten and a half acres of virgin forest "directly in front of thousands of acres of Bureau of Land Management land. . . . The trees, mostly fir and cedar, stretch endlessly upwards; the clouds rest in their tallest boughs. I would walk for hours through this peaceful setting of wooden monoliths and marvel at all this breath-taking beauty. I would sit transfixed and study these ancient wonders, tracing every crack that split each tree's bark. In some trees the bark is so thick you can put a yardstick into the crack and still not touch the inner wood."

Russell's early years were spent in far less serene and settled circumstances. Born in Chula Vista, California, in 1952, Russell passed her youth moving with her parents from one Navy post to another. She dropped out of high school in Houston, Texas, left home at seventeen to marry, and moved to Boston. After separating and eventually divorcing, Russell returned to the West Coast and remarried. Russell is now a student at Umpqua Community College in Oregon, where she plans to major in elementary education, hoping to make "a pivotal difference in children's impressionable lives by inciting them to read, write, and dream."

For a detailed analysis of Charlotte Russell's essay, see pages 220–242.

Logging: Then and Now

Logging in the Northwest in the 1880s was quiet and methodical compared 1 to the noisy, mechanical drone of the highly technical logging characteristic of the 1980s. It was by painstaking and tedious maneuvers that men and animals were able to drag fifteen thousand board feet of timber out of the forest. Today, with the aid of modern equipment, loggers can move millions of board feet of timber in a short period of time. In 1880, water was the method for transporting the logs to the sawmills, so only timber which was easily accessible to the shoreline was cut. Nowadays, machines make it possible for men to reach far inland and cut from the steep terrain common to the Northwest.

The mammoth firs and cedars growing a hundred years ago were so large 2 that often twenty men with outstretched arms could not encircle one. It wasn't a single man brandishing a motorized chain saw that felled one of these giants; instead, two men would usually spend eight days chopping, hacking, and sawing a chunk out, using their axes and cross-cut saw until finally, with a tremendous roar that echoed through the pristine forest, the virgin tree would fall heavily to the ground, crushing everything in its path. Back at the stump, the choppers would refill the bottle of kerosene that they hung inverted from their cross-cut saw and select another tree.

Periodically, the men would check this bottle of kerosene because not enough 3 kerosene dripping down over the cross cut would create drag from the sticky pitch. Pitch settled in the first ten to twelve feet of the tree, which made sawing at this level impossible. A method they used for getting above this pitch line was a springboard, a flat board with a metal hook on the end of it. They would jam this board into a notch they had made with their axes at about ten to twelve feet above the ground, each man having a springboard on his side of the tree. They would then "spring" onto this board and continue with their cross cut. Sometimes there was a third reason for the saw dragging, but that was probably due to one of the loggers falling asleep, rather than to a dull saw. That was called "riding the saw," and because cross cutting required precision teamwork, if one man didn't pull his own weight, he was quickly fired.

Once the sawyers were through, the buckers would come to saw the logs to 4 their desired size. Their job wasn't an easy one because they usually had to stand at tortuous angles balanced between several logs. After they were out of the way, the swampers would raise and flatten one side of the log, bevel one end so it wouldn't catch on the skids, and plow them out of the ground. Skids were roads made out of hand-hewn fir logs approximately ten to twelve feet long. One half their diameter would be embedded in the ground about nine feet apart, so a twenty-foot log would have a bearing on two skids. Young men, about thirteen years old, would run ahead of this train of logs with a swab and bucket of grease, liberally greasing each skid. Another skid, called a "brow skid," was constructed at the landing for transferring the logs to the water. In one week, an average of nine hundred cords was cut and dragged slowly by a team of sixteen oxen to the landing. For this grueling and hazardous work, the logger was paid $1.00 a day for a twelve-hour day. After putting in his twelve hours, the logger would trudge wearily back to camp, where he would make his home for the next six months. The ones that could walk back to camp were the lucky ones, because accidents in the 1880s were as common as ticks on a dog. Many a logger would walk past a dead man propped up against a stump, awaiting removal at the end of the day to a freshly dug grave back at camp.

Camp consisted of a group of seven to ten hastily built shacks. Twenty-five 5 loggers were housed in each one, and at 6:00 P.M. they would all be inside peeling off their soaked clothes and soggy boots, hanging them above a crackling fire in the wood stove. It was the bullcook's job to get the fires started in each cabin and feed these starving loggers. He was the most respected man in the camp. At his signal, the men would quietly filter into the dining hall and, at another signal, sit down to eat. There never seemed to be enough food, no matter how high the bullcook heaped each plate, but eventually every man would begin to stretch, rub his satisfied belly, and wander back to his cabin for a smoke, a story, or a song before the kerosene lamp was extinguished.

The logging camps disappeared long ago. The ringing of the axes and the 6 yells of the bullpuncher as he prodded the tired oxen to the landing have been replaced by the mechanical whine of the gasoline-powered chain saw and the noise and smell of diesel-driven yarders. Instead of taking days to fell a tree, it now takes minutes. The image of the "dumb country logger" has been transfigured into a new breed of professionals. It takes highly skilled men to run the complex machinery used in logging today. Million of dollars' worth of equipment are at stake, so the boss is very careful about whom he hires. Accidents are rare now, but should they occur, a helicopter would be summoned with a two-way radio for immediate removal of the injured. Cats, shovels, and skylines using various cables or lines are rigged to help log on steep terrain or in other inaccessible areas. These metal beasts use more fuel and spare parts in one day than the whole team of oxen ate in feed in one month. Myriad gauges, dials, and complicated whistle signals must be memorized by the yarder engineer, who is in charge of the lines that pull the logs out of the forest. From the yarder, the lines are strung to a D.A. cat with a C frame built on. From this line, another line, called a "carriage," drops down and pulls the log in place. This whole apparatus is called a "skyline."

Besides the yarder engineer, there's the hooktender, the rigging slinger, the 7 choke setter, and the chaser. The hooktender is the head man and oversees the entire logging operation. He's got to be able to splice a line quickly and make sure all the other lines are properly attached. He does whatever is necessary to keep the logging operation running smoothly. The rigging slinger is the man who sets the carriage in motion while simultaneously checking the quality of the logs. The choke setter then slips a line around the log and cinches it through an eye, much as the choker collar on a dog works. The chaser is the man who removes the log from the landing with the aid of a shovel attached to another yarder and loads it on a logging truck destined for the mills. These five men now do the job that used to take thirty. It's a new era of logging — fast and efficient. This new technology of man and machines has now been refined to a science that can rape an entire forest of its trees in days. The loggers, however, like to think of themselves as the gardeners of the forest, harvesting a crop of ripe timber.

It took a lot of strength and stamina to be a logger in the 1880s. Nothing 8
was easy. Each tree posed a new challenge and was conquered only through
sheer will, determination, and muscle. Today, the loggers have taken this
legacy for granted. Sadly, much of the romance that was a part of logging has
vanished and, like the virgin-growth timber, will never return.

QUESTIONS FOR READING AND REVISING

1. Charlotte Russell was asked to write a comparison and contrast essay. List all
   the points of contrast she presents on logging in the 1880s and 1980s. How do
   modern logging techniques differ from those of the 1880s? Does Russell organize
   these differences subject by subject, point by point, or a combination of the
   two? Explain.

2. How does Russell characterize logging in the 1880s? Point to specific words
   and phrases that establish her attitude toward logging in the late nineteenth
   century. How realistic is her description of old-time logging? Along with her
   earlier description, consider the last line of her essay.

3. Russell explains part of the purpose of her essay in the following terms: "My
   wanting to preserve that forest would be like someone's wanting to preserve
   that little church in the middle of downtown, or a little covered bridge somewhere, or a natural canyon, or some other nostalgic refuge." In what specific
   ways is this statement of purpose reflected in Charlotte Russell's tone, in the
   words and phrases she chooses to express her attitude toward both loggers of
   the 1880s and those of the 1980s? What word in the above quotation best
   characterizes Charlotte Russell's attitude toward logging in the 1880s? Which
   passages in her essay support your choice?

4. In the first draft of Russell's essay, the second sentence in paragraph 2 read:
   "A single man brandishing a motorized chain saw did not topple one of these
   giants; instead two men would usually spend eight days chopping, hacking, and
   sawing a chunk out, using their axes and cross-cut saws, until finally, with a
   tremendous roar that echoed through the pristine forest, the virgin tree would
   fall heavily to the ground, crushing anything in its path." Consider how Russell
   revised the sentence in her final draft: "It wasn't a single man brandishing a
   motorized chain saw that felled one of these giants; instead two men would
   usually spend eight days chopping, hacking, and sawing a chunk out, using
   their axes and crosscut saw, until finally, with a tremendous roar that echoed
   throughout the pristine forest, the virgin tree would fall heavily to the ground,
   crushing everything in its path." Explain how this revision strengthens or weak-
   ens the overall effect she is trying to create.

5. Russell offers the following explanation of her use of technical language to

describe logging: "One particular problem I had to work out was the modern, technical jargon that all of my readers might not understand. I didn't want to get into a lengthy and detailed explanation of what a cat or a yarder looked like, so I assumed instead a certain level of understanding from the readers (rather than bore them with a two-page description). Perhaps this is one of the weaknesses of my essay; it narrowed the audience." What effect does Russell's use of "technical jargon" have on your understanding of her essay? Should she have defined more of the logging terms or avoided them altogether? What revisions, if any, would you suggest she make in this aspect of her essay?

SUGGESTIONS FOR WRITING

1. Russell depicts a time when people and the natural world existed as coequals. In one respect, her essay is a plea for survival and an attack on waste. Barbara Howell makes a similar point in her essay "Survival and the Pig" (pp. 82–84). In an essay, describe an aspect of contemporary life that you feel still reflects the primal relationship between people and the environment.

2. Consider the process of doing some kind of work — or perhaps even an entire industry — that has been transformed in recent years by technological advances. Write an essay comparing and contrasting the past and the present processes. Exactly what changes in procedure have occurred, and what are the short-term and long-term consequences of those changes?

3. Apply the same principle and procedure as in question 2 to an essay about changes in your own life. Write an essay about some activity in your day-to-day life, describing and then evaluating how a new way of doing the activity has transformed your life. Explain as precisely as you can the nature of the changes in the activity and the extent of the changes it has prompted in your life.

LINNEA SAUKKO

Ohio State University
Columbus, Ohio
Toni Reed Bates, instructor

"The things I like to write about are inside of me, and when I write they pour out," Linnea Saukko explains. "I have always loved the outdoors and ever since I was in junior high school I have known that I wanted to do environmental work." Born in Warren, Ohio, in 1956, Linnea Saukko graduated from La Brae High School in Leavittsburg, Ohio, and went to work as a hazardous-waste laboratory technician. She later spent three years developing waste disposal and chemical safety programs for a large corporation. Saukko says her work made her "very aware of the shortage of safe methods and places to dispose of hazardous chemical waste. I continuously read about chemical dumps that were leaking and poisoning people and the environment. I became so concerned that I quit my job to go back to school to earn a degree in geology. Soon I will be able to help clean up some of the leaking dumps I have read about." Now a freshman at Ohio State University, Saukko plans to combine her interest in geology with technical writing.

Asked to write an essay on a specific process, Saukko resisted the obvious — sailing, photographing, and reading, her hobbies. "There are millions of papers on how to take pictures or how to sail a boat, but I aimed for something different," she says. "I thought this topic would be unique and wouldn't bore my readers." The result is an essay that satirically addresses the issue of threats to the environment.

How to Poison the Earth

Poisoning the earth can be difficult because the earth is always trying to cleanse and renew itself. Keeping this in mind, we should generate as much waste as possible from substances such as uranium-238, which has a half-life (the time it takes for half of the substance to decay) of 1 million years, or plutonium, which has a half-life of only 0.5 million years but is so toxic that if distributed evenly, 10 pounds of it could kill every person on the earth. Because the United States generates about 18 tons of plutonium per year, it is about the best substance for long-term poisoning of the earth. It would help if we would build more nuclear power plants because each one generates only 500 pounds of plutonium per year. Of course, we must include persistent toxic chemicals such as polychlorinated biphenyl (PCB) and dichlorodiphenyl trichloroethane (DDT) to make sure we have enough toxins to poison the earth from the core to the outer atmosphere. First, we must develop many different ways of putting the waste from these nuclear and chemical substances in, on, and around the earth.

Putting these substances in the earth is a most important step in the poi-   2
soning process. With deep-well injection we can ensure that the earth is poi-
soned all the way to the core. Deep-well injection involves drilling a hole that
is a few thousand feet deep and injecting toxic substances at extremely high
pressures so they will penetrate deep into the earth. According to the Environmental Protection Agency (EPA), there are about 360 such deep injection
wells in the United States. We cannot forget the groundwater aquifers that
are closer to the surface. These must also be contaminated. This is easily done
by shallow-well injection, which operates on the same principle as deep-well
injection only closer to the surface. The groundwater that has been injected
with toxins will spread the contamination beneath the earth. The EPA estimates that there are approximately 500,000 shallow injection wells in the
United States.

Burying the toxins in the earth is the next best method. The toxins from   3
landfills, dumps, and lagoons slowly seep into the earth, guaranteeing that
contamination will last a long time. Because the EPA estimates there are only
about 50,000 of these dumps in the United States, they should be located in
areas where they will leak to the surrounding ground and surface water.

Applying pesticides and other poisons on the earth is another part of the   4
poisoning process. This is good for coating the earth's surface so that the
poisons will be absorbed by plants, will seep into the ground, and will run off
into surface water.

Surface water is very important to contaminate because it will transport the   5
poisons to places that cannot be contaminated directly. Lakes are good for
long-term storage of pollutants while they release some of their contamination
to rivers. The only trouble with rivers is that they act as a natural cleansing
system for the earth. No matter how much poison is dumped into them, they
will try to transport it away to reach the ocean eventually.

The ocean is very hard to contaminate because it has such a large volume   6
and a natural buffering capacity that tends to neutralize some of the contamination. So in addition to the pollution from rivers, we must use the ocean as
a dumping place for as many toxins as possible. The ocean currents will help
transport the pollution to places that cannot otherwise be reached.

Now make sure that the air around the earth is very polluted. Combustion   7
and evaporation are major mechanisms for doing this. We must continuously
pollute because the wind will disperse the toxins while rain washes them from
the air. But this is good because a few lakes are stripped of all living animals
each year from acid rain. Because the lower atmosphere can cleanse itself fairly
easily, we must explode nuclear test bombs that shoot radioactive particles
high into the upper atmosphere where they will circle the earth for years.

Gravity may pull some of the particles to earth, so we must continue exploding these bombs.

So it is that easy. Just be sure to generate as many poisonous substances as possible and be sure they are distributed in, on, and around the entire earth at a greater rate than it can cleanse itself. By following these easy steps we can guarantee the poisoning of the earth.

QUESTIONS FOR READING AND REVISING

1. Linnea Saukko describes her writing process this way: "As soon as I decided on the topic, I made a list of all the types of pollution and I sat down and basically wrote the paper in less than two hours. The information seemed to pour from me onto the page. Of course I did a lot of editing afterward, but I never changed the idea and tone that I started with." Summarize Saukko's "idea" in her essay. What is her actual purpose in writing? How can you tell what her real purpose is? Does she aim to entertain us, to inform us of the dangers in our environment, to frighten us into action? Support your answer with examples from the essay.

2. How does Saukko go about achieving her desired effect? Consider, for example, paragraph 2. What are its strengths? What does Saukko accomplish in this paragraph? Point to other instances in her essay when she accomplishes her goal. Explain why you think her essay is effective at these points.

3. Why is Saukko's satiric approach (her efforts at ridicule) more convincing than if she had presented the same facts in a straightforward, serious tone?

4. In what specific ways do you think the technical details add to or detract from the success of the essay? Does Saukko's use of technical language increase or diminish the satiric effect of her essay? How does she make sure that her audience will not be bored or put off by this unfamiliar language?

5. Which of Saukko's points about "poisoning the earth" are supported by factual information and statistics? Are there any points that could be strengthened with such support? Explain.

6. Consider the structure of Saukko's essay. What kind of order does she establish? Increasing importance, increasing complexity, specific to general, general to specific, step by step, something else? Explain.

7. Show how Saukko's opening paragraph does or does not provide enough evidence of her satiric tone for her readers to grasp her purpose. Suggest how Saukko could revise this paragraph to signal her satiric intention.

8. Compare Saukko's essay with Virginia Bean's "Bitter Sitter" (pp. 31–33) and Allison Rolls's "Lady Diana: He Married the Wrong Woman" (pp. 115–18). Examine how each writer uses irony or satire differently to present her point. Which writer most clearly relates her ironic or satiric tone to her purpose?

SUGGESTIONS FOR WRITING

1. Read through a few past issues of your local newspapers. In addition to environmental pollution, identify three issues that receive prominent attention because they pose serious threats to the public welfare. Choose the issue that interests you most and write a satiric essay proposing a solution to the problem.

2. Choose some current topic (such as vivisection, abortion, state and local income or sales taxes) and write a "proposal" that ostensibly encourages the activity but actually underscores its illegality or inappropriateness.

JACKIE SCANNELL

East Central College
Union, Missouri
Mark Rockhold, instructor

Jackie Scannell reports that the most difficult aspect of writing is selecting a topic: "If the topic is assigned, I can usually concoct something to say about it, but being given a choice of subjects may leave me blank. However, once an idea 'clicks,' writing is easy and fun." Asked to write an example paper, Scannell never even flinched. "After reading several thousand romantic novels, I noticed the similarities," she explains. "I realized that this topic fit the assignment perfectly."

Scannell was born in Louisville, Kentucky, in 1948, graduated from high school in St. Louis, Missouri, and lives with her husband and three children in Washington, Missouri. She has been employed by a government agency, a major department store, a hospital, and a crafts shop. Currently, she is the secretary/rental manager of a car dealership and also attends East Central College, where she is working toward a degree in business management. In her "spare" time, Scannell enjoys camping, wood carving, oil painting, coaching a women's soccer team, and reading popular satirists such as Erma Bombeck, Art Buchwald, and Andy Rooney. "For pure relaxation, I read locks-and-tresses novels," she says.

Locks and Tresses

The shelves in libraries and bookstores are laden with locks-and-tresses 1
novels. A locks-and-tresses novel is a history-based romantic fiction, usually
with a provocative title such as *Dark Fires, Sweet Savage Love, Dangerous Obsession,* or *Forbidden Passion.* In a true locks-and-tresses novel, the heroine
never has just hair; she has "a golden mane" (blond hair), "flaming locks"
(red hair), or "raven tresses" (black hair). These books are a real literary
adventure; they are also all quite similar. On page 83 the main characters are
always doing the same thing.

The heroine of the story is a young, naive maiden of the eighteenth century, 2
usually age sixteen. She has a well-developed, voluptuous body, but when she
dons men's clothing, as she invariably does, everyone mistakes her for a boy.
(Any woman who is built like a boy knows this to be an impossibility.) She
is an incredibly beautiful girl who always retains her fierce pride and self-
confidence, and no matter how often she is raped, abused, or beaten, as she
invariably is, she remains virginal. Her eyes are always "flashing" with anger,
lust, or hatred. She is usually scheduled to be sacrificed in marriage to a short,
fat, bald, rich old man.

The hero is unfailingly handsome. He has broad, muscular shoulders, narrow   3
hips, and thick wavy hair. The color of his hair may vary, but it's usually
falling in his eyes. He undoubtedly has cold, steel-gray, flintlike eyes that are
capable of "smoldering with passion." He is several years older than our maiden.
He's been around. He is a man of adventure, usually a pirate or spy, and
although he appears to be a rogue, when his true motives are revealed he
proves to be quite gallant.

The plot of a locks-and-tresses novel is quite standardized. The story begins   4
with the heroine cavorting in wild abandon about her family estate, a lush
Tudor manor. Our hero finds the maiden in a secluded glen and ravishes her
(page 83), thinking her to be a common wench when in actuality she is a
high-bred lady. (Apparently, in the eighteenth century it was acceptable to
rape wenches.) This attack awakens in our lady fires of passion hitherto unknown. However, it also arouses hatred for our hero as well as anger at him
for ruining her life. Shamed forever, madame runs away from her beloved
family, rich old husband-to-be, and ancestral home. After traveling across the
countryside disguised as a boy, she usually ends up at sea, where she suffers
many terrible misadventures, all of which she blames on our hero. However,
our adventurous rogue is on a parallel course across the sea, and he is suffering
imprisonment or slavery, usually caused by his efforts to find the lady.

Midway through the book, fate throws them together in a twist of irony.   5
The hero rescues the maiden, a confrontation occurs between the two, and
the fires of passion are rekindled (page 157), in spite of her hatred for him.
At this point, the "happy couple" is separated, and the heroine is usually
abducted and raped by the villains. Through her own daring and cunning, she
escapes from this peril only to discover that she is pregnant. This, too, she
blames on our hero, not on the ruffians who attacked her. She resolves never
to see him again, runs away, gives birth to twins, immediately regains her
beautiful and voluptuous body, and runs away again — this time with her
children. In the heart-wrenching conclusion, our hero finds the maiden, claims
the children as his own (undoubtedly, the babies have his flintlike eyes), and
declares his undying love for all of them, and the fires of passion are again
rekindled to burn forever on the library shelves.

QUESTIONS FOR READING AND REVISING

1. According to Jackie Scannell, what are the essential traits of a locks-and-tresses
   novel? If you have never read such a novel, are you given enough information
   and examples in this essay to understand the distinctive nature of this form of

fiction? Which of her detailed examples are particularly vivid or memorable? Does Scannell make you want to read a locks-and-tresses novel? Why or why not?

2. In what ways does the purpose of this essay extend beyond defining and illustrating the essential features of a locks-and-tresses novel? Do any larger points emerge about the general appeal of romantic fiction and about the audience for such literature? What are the cultural implications of this essay? What is its unstated purpose?

3. Jackie Scannell uses a good deal of irony in her essay. (*Webster's* defines irony as an "incongruity between a situation and the accompanying words or actions that is understood by the audience but not by the characters.") Find instances of irony in Scannell's essay and evaluate the effectiveness of each. What, for example, is the function of the parenthetical commentary in paragraphs 2 and 4 of this essay? How does Scannell's use of irony add to or detract from the success of the essay?

4. The first draft of Scannell's essay contained the following opening sentences:

> The history-based, romantic novel is my favorite type of reading material. The shelves in bookstores are laden with this type of book, which I call a "locks-and-tresses" novel.

Compare and contrast this version with her final draft:

> The shelves in libraries are laden with locks-and-tresses novels. A locks-and-tresses novel is a history-based romantic fiction, usually with provocative titles such as *Dark Fires, Sweet Savage Love, Dangerous Obsession,* or *Forbidden Passion.*

Describe the nature of the revisions Scannell has made here. Which version is more effective? Why?

SUGGESTIONS FOR WRITING

1. Examine Scannell's use of the word *heart-wrenching* in paragraph 5. The word called for here normally would be *heartrending.* Which of the two words is more appropriate in the essay? Write a paragraph making a convincing case for the use of one phrase or the other.

2. How would you classify by genre the books you have read or the films you have seen recently? Are they mostly horror stories, spy thrillers, tales of extraterrestrials? What essential features do they share? Write an essay defining the essential ingredients of one such genre and explain why the books or films in that genre appeal to a particular segment of the American public.

JAMES M. SEILSOPOUR

Riverside City College
Riverside, California
William F. Hunt, instructor

James Seilsopour was born in Anaheim, California, in 1962 but spent most of his childhood and adolescence living in Teheran, until the Iranian revolution forced his family to return to the United States in 1979. He graduated from high school in Norco, California, in 1982 and enrolled in Riverside City College, where he is now working toward a major in English.

James Seilsopour says he did not plan "I Forgot the Words to the National Anthem" as a response to a specific course assignment but as a means "to talk about that part of my life." When he returned from Teheran, he was alienated from many of his American peers and ridiculed at times for his Iranian heritage, and he decided to write some poetry about these experiences. But then, as he explains, "I had fallen behind in my English class and needed a paper to turn in." Encouraged by his instructor to "write for publication," Seilsopour revised the essay several times ("Revisions are painful—like cutting yourself with a hot blade"), eventually pleased that his story "will finally get told."

"When people read my essay, I want them to imagine themselves in my place for just a moment—then never think about it again."

I Forgot the Words
to the National Anthem

The bumper sticker read, "Piss on Iran." 1

To me, a fourteen-year-old living in Teheran, the Iranian revolution was 2 nothing more than an inconvenience. Although the riots were just around the corner, although the tanks lined the streets, although a stray bullet went through my sister's bedroom window, I was upset because I could not ride at the Royal Stable as often as I used to. In the summer of 1979, my family— father, mother, brothers, sister, aunt, and two cousins—were forced into exile. We came to Norco, California.

In Iran, I was an American citizen and considered myself an American, 3 even though my father was Iranian. I loved baseball and apple pie and knew the words to the "Star-Spangled Banner." That summer before high school, I was like any other kid my age; I listened to rock 'n' roll, liked fast cars, and thought Farrah Fawcett was a fox. Excited about going to high school, I was looking forward to football games and school dances. But I learned that it was not meant to be. I was not like other kids, and it was a long, painful road I traveled as I found this out.

The American embassy in Iran was seized the fall I started high school. I 4 did not realize my life would be affected until I read that bumper sticker in the high school parking lot which read, "Piss on Iran." At that moment I knew there would be no football games or school dances. For me, Norco High consisted of the goat ropers, the dopers, the jocks, the brains, and one quiet Iranian.

I was sitting in my photography class after the hostages were taken. The 5 photography teacher was fond of showing travel films. On this particular day, he decided to show a film about Iran, knowing full well that my father was Iranian and that I grew up in Iran. During the movie, this teacher encouraged the students to make comments. Around the room, I could hear "Drop the bomb" and "Deport the mothers." Those words hurt. I felt dirty, guilty. However, I managed to laugh and assure the students I realized they were just joking. I went home that afternoon and cried. I have long since forgiven those students, but I have not and can never forgive that teacher. Paranoia set in. From then on, every whisper was about me: "You see that lousy son of a bitch? He's Iranian." When I was not looking, I could feel their pointing fingers in my back like arrows. Because I was absent one day, the next day I brought a note to the attendance office. The secretary read the note, then looked at me. "So you're Jim Seilsopour?" I couldn't answer. As I walked away, I thought I heard her whisper to her co-worker, "You see that lousy son of a bitch? He's Iranian." I missed thirty-five days of school that year.

My problems were small compared to those of my parents. In Teheran, my 6 mother had been a lady of society. We had a palatial house and a maid. Belonging to the women's club, she collected clothes for the poor and arranged Christmas parties for the young American kids. She and my father dined with high government officials. But back in the States, when my father could not find a job, she had to work at a fast-food restaurant. She was the proverbial pillar of strength. My mother worked seventy hours a week for two years. I never heard her complain. I could see the toll the entire situation was taking on her. One day my mother and I went grocery shopping at Stater Brothers Market. After an hour of carefully picking our food, we proceeded to the cashier. The cashier was friendly and began a conversation with my mother. They spoke briefly of the weather as my mother wrote the check. The cashier looked at the check and casually asked, "What kind of name is that?" My mother said, "Italian." We exchanged glances for just a second. I could see the pain in her eyes. She offered no excuses; I asked for none.

Because of my father's birthplace, he was unable to obtain a job. A natu- 7
ralized American citizen with a master's degree in aircraft maintenance engineering from the Northrop Institute of Technology, he had never been out of
work in his life. My father had worked for Bell Helicopter International, Flying
Tigers, and McDonnell Douglas. Suddenly, a man who literally was at the top
of his field was unemployable. There is one incident that haunts me even
today. My mother had gone to work, and all the kids had gone to school
except me. I was in the bathroom washing my face. The door was open, and
I could see my father's reflection in the mirror. For no particular reason I
watched him. He was glancing at a newspaper. He carefully folded the paper
and set it aside. For several long moments he stared blankly into space. With
a resigned sigh, he got up, went into the kitchen, and began doing the dishes.
On that day, I know I watched a part of my father die.

My father did get a job. However, he was forced to leave the country. He 8
is a quality control inspector for Saudi Arabian Airlines in Jeddah, Saudi
Arabia. My mother works only forty hours a week now. My family has survived,
financially and emotionally. I am not bitter, but the memories are. I have not
recovered totally; I can never do that.

And no, I have never been to a high school football game or dance. The 9
strike really turned me off to baseball. I have been on a diet for the last year,
so I don't eat apple pie much anymore. And I have forgotten the words to the
national anthem.

QUESTIONS FOR READING AND REVISING

1. James Seilsopour explains that the only problem he had was "toning the paper
   down from an angry commentary to a straightforward personal essay." How
   does he maintain control of his anger? Consider, for example, paragraph 5.
   How does he restrain his emotions? What is the effect of the final sentence in
   this paragraph?

2. What does James Seilsopour tell us about himself in paragraphs 2 and 3? Why
   do these two paragraphs make the rest of his essay more powerful?

3. What kind of relationship does James Seilsopour establish with his audience?
   Point to specific words and phrases to verify your response. How does he elicit
   his readers' sympathy for himself and his family?

4. Identify the three distinct anecdotes in this essay. What point does each anecdote make? Explain how Seilsopour uses these anecdotes to unify his essay.

5. What is Seilsopour's objective in writing this essay? Considering his overall
   purpose and organization, would this essay be more effective if it ended with

his mother's denial of Seilsopour as an Iranian name? What do the final three paragraphs add to his essay?

6. What is the function of the opening line in the essay? Seilsopour quotes the bumper sticker again in paragraph 4. Does his use of it at the beginning of the essay strengthen or weaken its impact later?

7. In his first draft, Seilsopour ended paragraph 7 with the following sentence: "To this day we have never spoken of that incident." Does Seilsopour's decision to omit this line from his final draft improve or damage the effect of this paragraph?

SUGGESTIONS FOR WRITING

1. James Seilsopour and Annie Glaven describe in detail their struggles to live with the consequences of being different from most of their peers. Compare and contrast their situations, their approaches to their lives, and their responses. What inferences can you draw about the American character from their stories?

2. Imagine that you are a diplomatic representative of the United States government responsible for writing a letter to James Seilsopour in response to his essay. In writing the letter, you must decide whether you should explain, justify, or apologize for the treatment he and his family have received since their return to the United States. What action, if any, will you take? Or imagine that you are a student at the high school Seilsopour attended. Write a letter in response to Seilsopour's essay. Will you explain, justify, or apologize on behalf of other students for the ways in which Seilsopour and his family have been mistreated? What action, if any, will you take?

3. A particularly painful episode in James Seilsopour's narrative is the humiliation he suffers in his high school class. Write an essay in which you use either the first or the third person to recount a humiliating or embarrassing incident in high school or college. Describe the motives and the responses of those involved. What lasting effects did the incident have?

TODD ALEXANDER SENTURIA

Harvard University
Cambridge, Massachusetts
Victor Kantor Burg, instructor

Todd Senturia was born in Boston in 1965, graduated from Commonwealth High School there, and enrolled in Harvard University in 1982. A nationally ranked junior squash player and a freshman member of Harvard's NCAA championship squash team, Senturia is also an avid reader of detective fiction and a student of the Lao and Khmer (Cambodian) languages.

Senturia traces his interest in foreign cultures to the year he spent living in Europe. A summer job teaching sports to teenage Laotian and Cambodian refugees has become, as he notes, "the major motivation in my life over the past few years" and one of the reasons he has decided to major in East Asian studies. He currently serves as the deputy director of the Asian Newcomer Youth Program in Boston and plans to use his writing to call the public's attention to the efforts of East Asian refugees to adjust to life in the United States.

Asked to write a descriptive essay, Senturia decided to focus on the national customs of a Cambodian family in strikingly different circumstances — a working-class Boston neighborhood. His essay presents a vivid description of how, as he says, "two very different worlds are so arbitrarily juxtaposed."

At Home in America

Chindaree's delicate oval face is framed by thick black hair which flows in shifting waves down across her shoulders and back. As she leans forward, a wrinkle of concern shades her forehead for the tendril of hair which curls across one eye. She brushes the lock away with her forearm. The pan on the burner fills the small kitchen with smells recognizable to my American senses only as delicious. The aromas somehow match the brightly colored flower pattern of the cotton sarong wrapped tightly around the girl's waist.

Something in the pan displeases her, and she crosses the tiny space in search of additional spices. In one fluid motion, she slips from a standing position into a squat which would look ugly and awkward on an American but graces the full figure of this eighteen-year-old Cambodian woman-child. She rummages briefly in the cabinet and rises triumphant, holding a bottle whose label boasts no English, only the decorative scripts of the Khmer and Thai languages. She adds a certain amount from this new bottle, the tendons in her wrist standing out as she stirs the liquid in with a spoon. She smiles lightly as the results meet with her approval, then winces as a drop of fat pops, spattering her arm. A single bead of sweat gathers on her nose, glinting in the light.

Exotic and familiar sounds crowd the small apartment in a clashing of cultures. Occasionally the popping from the stove punctuates the rhythmic melodies of the *romvong*, Cambodian dance music which accompanies Chindaree's efforts on a cassette recorder. Much of her family sits in the next room. Their conversation, of which I can understand only a few words — "maa," mother; "ñam baay," eat rice; "tiv salaa," go to school — contends with the babble of the television set. Chindaree's baby niece cries in no particular language at all. Outside, of course, the sounds of an East Boston neighborhood preside: cars honking, dogs barking, and residents hanging out of windows shouting the latest gossip back and forth.

One of Chindaree's sisters, Pharee, lured by the aroma of lunch, slips past where I stand and into the kitchen. Pharee is only fifteen, thin and lithe, not as fully figured as her older sister but with the same oval face and rich black hair. She carries herself as regally here at home in blue jeans and sneakers as when she performs the ancient Khmer classical dances up on stage in front of hundreds of people. She leans over her sister and asks a question in the jarring syllables of their language. As the two talk, Pharee slips her arm around her sister's waist and rests her head upon Chindaree's shoulder.

The telephone shatters the moment, and Pharee picks it up with a cautious "Allo . . . ?" She listens briefly, then puts the phone down on the table, calling, "Nee, mao nih, Theavy . . ." Phanee, the youngest girl, bounds in, all smiles. Only thirteen, boyish and energetic, her hair pulled back from her face in a pony tail, Phanee nonetheless unmistakably resembles her sisters. The oval features which in Chindaree's face are subdued and unassuming, and in Pharee's regal and almost haughty, come out in Phanee as impishly angelic. The glint in her dark eyes and the slight smile playing around the corners of her mouth hint at some secret joke which she might tell you, and then again might not.

Later, Chindaree and I eat at the table. A bowl of white rice sits at each place, along with fork, spoon, and chopsticks, as the different plates of food vie for attention. A beef and vegetable dish seasoned heavily with ginger proves itself magnificent. A cold, spicy cucumber salad which looks somewhat dubious conquers me as well, and I eat nearly the whole bowl. Another plate, filled with strips of cooked pork and beef, sits next to a small saucer holding an innocuous-looking red sauce. Chindaree takes a strip of meat from the platter with her chopsticks, dips it into the sauce, and brings it directly to her mouth. I copy her example, but as I'm about to open my mouth, she warns, "Kdav nah" — very spicy. It is, but equally delicious, and she and I share a companionable time of alternating bites. Chindaree eats as gracefully as she does everything else, a slight frown of concentration between her arched eyebrows as she manipulates her chopsticks or spoons up the last bit of rice from her bowl.

As we sit at the table, the other members of the household drift in and 7
out, serving themselves food and then going to sit either outside on the porch, which looks out over clotheslines and backyard lots, or back into the room with the TV. Pharee, Phanee, and a girl from downstairs, fresh-faced and bright, troop in, take their food, and settle on the porch for a playful meal full of shrieks and laughter.

Vuthy and Chindee, the two older boys in the family, come in to take their 8
share. Vuthy, seventeen years old, tall and well proportioned, wears just shorts, and the hairless skin of his chest and arms gleams slightly with sweat. He carries a hand exerciser and a pair of nunchuks. His regal bearing recalls Pharee, and, indeed, Vuthy often dances the male lead opposite his sister. Chindee, twenty years old, is darkly handsome, with a flash of white smile. His button-down shirt, open at the neck, shows a densely muscled chest, and as he spoons rice from the stove into a bowl, his biceps bulge. His left eye doesn't focus very well, though, as he's not yet fully recovered from the beating he took at the hands of six East Boston kids. His broken nose has healed, but his tentative, gloomy, smileless air contrasts sadly with his previous cheerful spirit.

The door to the porch bounds open, and in struts the youngest family 9
member. Pausing for a moment in the doorway, he poses in his Superman T-shirt, flexing an imagined bicep. Finding the beat in the *romvong*, he dances wildly across the small floor to the stove. His name is Chearee, and at twelve years old he already speaks more English than anyone in the family except Chindaree. He departs as dramatically as he entered, holding his bowl aloft as if it were an offering to Buddha. He disappears into the TV room, and soon his accented voice raises in song, accompanying the commercials—"What a great place, it's a great place to start."

As my hostess washes the dishes, humming to herself in Khmer, she glows 10
with life and color against the stark, dingy kitchen. Her bright green sarong, wrapped around her waist, fits snugly about her hips and falls in folds nearly to the floor. Her sandals peek out from beneath the swaying fabric as she moves back and forth. A cockroach scurries out from beneath the sink, and Chindaree casually stamps on it with her sandal, briefly exposing an ankle and lower calf. Her hair, held away from her face now by a pair of enameled combs, cascades down her back, almost to her waist, starkly black against the greens of her shirt and sarong. Her breasts stretch the fabric of the shirt, lengthening

the slight V-neck to expose the smooth white skin of her neck and collarbone. Droplets of water cling to the down on her arms, darkening it slightly. The steam from the sink colors Chindaree's cheeks and dampens the stray strands of hair on her forehead. That same bead of sweat forms at the tip of her nose. Her long eyelashes highlight the color of her eyes against the fairness of her skin, which is especially light for a Khmer.

She turns her head suddenly and catches me watching her. She smiles at 11 me briefly from the depths of her dark eyes, then turns back away from me, a slight blush heightening the color in her cheeks and even tinting her throat. She begins to hum again. Among the chaotic sounds of laughing, crying, music playing, and dogs barking, she appears calm and composed. Against the backdrop of bare pipes and peeling paint, she sparkles with an innocent beauty. Even her name, Chindaree, suits the image of this delicate, exotic Cambodian flower flourishing here in the poverty and dirt of East Boston's slums.

QUESTIONS FOR READING AND REVISING

1. What overall impression does Todd Senturia create of Chindaree and her family? How well have they adjusted to life in the United States? What is the significance of the youngest child's singing television commercials? What is the effect of Chindee's having been beaten up by "six East Boston kids"?

2. One distinguishing feature of effective description is the use of concrete, sensory details. List the instances when Senturia appeals to each of his readers' five senses.

3. Another prominent feature of effective description is a clear point of view, the physical perspective from which a story is told or a scene is described. What is Senturia's point of view in the essay? Show how his point of view either changes or remains consistent as the essay proceeds.

4. How does Senturia establish the contrast between American and Cambodian cultures in the opening paragraph? How does he sustain this contrast in each of the following paragraphs? Consider, for example, the contrast in the final paragraph, where, "against the backdrop of bare pipes and peeling paint" Chindaree "sparkles with an innocent beauty . . . [a] delicate exotic Cambodian flower flourishing here in the poverty and dirt of East Boston's slums." In light of this contrast, explain whether the impact of the essay is strengthened or weakened by the previous mention of the slum and the beating of Chindaree's brother.

5. What aspect of this family's home life does Senturia use to unify his description? Show how this activity serves as a background for his description of each family

member. Why do you suppose Senturia chose this aspect of the family's life to unify his essay?

6. This essay is rich in detail. Readers can sense the presence of a writer working hard — and quite consciously — at description. Yet one of the risks of writing descriptive essays is the possibility of allowing adjectives or other modifiers to get in the way of meaning. Consider these sentences from paragraph 5:

> The oval features which in Chindaree's face are subdued
> and unassuming, and in Pharee's regal and almost haughty,
> come out in Phanee as impishly angelic. The glint in her
> dark eyes and the slight smile playing around the corners
> of her mouth hint at some secret joke which she might tell
> you, and then again might not.

What are the specific strengths and weaknesses of these sentences? What advice would you give Todd Senturia about revising them? Locate similar descriptive passages, consider their strengths and weaknesses, and, if appropriate, draft a new version of each.

7. Paragraphs 1 and 10 present physical descriptions of Chindaree. Which details does Senturia repeat and with what effect? Does he need to repeat these details? What would he gain or lose by eliminating the repetition?

SUGGESTIONS FOR WRITING

1. Prepare a detailed set of notes comparing and contrasting the experiences of Chindaree and her family in the United States with those of James Seilsopour and his family in "I Forgot the Words to the National Anthem" (pp. 132 – 34). Add to these notes your own view of the experience of recent immigrants to this country. Write an essay describing the pleasures and perils immigrants face in adjusting to life in the United States.

2. Write an essay in which you describe your first encounter with a foreign culture through its food (or through an item of clothing, a particular mannerism, or some other aspect of the culture). Explain the inferences you drew about the foreign culture — and, by contrast, about your own — as a result of this encounter. Evaluate your response at the time. How was your response different from your current perspective on the experience?

3. An "oasis" can take many forms: a striking person (physically or spiritually) in an otherwise dull crowd, a clearing in a dense forest, an event that distinguishes itself from daily life. An oasis can also be discovered in many places: a desolate rural landscape, a crowded city. Todd Senturia describes one such oasis. Describe an oasis you have encountered, using vivid details, as Senturia does, to re-create the vitality, mystery, and wonder of your oasis. Place your readers right on the spot. Make them see exactly what is so special about this place.

MEL TENNANT

University of Colorado at Denver
Denver, Colorado
Carolyn Kallemeyn, instructor

Mel Tennant's earliest recollection of writing is of "a short story I wrote in grade school. All I remember is that it was a fantasy in which I died at the end, making a statement that the story was 'ghost-written.' " Born into a military family in 1950 in Los Angeles, Tennant spent much of his youth moving from one base to another, acclimating himself to ever-changing cultural and social circumstances. He graduated from Central High School in Aurora, Colorado, in 1968 and spent the next eight years in the Army at several domestic and foreign posts, including Korea. He held various jobs before enrolling at the University of Colorado.

Asked to write a comparison and contrast essay, Tennant wrote his essay to show how it felt to return home to the United States after adapting to an alien environment as well as "to make a statement about the many unappreciated benefits we enjoy in this country." He did a great deal of free writing and brainstorming to help shape his idea and then prepared an outline and three drafts: "rough, polished, and final." In each, he strove to "show my audience something they hadn't seen before, some place they had never been. I wanted them to feel what I felt and understand what the experience meant to me. . . . I tried both to compare Korea with the United States and to contrast the way America seemed after my tour with the way it seemed before I left."

A Stranger's Eyes

I had never seen military checkpoints or anti-aircraft batteries along I-25; yet, as I drove toward the dirty brown haze that enveloped Denver, it seemed odd *not* to see them. Upon my return from Asia, it was not the road which had changed; it was my viewpoint. During my thirteen months overseas, I had become acclimated to that environment, and now, to metaphrase Heinlein, I was a stranger in a familiar land.

Physically, Denver was much the same as I had left it. The traffic I had so often cursed for its unthinking, discourteous drivers and undisciplined flow still inched along at its nerve-fraying pace. Instead of being irritated, however, I was fascinated with the traffic's orderly movement. Only a few days before, I had been in a tiny cab, hurtling through the densely packed streets of downtown Seoul. I had clung desperately to the handle above the door as the taxi weaved violently around motorcycles, pushcarts, buses, bicycles, small three-wheeled trucks, and fellow maniacs. These disparate components crowded together to make an eight- or nine-lane asylum out of a four-lane road. Com-

pared with the oriental version of Mr. Toad's Wild Ride, Denver's traffic was
as orderly and regimented as a military dress parade.

The traffic slowly began to disperse as I reached the accident that had caused   3
the congestion. A police cruiser was at the scene, and a uniformed officer
waved traffic around the blockage. The patrol car looked enormous, as did the
other American cars. I had previously considered policemen to be heavily
armed, but compared to the automatic weapons carried by Korean police, the
handgun, mace, and baton of our patrolmen appeared almost benign.

I felt great joy, as I drove, in being able to read signs again. Store, street,   4
and advertising signs were gloriously legible rather than undecipherable ideo-
grams. I felt a peculiar security in knowing what a building was without looking
inside. I could now identify a pharmacy without looking for jars of pickled
snakes or ginseng. The many signs I had once ignored I now read with unre-
served relish.

These signs and other sights made the societal wealth I had once taken for   5
granted shockingly conspicuous. Large cars, new clothes, giant food stores,
and innumerable entertainment spots assaulted eyes that had become accustomed to poverty and frugality. I saw trash bins full of cardboard boxes, old
clothes, broken furniture, and even unopened containers of food. What had
been discarded as garbage and junk would be a treasure trove to the many
destitute people overseas. Cardboard boxes could repair, or be, a dwelling; old
clothes could be sewn and worn, broken furniture repaired and used, and the
discarded food would help them survive. Even what is, to us, the most useless
of trash was recycled in Korea. In the village near my base, a street vendor
sold fried shrimp served in paper bags made from our discarded daily reports.

The contrasts between our societies was further illuminated by a construc-   6
tion site I passed. The equipment and construction methods seemed almost
futuristic when compared to the primitive manual labor I had so often encountered. Giant power shovels excavated the foundations, rather than men
and women laboring with hand tools. Dump trucks were filled by bulldozers
instead of hunched-over men with wooden boxes strapped on their backs.

As the very thought of intense physical labor can make me tired and thirsty,   7
I readjusted my course toward my old watering hole. I arrived at the Great
Divide Bar and found it little changed. The same weathered antique signs
decorated the same bare, rough wood walls. The pool table, chairs, and bar-
stools were still in dire need of recovering. The jukebox's limited repertoire
also remained unchanged, much to my disappointment. I ordered a brew and
noted how odd it was to be in a bar and not be descended upon by a horde
of women, each vying for the dubious pleasure of trying to separate me from
the contents of my wallet. The icy Michelob tasted sweet compared to the

carbonated formaldehyde that the Korean breweries tried to pass off as beer. Led Zeppelin sang "Stairway to Heaven" from somewhere inside the aging jukebox. I had heard it sung phonetically by oriental club bands so many times that the original version sounded queer.

Over the music, I overheard two other customers complaining loudly about 8 how hard their jobs were:

"Runnin' that paint gun for eight hours sure wears ya down."   9

"Yeah, and for a lousy $10.75 an hour. We should get extra just for putting 10 up with that foreman."

The first man laughed, laid a fresh twenty on the bar for the next round, 11 and said: "I get tired of not havin' nothin'. After I make the payments on my car an' the truck an' the house, I hardly got nothin' left at all."

As the two men continued their diatribe, I found myself thinking of a man 12 I once saw laboriously pedaling up a steep hill, his battered old bicycle laden with 18 fifty-five-gallon drums. I recalled images of old people, cruelly and permanently bent from a lifetime of toiling in rice paddies. I was angered by the arguing men's ignorance of the true quality of their lives. I guess I was angered most by the realization of the many times I had engaged in the same conversation.

Rather than endure further exposure to the men's drunken lamentations, I 13 decided to finish my beer and find a room for the night. While on my way, I realized that people were not leaving the streets. I was so used to my old schedule that I'd forgotten that Denver didn't have a curfew. For over a year I had had to be inside by midnight or risk being shot by the local constabulary. But tonight there was no curfew, no barbed wire, and no machine guns. The city seemed wondrously alive and unrestricted. I felt as though I had just been released from prison. I would find a room later; it was time to look up a few friends and see if anyone else wanted to party.

The welcome-back parties soon passed, and although I rapidly regained my 14 familiarity with this strange land, my view of life in this country was changed forever. I gained a great deal from my experiences overseas, the most valuable of which was the opportunity to see my life through a stranger's eyes.

QUESTIONS FOR READING AND REVISING

1. In the final paragraph, Mel Tennant reports that his "view of life in this country was changed forever." What new perspective has he gained on America? Summarize his attitude toward life in the United States.

2. After listening to the complaining of two men in a Denver bar Tennant was

angered by their ignorance of the true quality of their lives in this country but even more by his own previous ignorance. Why does he respond this way? Support your answer with specific details and examples from the essay.

3. Tennant explains that he was eager to "make a statement about the many unappreciated benefits we enjoy in this country." To avoid sounding moralistic, he packed his essay with details and subtle humor. Where is Tennant most refreshingly specific? Where are his details and language most inventively precise?

4. How does Tennant organize his essay? Does he develop his comparison and contrast point by point? Subject by subject? In some other way? Explain.

5. List the features of life Tennant contrasts in Seoul and Denver. What sense of order and progression does he establish among the details he introduces?

6. How do Tennant's verbal snapshots of life in Seoul underscore his sense of dislocation in Denver? What does he state and what does he imply about the economic and cultural differences between the two societies?

7. Tennant wrote several drafts of this essay. The following are his first and second drafts, respectively, of the opening paragraph.

> The lack of checkpoints and their attendant armed guards seemed strange to me. Camouflaged anti-aircraft gun emplacements were also conspicuously absent from the long stretch of I-25 that snaked into the brown haze which hid Denver from view.

> I have never seen military checkpoints or anti-aircraft batteries on I-25 and there weren't any now. Yet as I drove toward the brown haze that enveloped Denver, after thirteen months overseas, it seemed odd not to see them. Upon my return from Southeast Asia, it was not the road that had changed, it was my viewpoint. During my thirteen months overseas, I had become acclimated to that environment and the once familiar now looked strange and foreign.

Compare the two drafts with each other and with the final version. What specific changes do you notice? Comment on the effectiveness of each change.

8. Tennant says that "determining when the essay is properly finished is the hardest thing to do in writing." Apply his comment to the final paragraphs of his essay. In what specific ways might the ending of his essay be improved? Consider, for example, the possibility of finishing the essay with the next-to-last sentence in paragraph 13 ("I felt as though I had just been released from prison."). What would Tennant gain or lose if he were to make such a change?

9. Make a detailed set of notes recalling a time when you felt a sense of dislo-

cation on returning home from a vacation or from school, or when you found you had little to say to someone you used to know well but had not seen in a long time. How did the previously familiar seem strange?

10. Read William Hill's essay "Returning Home" (pp. 73 – 74). Compare and contrast what it means for the two writers to return home. How similar are the adjustments they must make? In what ways are their problems different? What conclusions can you draw about the common elements of their experiences?

SUGGESTIONS FOR WRITING

1. Write an essay recounting the process you went through when trying to adapt to a move from one town to another or from one school to another or from one social context to another. Be sure to provide your readers with as much detail as possible to help them appreciate fully your process of adjustment in light of the contrast between both sides of the change.

JOHN CLYDE THATCHER

Otterbein College
Westerville, Ohio
Sylvia Vance, instructor

"I am a famous procrastinator. I had put off writing my essay until the night before it was to be turned in," John Thatcher reveals. "This, however, is not unusual, for it seems I can write only under tremendous pressure. I seem to take perverse delight in watching the time slip by until it is almost too late to begin writing. It is like a game of literary Russian roulette. The hammer clicks as the cylinder revolves and time rushes by. And I pray that inspiration will come before the occupied cylinder snaps into place and the hammer poises above the pin. This essay was begun at 11:00 P.M. and finished around 4:00 A.M. I by no means endorse this method, but that is what works for me. So far."

Born in Galion, Ohio, in 1963, Thatcher was raised in his family's five-generation home outside Mt. Liberty, Ohio. He has worked part time as an assistant in both a nursing home and his father's electrical engineering business. He credits his parents and teachers for nurturing his interest in writing and reading, and he recalls that as a child "books were more important than toys." With a double major in political science and history, Thatcher intends to go on to law school after graduation.

Thatcher reports that he wrote his essay "during my first term of college and first long period away from home. I didn't get as homesick as the rest of my freshman friends because if I wanted to go home all I had to do was sit down and write about the things that happened when I was at home and what it was like to be there." In the following essay, Thatcher records the impact of what he calls his "brief trapping career."

For an extended discussion of John Thatcher's essay, see pages 271–286.

On Killing the Man

I wanted to trap! All of the other boys did. Certainly that was reason enough 1
for me. And what about the stacks of money to be made through this time-honored trade? Why, boys had been known to make a small fortune in one season. Boys that wished to become young men required inordinate amounts of money, and for those that live out of town, on a farm with a woods and small creek, trapping during the winter is a most convenient means to an end. The end being, in most cases, the all-important automobile. So I began trapping in the winter of my seventeenth year. I felt as if I were pleasing generations of woodsmen; the pioneer spirit raged in my blood. I would soon be a man. Whose man?

One goes about trapping in this manner. At the very outset one acquires a   2
"trapping" state of mind. This entails several steps. The purchase of as many
traps as one might need is first. A pair of rubber gloves, waterproof boots, and
the grubbiest clothes capable of withstanding human use come next to outfit
the trapper for his adventure. A library of books must be read, and preferably
someone with experience is needed to educate the novice. The decision has
to be made on just what kinds of animals to go after, what sort of bait to use,
and where to place the traps for highest yield. Finally, the trapper needs a
heavy stick. Often a trap set to drown the animal once caught fails to do so.
Then it is necessary to club the animal and drown him. A blow with a club
will not damage a pelt the way a gunshot would. A club is a most necessary
piece of equipment for the trapper.

So I set out on my wilderness adventure. My booted feet scarred the frosted   3
grass. The traps slung over my shoulder tolled a death knell as they slapped
against my back, and the oaken club rapped a steady drumbeat on my thigh.
I had my chance to become a man, a real man in the old sense of the word.
I was the French voyageur trapping lands no white man had ever seen before.
I was Dan'l Boone about to catch my famous coonskin cap. I was the Hudson
Bay Company trapper, trading axes and blankets with the Indians and sending
beaver pelts to London for a gentleman's top hat. I was my father too. I was
he and he was me as the two of us set out together for the great woods. This
was truly the way men should live.

The actual work of trapping can be completed only after the trapper has   4
suffered as much as possible. It is cold, tedious, backbreaking, finger- and toe-
numbing, infuriating torture often described as exciting and fun by someone
who really enjoys trapping. In my case the traps were mostly set in the water.
This is done in the hopes of catching muskrats, raccoons, and possibly a mink
or two. It is also done to enhance the feeling of already numb fingers by
immersing them in freezing water. It is a most difficult task becoming a man,
even more difficult to enjoy doing it.

· Once the animal is caught it must be skinned. This involves cutting the   5
pelt away from the body, scraping off the fatty deposits from the underside,
and stretching the skin on a board until it is dry. All in all a great amount of
work for a twenty-five-dollar pelt. Twenty-five dollars, that is, if the pelt is
large for a raccoon, if it is in good condition, and if the dealer you go to is a
generous man. But who can deny the sense of accomplishment a man feels
when he sells his pelts? Only he can know the great satisfaction felt by outsmarting small animals through catching and killing them in traps they could
not smell or see. What joy is felt when a man can say he has beaten nature
with only his quick mind, traps of spring steel, rubberized gloves that leave no

betraying scent, scientifically tested lures and baits, and clever sets that catch the animals and sink them to their deaths as they struggle to get away while water fills their small, gasping lungs.

But often the novice does not succeed in making a "water set" that quickly 6 drowns the animal.

One cold morning I stayed home from school, and though sick with a cold 7 I checked my trapline like any humane trapper. My "water sets" had not worked the night before. I walked in the direction of a trap anchored to a fallen log that was intended to encourage a trapped animal to escape by swimming across the creek and thus drown itself. As I neared the trap I immediately saw that it had been disturbed but didn't see an animal. "Drowned," I thought. When I was very close to the set I realized the animal was not drowned and underwater; hopelessly entangled around a limb of the log was a large male raccoon.

Now I had a problem. The raccoon must be knocked senseless and drowned. 8 The club that hung around my wrist had grown very heavy all of a sudden and my stomach knotted at the thought of what I had to do. I was torn between wanting to absolve myself by setting him free (although I knew he would suffer a horrible death) and doing what it was I had worked so hard to come to. I wanted to be a man but also wanted to run away from what I'd done and cry into my mother's breast. My hand, however, was forced by my earlier actions, and now I had to take this creature's life to end the suffering I had caused it. The bile rose in my throat as I raised the club.

At that moment I knew what an awful thing it is to be hated, violently 9 hated by another living thing. He looked at me and not the club. He looked at me with his trap-torn flesh bleeding away his fear, leaving only raging hate. He barely paused in his screamed hiss as the club came down, again and again, on his skull. I didn't kill him well because he was my first murder, and the hot tears that burst from me blinded my eyes, making the blows poorly aimed.

Once that hideous screaming stopped and the despising, damning eyes rolled 10 back into their sockets, I drowned him. As I watched the water fill him up and the bubbles and blood float up from his nostrils, I wondered if I was now the man I had wanted to be. Whose man? I decided then that the boy who was responsible for this wretched thing was not ready to be a man because he had aspired to be someone else and not himself. I knew then that I would never do this despicable thing again and never have since. To reach manhood is a wonderful thing, but this happens only when the man can look at himself and recognize what he sees. A boy must kill "the man," the one he has dreamed for himself in his head, in order to let out the one inside that patiently bides his time until the boy is ready to accept what he is. It takes a significant event to make the change. In my case it took the murder of an animal. Life is not always clean and bloodless. If I could have killed my "man" with a swift rapier thrust I would have done it. Instead I am left with the memory of blow after blow on a tiny head. I still see the bared teeth and still hear the wild snarling. My "man" died especially hard in bloody frothing waters. I have learned from that and will never forget.

QUESTIONS FOR READING AND REVISING

1. What has John Thatcher learned about being a man from his brief trapping career? What does he mean when he writes: "A boy must kill the man, the one he has dreamed for himself"?

2. What is the " 'trapping' state of mind" (paragraph 2)? What did trapping represent to Thatcher before and after his experience? Did the ending surprise you?

3. Thatcher's essay is solidly based on a personal experience. We can tell from the powerful details that he is writing about an experience of some real importance. List specific details in the essay that you find especially compelling and powerful.

4. From paragraph 7 to the end, Thatcher uses narration to tell us about killing his first animal. Why is this narration effective? What is his purpose in relating this incident?

5. What is the purpose of paragraphs 2, 4, and 5, which analyze the process of trapping? How do they introduce the narrative?

6. Because Thatcher's personal narrative does not go beyond killing the raccoon, does he need the information on skinning and selling pelts in paragraph 5? What would be the effect of deleting paragraph 5?

7. How would you characterize Thatcher's tone? Does it remain consistent throughout the essay? Is there anything confusing about his tone?

SUGGESTIONS FOR WRITING

1. Choose an incident in your own life or the life of someone you know well that marked the turning point between childhood and adulthood. In an essay, describe the incident and explain its significance.

2. Think of an ideal image you cherished as a child (the ideal mother or father, the ideal friend, the ideal family, the ideal wife or husband). Write an essay describing how that image is similar to and different from your view of the ideal

today. Try to focus on one incident that will demonstrate how and why your view has developed to its present form.

3. When John Thatcher set out to trap, he saw himself as a follower of "Dan'l Boone" and the "Hudson Bay Company trapper" until that myth was dispelled by reality. Have you ever been in a similar situation where reality intruded on fantasy? Describe the fantasy, why you believed in it, and how it came to be dispelled. Did you come to any better understanding as a result?

CYNTHIA JANE THOMPSON

University of North Carolina at Chapel Hill
Chapel Hill, North Carolina
Helen Jacqueline Gray, instructor

Cynthia Jane Thompson describes herself as a productive and motivated writer. She writes whenever she feels the need to express herself because, as she reports, "I can express my ideas in writing better than I can vocalize them." But she cannot write in silence: "I need some type of noise in the background so that I can concentrate." She normally writes amid what might be called a focused state of rhythmic disarray: "Lying stretched across my bed, I can sense my mind thump thesis sentences with each beat of my blaring stereo. Wadded balls of paper lie scattered over the floor beneath me, along with Reese's Cup wrappers and a few stray kernels of popcorn."

Thompson was born in Mecklenburg County, North Carolina, in 1963, and was raised by her adopted parents in Charlotte, North Carolina. She graduated first in her high school class and was named one of Charlotte's All-Star Scholars. Now a biology major at the University of North Carolina and a "Shakespeare fanatic," she plans to go on to medical school.

Asked to write a "researched argument," Thompson summarizes the issues surrounding the legal restrictions adopted children face in searching public records to identify their biological parents. The goal of her essay, she reports, is "to make the reader aware of an adoptee's feelings toward the matter of opening the sealed files. I directed my essay to the adoptive parents. I want them to realize that if adopted children decide to search for their biological parents, it does not mean they love their adopted parents any less. I also want adopted children to understand that searching is not always necessary to find their inner peace."

To Search Is to Grow

In Sophocles' classic *Oedipus Rex*, the downfall of the adopted King Oedipus 1 is directly related to his ignorance about his origins. Although Oedipus was curious about his descent as a child, his parents forbade any investigation.

Instinctively, a person wants to know about his origins, his background, 2 and his genealogy. But in the United States, adoptees, like Oedipus, are not able to explore their roots because of the government's sealed-record policy. Many adoptees are now wanting to find the missing links in their lives by opening the sealed records of their adoptions. These activists, however, are being opposed by other adoptees, natural parents, adoptive parents, and state governments who do not realize the full emotional, and sometimes physical, compulsion to violate the confidentiality of the closed files. Prohibiting the records to be opened not only infringes on the constitutionally based personal rights of the adoptee, but often creates a vortex of frustration and emotional controversy for the adoptee, his adoptive parents, and his natural parents.

To completely understand the view of the activists, one must first know   3 what the sealed records contain and understand the laws regarding their release. When a child is adopted, the adoptive parents are told everything about him, including his medical history, except the identity of the natural parents.[1] At birth the child is issued a birth certificate with the names of his natural parents. The child retains their name until the judge issues an adoption decree and orders a new birth certificate with the names of the adoptive parents. At this time, the original birth certificate is removed and placed on file at the bureau of vital statistics in each state. It is this original birth certificate which the activists are seeking to obtain.[2] Here in North Carolina, as in most states, a court order must be approved by a judge for the parent or adoptee to open the record. Yet any medical record regarding the physical or mental health of the adopted child may be revealed upon written request by an adopted child who is eighteen or older or by his parents, provided that any information about identity is deleted.[3]

It is only natural for the adopted person to show an interest in his genealogy.   4 Unless he has compelling reasons, an adoptee is deprived of information such as whether he will have a weight problem, turn bald, or have a short life span. Adopted females often wonder during pregnancy about whom their baby will resemble or if he will have some type of handicap. In a case of Dr. Arthur Sorosky, physician and coauthor of *The Adoption Triangle*, a pregnant woman worried all through her pregnancy that her baby would look like her unknown family and would not be able to identify with a group. When the child was finally delivered, her first question to her husband was, "Is it all right if he has black hair?"[4] It seems as if this woman became preoccupied with her child's physical appearance rather than his well-being. A search into her genealogical history would have removed many needless fears during her pregnancy. This would have allowed her to review the physical traits that run in her biological family and would have given her time to realize that these characteristics are acceptable.

---

[1]Ruby Lee Piester, "For Ruby Lee Piester, the First and Last Word on Adoption Is 'Confidential,' " *People*, 18 May 1981, p. 60.

[2]Arthur D. Sorosky, Annette Baran, and Reuben Pannor, *The Adoption Triangle* (Garden City, N.Y.: Doubleday, 1978), pp. 19–20.

[3]Jayne Askin, *Search: A Handbook for Adoptees and Birthparents* (New York: Harper and Row, 1982), pp. 260–61.

[4]Sorosky, pp. 124–25.

Innate curiosity and personal fears are not the only reasons that inspire 5
adoptees to search for their natural parents. A search is often the result of
tragic misfortune, as in the case of Jim George. George, age thirty-four, suffers
from chronic myelocytic leukemia and needs to contact a blood relative to
donate bone marrow so he may survive. The operation will be of no more risk
to the donor than the hazards of general anesthesia. Yet Missouri's justice
system will not allow him to open the files. *Science News* explains that the
state of Missouri does not consider his case a sufficiently "compelling circum-
stance" to have the records opened; therefore, he cannot locate the donor he
so badly needs to save his life.[5] If the files were opened, George might find a
donor and live the rest of his life as a healthy individual, but because of the
statutes of Missouri, he must live with the fear of dying.

Other adoptees, however, feel it is unnecessary to open the sealed records. 6
Although curious, most assume their natural parents acted in their best interest. Those with this point of view do not want to disturb old memories and
create needless pain for their adoptive parents and their biological parents.
According to an editorial in *Ms.* magazine by adoptee Cynthia Jones, opening
the records would be an insult to her adoptive parents:

> To go in search of a woman, who is to me a total stranger,
> and claim her as my mother simply because of her biological
> function of some twenty-odd years ago, is to deny the many
> years of love, care, and devotion my real parents have given
> me.[6]

When an adopted child shows interest in searching for his origins, many 7
adoptive parents unduly feel as though they have failed. It is not easy to
understand the intrinsic desire of some adoptees to explore their heritage, but
activist Lorraine Dusky, natural mother of an adopted child and author of
several books about searching for biological parents, believes "the bond of
birth is in our genes."[7] That an adoptee wants to examine his biological background does not necessarily mean his adoptive parents have failed, but if the
records are opened the threat of losing the affection of an adopted child is
ominously present to the adoptive parents. Before an adoption, according to
Ruby Lee Piester, the executive director of the country's largest maternity
center and adoption agency, the adoptive parents want to know how the
mother feels about giving up her child; they want an assurance she will not

[5]"Birth Rights," *Science News*, 17 Oct. 1981, p. 249.
[6]Cynthia Schatz Jones, "I Hold No Resentment Toward My Natural Mother for Not Wanting
Me," *Ms.*, Apr. 1976, p. 8.
[7]Lorraine Dusky, "Who Is My Daughter?" *Newsweek*, 15 Oct. 1979, p. 27.

change her mind.[8] Even if there is confidence in the parent-child relationship, biased emotional overtones surround the adopted child and his decision about investigating his biological history.

Occasionally an adoptive parent will want to seek the natural parents of his child for himself. Some adopted children experience sensations of alienation, shame, and guilt because of their adoptive status.[9] In the book *The Adoption Triangle*, clinical studies of adopted children in psychotherapy show that behavior problems and delinquency occur more frequently in adopted children than in children living with their natural parents.[10] In another case of Dr. Sorosky's, a parent wanted to look into the background of her delinquent son to try to understand him better and to give him the help he needed.[11] Because of the sealed records, she was unable to succeed in gaining the necessary information about her son's history. Without this vital information, she could not help him to her fullest potential.

Beneficial insights may be gained by opening the sealed records, but the natural parents of adopted children have mixed opinions about the proposal of such a policy. Coauthor of *The Adoption Triangle* Annette Baran says adoption agencies feel a mother's right to privacy will be invaded if her identity should become known:

> Adoption agencies have insisted that the birth mother's permanent anonymity and privacy were vital to her survival. She had sinned and suffered, paid dearly, and deserved to be left alone. No one had a right to barge into her life and ruin it; she had been promised freedom from fear, and the adoption agency could not violate this sacred oath.[12]

Ruby Lee Piester declares the first question pregnant girls ask regarding adoption is about confidentiality. They look forward to the time when they can reorganize their lives and start over.[13] If the sealed files are opened, natural parents will face the risk of having their identities revealed.

Some natural parents are not as concerned about this risk. In a poll taken by the American Psychological Association in 1976, fifty percent of thirty-eight birth parents interviewed had feelings of loss and pain. Desires to know

---

[8]Piester, pp. 60–62.

[9]John Triseliotis, *In Search of Origins: The Experiences of Adopted People* (Boston: Routledge and Kegan Paul, 1973), p. 91.

[10]Sorosky, p. 101.

[11]Sorosky, p. 111.

[12]Sorosky, p.50.

[13]Piester, p. 59.

about their children were expressed by the group, but none of them envisioned parental relationships with the adoptees.[14] In most cases the natural mother just wanted to explain to the child why she gave it up for adoption. If the files are not opened, the natural parent may never have the opportunity to unleash these feelings of loss and pain.

As an adopted child, I am not opposed to the opening of the sealed files. [11] Personally I have no desire to speak with my biological parents, but unlike many adoptees I have been exposed to information about their existence and the reasons behind my relinquishment. I would, however, be interested in knowing more about my genealogical descent. It would be comforting to be aware, if possible, of any diseases, such as cancer or leukemia, that might run in my family. Before beginning a search for his natural parents, an adoptee should carefully analyze his reasons for doing so, respecting the feelings of all involved. The decision to search should reflect speculation and maturity. I have chosen not to search, but I feel the present laws infringe upon the constitutional and personal rights of the adoptee who wants to find the missing links in his heritage. Ultimately, the decision should be the mature decision of the adoptee.

[14]Sorosky, pp. 50–53.

Bibliography

Askin, Jayne. *Search: A Handbook for Adoptees and Birthparents.* New York: Harper and Row, 1982.
"Birth Rights." *Science News,* 17 Oct. 1981, p. 249.
Dusky, Lorraine. "Who Is My Daughter?" *Newsweek,* 15 Oct. 1979, p. 27.
Jones, Cynthia Schatz. "I Hold No Resentment Toward My Natural Mother for Not Wanting Me." *Ms.,* Apr. 1976, p. 8.
Piester, Ruby Lee. "For Ruby Lee Piester, the First and Last Word on Adoption Is 'Confidential.' " *People,* 18 May 1981, pp. 55, 59–62.
Sorosky, Arthur D., Annette Baran, and Reuben Pannor. *The Adoption Triangle.* Garden City, N.Y.: Doubleday, 1978.
Triseliotis, John. *In Search of Origins: The Experiences of Adopted People.* Boston: Routledge and Kegan Paul, 1973.

QUESTIONS FOR READING AND REVISING

1. Cynthia Jane Thompson does not explicitly mention until the last paragraph that she is adopted. But where do we see signs of her personal involvement

with her topic earlier in the essay? How does she manage to keep her own experiences from dominating the essay?

2. Summarize the main points of Thompson's essay. What is Thompson's thesis? In light of the information given in the essay, how would each of the concerned groups (adoptees, biological parents, adoptive parents) respond to her thesis?

3. Examine Thompson's handling of the legally tangled issue of privacy. Whose privacy is at stake? How does she deal with each aspect of the privacy issue in adoption situations?

4. What is Thompson's assumption about her audience's knowledge of her subject? Why does she include a description of the sealed records in paragraph 3? How does she provide her readers with information that they are unlikely to know but that they need to understand her argument?

5. When commenting on her method of organizing her thoughts, Thompson explains: "I prefer to outline my paper before I write it. Outlining keeps me from straying from the subject and enables me to make the transitions from one paragraph to the next." Outline each paragraph of the essay and show how Thompson constructs a logical argument. How does she clearly connect each point to the point that precedes it and the one that follows it?

6. Thompson's essay successfully combines research and personal experience. Point to specific paragraphs where she effectively integrates the two. How does she accomplish this? In which paragraphs does she use direct quotation and paraphrase most effectively?

7. Consideration of opposing views is an essential feature of a successful argument. Where and how does Thompson explain and then refute opposing arguments? How does she respond to each objection she raises in paragraphs 6 and 7?

8. Thompson's first draft of paragraph 2 read this way:

> It is a natural instinct to want to explore your origins, but adoptees are deprived of this knowledge because after the adoption the identity of the natural parent is never revealed. If the sealed records were opened, the genealogical bewilderments some adoptees express would be cleared up.

In what specific ways does Thompson's revised version more successfully support her thesis? How might her final draft be improved?

9. Reread paragraph 11, paying particular attention to the fourth sentence ("It would be comforting to be aware, if possible, of any diseases, such as cancer or leukemia, that might run in my family"). What are the specific strengths and weaknesses of this sentence? Consider the following revision: "It would

be comforting to know, for instance, that no inherited diseases such as cancer or leukemia run in my biological family." In what specific ways does this revision improve or damage the original? Which version more effectively supports Thompson's thesis? What other alternative revisions can you think of?

10. In what ways does the title of the essay reflect the essay's contents and the author's position on the issue? Where have you heard this phrase — or a version of it — before? What associations does the title call to mind? In what ways, if any, might the title be changed to make it anticipate more effectively the substance of the essay and Thompson's thesis?

SUGGESTIONS FOR WRITING

1. The popular television film *Roots* focused national attention on tracing one's origins. Since the showings of that film, many psychologists and sociologists have supported author Alex Haley's contention that people need to know about their ancestors. Write an essay in which you endorse or refute this idea. Draw on library research as well as on your own experiences or those of people you know to support your point.

2. Cynthia Jane Thompson successfully blends common sense, sensitivity to human nature, and careful research to present her argument. Choose one of the following laws, research it, take a position on the issues it creates, and argue either for or against its retention: (a) local or state "blue laws" (which require that stores close on Sundays or that bars close at certain hours); (b) laws on gambling; (c) laws regulating highway speed limits; (d) some other controversial statute.

JOHN ROSS THOMPSON

Highland Community College
Highland, Kansas
Daniel Glynn, instructor

John Ross Thompson describes himself as a "survivalist" who enjoys hunting, fishing, swimming, boating, skydiving, and mountain climbing. One of eight children, he was born in Richmond, Virginia, in 1956 but moved to Kansas at age nine, soon after his father and sister died at sea. He quit high school in Concordia, Kansas, at seventeen and enlisted in the Army. He served in Kansas, Korea, and California, earning a general education diploma along the way. Since leaving the Army, Thompson has worked as a construction laborer and a crane operator. Now a full-time student at Highland Community College, he is considering both law enforcement and writing as career goals.

His earliest recollections of writing are as a form of punishment. He remembers writing "I will not tease my younger brother" five hundred times and hearing, "If you don't do your studies, you're going to grow up to be a writer." But with the encouragement and assistance of his eighth-grade teacher and his college composition instructor, Thompson is now far more practiced and relaxed at writing. He describes his ideal writing environment in these terms: "Kicked back in my chair, feet on the desk, dictionary in my lap, thesaurus on the shelf or on the floor within easy reach of my hand, notebook on my knee, Kool-Aid on the table, books surrounding me—at home alone, with no distractions and a deadline to meet. If I didn't have the deadline, I'd never get anything done."

A Frozen Night

With an M-16 rifle slung over my shoulder and my parka hood drawn tightly 1
about my face, I fumbled clumsily for a cigarette which would provide me with
an illusion of warmth against the crisp night air. Distant laughter and the soft
gentle flow of music drifted faintly over the compound from the frozen river
below. Through twisted coils of concertina wire I could see the shadows of the
skaters dancing in the flickering fire light like lost souls searching in vain for
eternal rest. It was Christmas Eve in Korea, 1976.

I was a lone sentry on foreign soil, thousands of miles from home and loved 2
ones, guarding my post against improbable evils lurking in the darkness. Faced
with countless hours of solitude and incredible loneliness, my mind might have
wandered through the infinite realms of space and time to the solace of the
spirits of Christmas past. Yet my thoughts were not of home. They were
overshadowed by the events of the previous night.

It was two days before Christmas and darkness had long set as I walked 3 across the compound toward the dilapidated olive-drab Quonset hut that had faithfully served as an N.C.O. club since the close of the Korean war. A single glaring light bulb marked the entrance. As I approached, the muffled pounding of the jukebox was the only sound to be heard save for the rime-coated tree branches tinkling like oriental wind chimes in the northern breeze. My frozen breath hung heavily in the ice-chilled air as I hurried for the door that would provide warmth and protection against the adversity of the winter night.

Stepping inside was like entering another world. Raucous laughter, loud 4 music, and clinking glasses produced a festive atmosphere not unlike that of an Irish pub on St. Patrick's Day. Shaking off the cold, I wended my way toward the space heater stationed in the center of the room. After warming my stiff, frozen fingers, I lit a cigarette on the glowing surface of the stove, turned my back to the heat and scanned the room searching for the new recruit whom I'd promised a night on the town.

I found him seated at the bar with a man for whom I felt nothing but 5 contempt. The members of my platoon had nicknamed him Whimpy as he was inclined toward the perversion of the truth and querulousness. I was somewhat surprised to see him in the club since he was not one given to socializing and spent most of his leisure time in a spare room behind Rosie's bordello, drowning all visions of reality in the native spirits of jin-ro-soju and moguli. Since the man appeared to be somewhat peculiar, we simply avoided him whenever possible. After crossing the room and listening to Whimpy telling his war stories to the young teenage soldier, I felt anger welling inside me. It was bad enough that the boy had to be there in the first place without this oaf terrifying him with tales of death and destruction. True, we had lost men in unfortunate confrontations with the North Koreans, but those were rare, isolated instances. To hear him talk one would have thought we were in the Mekong Delta.

Rudely interrupting him in mid-sentence, I unloaded all the foul, despicable 6 language I had acquired through my years as a soldier. With the fury of a machine gunner inflicting his wrath upon those who had tortured and mutilated his comrades, I assaulted him with insult upon insult. As my voice reached shouting proportions I told him that his mother should have killed him when he was a baby, that every time he opened his mouth I mistook it for his moving bowels, and that he was full of enough shit to fertilize all the rice paddies in Korea for eternity. He sat in dumb silence. Having exhausted my repertoire of verbal abuse, and feeling the need to insult him further, I extinguished my cigarette in his drink. I left Whimpy, taking the bewildered young soldier with me. As I shouldered my way through the crowd, the quiet, which had enshrouded the room in anticipation of a fight, broke. Conversations resumed, as did the movement of bodies in chairs and the scraping of mugs, pitchers, and glasses on table tops.

The next morning, as the dawn's first light outlined the jagged cliffs that   7
loomed over the still-dark village below, I was approaching the gate when an extremely distraught old Korean woman ran up to me. Gesturing wildly and lamenting in a language I could not understand, she led me to an enclosed courtyard behind Rosie's. Several working girls were pacing nervously back and forth. One of them ran up to me pointing frantically toward a small door constructed of balsa wood and rice paper and exclaimed, "I smell charcoal!" She needed to say no more, for I knew full well of the dangers of carbon monoxide fumes emitted from the small pot-bellied stoves used to heat the homes. I rattled the door and hollered. Not receiving an immediate response, I kicked the door, splintering it into innumerable pieces. Slapping the remains out of the way, I took a deep breath and entered the room.

The fumes were overwhelming. As my eyes adjusted to the darkness I saw   8
a figure lying on the bed. As I crossed the room I stumbled on something. Something large and soft, yet slippery under foot. It was a man; he was cold and lifeless. I then turned to the bed and discovered that the figure lying on it was a guitar. I hurried outside and sent one of the girls for the M.P.'s. After catching my breath I returned to the room and looked around. The window and door had been taped shut. The lid to the stove had been carefully placed on a mat beside it. Lying on the floor as if in sleep was the body of an American soldier with a bottle of jin-ro beside his head and a photograph of his wife and children across his heart. The realization and horror of what had happened swept over me. This man had killed himself. I knew this man as Whimpy.

Readjusting the rifle sling on my shoulder, I shivered at the sudden chill   9
that swept through my entire being. I found little consolation as I attempted to fight off feelings of guilt with the thought that I could not change those things which had already come to pass. Turning my back to the cold, I watched as the wind spun the glowing coal of my discarded cigarette through the air in a fiery trail. Then it dropped to the ground in a burst of tiny sparks and disappeared into the blackness.

QUESTIONS FOR READING AND REVISING

1. What is the point of John Ross Thompson's essay? What significance does he suggest — either explicitly or implicitly — for his essay? How effectively does he make his point?

2. What do we learn from the essay about an American soldier's life in Korea?

What feeling does Thompson create of being outside on guard duty (paragraphs 1 and 2), in the N.C.O. club (paragraphs 3 and 4), and in the spare room behind Rosie's bordello (paragraphs 5 and 7)? What contrasts does Thompson set up among the three places? How effectively does he distinguish each?

3. Characterize the narrator. What is your attitude toward him? How do the details he presents of life in Korea influence your response to him? What do you think of Whimpy? Does Thompson provide sufficient evidence for Whimpy's motivation to commit suicide? Support your answer with examples from the text.

4. The main narrative occurs in paragraphs 3–8. What is the purpose of paragraphs 1, 2, and 9? How are they connected to the main narrative?

5. Thompson uses a cigarette as a repeated image. Where does he first set up this image and with what effect? What symbolic significance does the image take on in the final pargaraph?

6. Paragraph 4 appeared this way in a previous draft:

> Inside was like entering another world. With the bar maids prancing around in mini-skirts, serving the crowd of rowdy G.I.'s, one could almost forget the frigid, desolate land outside. Shaking off the cold, I scanned the room searching for the new recruit whom I'd promised a night on the town.

How do the additional details in the final draft help draw a contrast to the preceding scene? Rather than telling us about the "frigid, desolate land outside," how does Thompson evoke the same effect and more in the final draft? Which details, if any, from this earlier draft would strengthen the final draft?

7. An earlier draft contained the following paragraph, which Thompson expanded into paragraphs 7 and 8 in the final draft:

> Early in this morning an extremely distraught old woman led me to the body of an American soldier who had taken his life in the Korean tradition of asphyxiation through carbon-monoxide poisoning, a slow, quiet, yet painless death. With a bottle of jin-ro beside his head and a photograph of his beloved wife and children across his heart, this disconsolate man had passed from our world into the next undetected and undisturbed with the dignity and honor of those who hold no other course but to walk with Buddha along the gentle slopes of Happy Mountain. This man I knew as Whimpy.

How has Thompson changed the sequence of his narrative in the final draft of this section? In what specific ways is the final draft more effective?

SUGGESTIONS FOR WRITING

1. Reread Thompson's essay carefully, noting its basic story line and its distinctive details. Rewrite the story as it might have been told by the young recruit, by Whimpy, or by a Korean waitress who works at the N.C.O. club and lives near Rosie's place.

2. Consider Thompson's "philosophy of life": "Everything a person does, whether he or she realizes it or not, affects someone somehow. It's possible that a person could be saving lives and never know it. It can also be the other way around. . . . I feel as long as a person is helping others and not doing anything to hurt anyone, chances are he or she is on the right track." Write an essay that illustrates or refutes such a philosophy.

PAIGE TURNER

Tufts University
Medford, Massachusetts
Phyllis Kutt Leith, instructor

Paige Turner's earliest recognition as a writer came at the age of eight or nine when she wrote a poem about a lake. "I remember my father's liking it so much that he had it typed so that he could keep a copy." Born in Charlottesville, Virginia, in 1964, Turner attended the Tandem School there, where she won the eleventh-grade English award. She is now a student at Tufts University and plans to major in international relations and to pursue a career as a foreign correspondent or a magazine editor.

In her essay on Francisco Goya's painting El amor y la muerte, *Turner demonstrates that she enjoys thinking and writing about original ways of seeing. Asked to respond to a comparison and contrast exercise presented in Barnet and Stubbs's A Practical Guide to Writing, Turner set as the goal of her essay "to show the effects of Goya's switch from watercolor to chalk and how this affected the feeling of the piece. I wanted the reader to realize that Goya's change in medium was a result of a change in perception—from an optimistic feeling about the scene to a gloomy, darkened one."*

The assignment reads:

> Study the two drawings [on pages 166 and 167], by Francisco Goya (1746–1828), entitled "El amor y la muerte" (Love and Death). They show a woman holding a dying lover, who has fought a duel for her. The first version [page 166] is a watercolor; the revised version [page 167] is in chalk. Write a brief essay . . . comparing the drawings.

El amor y la muerte:
An Interpretation

Francisco Goya's vision of the two lovers changes dramatically from his original watercolor of *El amor y la muerte* to his revised interpretation of the scene in chalk. In the two drawings, Goya manipulates his medium in an effort to obtain a desired effect. By discarding the unbending and restrictive quality of watercolor, Goya finds a more pliable tool with which to express himself in his use of chalk. The substance of the two versions remains the same, with little change in the position of the objects. Goya's manipulations, however slight, succeed in transforming the complacent mood of the first work into the startlingly realistic feeling of the chalk portrayal.

In the watercolor version of *El amor y la muerte*, Goya's use of shadows and light gives the picture a sense of stability and control. Instead of suggesting a wavering translucence, the harsh treatment of the sunlight creates concrete images that appear undaunted by the surrounding tragedy. As the dying man leans against his lover's chest for his last moments of support, his weakness evidences only physically, while the spiritual tone of the piece retains its decision and strength. The metaphysical implications of Goya's work suggest that the two lovers are in control of their tragedy and that they have a firm grip on their fates. The brightness of the male figure's clothing lends itself to the overall optimistic feeling of the drawing as well. The garments of both figures are crisp and clear, making the final tone one of untouchable sorrow, as if even in their last pain the two lovers are able to rise above the realm of despairing grief. Their unruffled appearance renders them almost otherworldly as they stand up majestically in the face of their sorrow.

In his chalk representation of the scene, Goya manipulates the light and   3 dark images in an entirely different manner. Again the shadow on the wall suggests the existence of two concrete figures, but in this version of the piece there is no definite sense of where the people end and where the wall begins. The viewer is given only an impressionistic sense of three dimensions instead of a distinguishable picture of the two lovers against the wall. The murky, dingy effect of the chalk on the canvas causes the individual elements of the picture to dissolve into one despairing mass, the female and male appearing to crumble as they melt into the confusion of the black wall behind them. The color tone is constant in the piece — the figures' garments, the sky, the ground, and the wall each treated with an even bleakness. The resulting gloom intensifies the "gray" inescapable emotion that hangs over the drawing, and the figures seem trapped by their insurmountable grief.

In Goya's original version of the scene, the woman seems strong and hopeful   4 as she holds her lover up against his inevitable death. This strength comes from her body's position slightly forward of the male yet still partially behind his swaying body in an all-consuming, embracing stance. The viewer is drawn from the left foreground, up the curve of the male's torso, and up to the sky where the woman is gazing so dutifully. The discarded sword and hat are strategically pointed toward the two bodies, causing the viewer's eye to be directed to the center of the piece and then from that strength upward to the equally immortal world beyond. The created curve has a concentrating effect, and it gives the figures the greatest importance, with the other objects acting only as supportive props. Goya's portrayal of the wall, for example, adds to the piece's sense of boundary. The wall is totally intact, and, as a consequence, renders the two figures more stable and self-sufficient.

The chalk rendition is treated in a much less partitioned fashion. The hat   5 and sword are strewn about the ground, encircling the lovers' feet as if to remind them that they were the very devices of the love that trapped and consumed them. The wall is in shambles, leaving the figures with no stability and no protective support. The lines of the piece fail to guide the viewer as he attempts to follow them. One searches from the anguished faces of the lovers to the foreground and background, unable to find any sort of directive optimism. The woman is no longer able to sustain what has become the burden of her dissolving lover and tries unsuccessfully to place all her strength behind his collapsing figure.

The figures themselves in the watercolor are detailed and accurate. The hair of the woman is intact, and her lover is equally unruffled by his battle. Only the man's hand is visible, suggesting the power of the immortal who need not cling to anything in expectant hope. The man's finger is extended from his hand, not from exhaustion, but in a calculated act of gallantry. Both of the figures' feet are planted firmly on the ground, their shoes easily distinguishable from the earth beneath them. They seem to be positioned almost as pieces in a puzzle, and their bodies fit together in an almost too-perfect embrace. Their faces appear serene; the man's lips are closed as if he were merely dreaming. The absence of any harsh contours in their faces makes them seem smooth and untroubled. 6

Goya treats the figures with much more compassion in his chalk version. Although the figures lose much of their physical definition, the pain in their faces gives the piece a more graspable meaning. Shaded contours make the faces seem hollow and deathly, and their mouths hang agape in agony. Their eyebrows are only tortured dots above their eyes, offering their faces no lines of comfortable expression. The two figures seem to be struggling to remain interlocked, fighting against the inevitable separation that is forthcoming. Nothing in this version of *El amor y la muerte* is orderly or comfortable. The figures are drawn together in a fit of insurmountable anguish, only to be torn from their embrace by an unavoidable doom. 7

The ultimate effect of Goya's switch from watercolor to chalk is that the second version of the scene is much more expressive. While the watercolor is well executed and painfully detailed, it loses emotional impact when the weaker medium is used. By using chalk, Goya is able to create more of a mood, not just a situation. Goya's emotional ties to the two drawings are dramatically different. The watercolor seems to be a product of detached objectivity, while the chalk seems to reveal an integral part of Goya's soul. 8

A personality deviation appears to have overtaken Goya in the period between the two drawings, Goya emerging with a much more individual interpretation of the scenario. The feeling of newfound realism is, then, not only a victory of honesty over bravado in interpretation but a reawakening of Goya's emotional center as well. 9

QUESTIONS FOR READING AND REVISING

1. How does Paige Turner organize her comparison and contrast essay? Does she develop it point by point or subject by subject? What are the points of comparison that Turner sets up in paragraphs 2 and 3, 4 and 5, 6 and 7? What aspect of the two pictures does Turner consider in each phase of her comparison?

2. Outline Turner's major points along with the specific evidence from Goya's works that she uses to support her interpretations. Is her evidence convincing in each instance?

3. What is Turner's thesis? Where does she state it? After studying the two Goya prints yourself, do you agree or disagree with her conclusions?

4. Roughly what percentage of Turner's essay is devoted to observing the two versions of Goya's work? What percentage is devoted to drawing inferences from these observations? Show how the proportionate attention to observation and inference in paragraphs 2 and 3, for example, is or is not representative of the rest of the essay.

5. Examine carefully the reproductions of Goya's work on pages 166–67. Which aspects of these works does Turner seem to overlook or pay proportionately less attention to? Explain why she should or should not have given them more attention.

6. Characterize Turner's point of view in this essay. Is she detached and objective? Involved and subjective? Some other combination? Support your response with an analysis of specific words and phrases from the essay. How appropriate is her point of view to her purpose? To the works of art she is discussing?

7. Which of Turner's points would you like to see clarified, expanded, or deleted? What does she mean, for example, when she says, "The garments of both figures are crisp and clear, creating a sense of untouchable sorrow" in paragraph 2? In what sense does she mean "directive optimism" in paragraph 5? How would you suggest that Turner revise this sentence and phrase? Locate and suggest possible revisions for similar sentences in the essay.

SUGGESTIONS FOR WRITING

1. Browse through the art history section of your library and choose — and then examine — a collection of the works of an artist whose paintings you admire. Select a work that was first prepared in one medium and then later done in another. Write an essay comparing and contrasting the most prominent features of each. Include your conclusions about the development of the artist's skill as he or she shifted from one medium to another.

2. Select a poem or short story for which previous drafts exist (such as Robert Frost's poem "Design" or D. H. Lawrence's short story "The Odour of the Chrysanthemums"), and write an essay comparing and contrasting earlier draft(s) with the final version. What changes did the author make from one draft to the next? What are the specific effects of each revision? Based on the cumulative evidence of these drafts, what conclusions can you draw about the development of this writer's craft?

SUSAN ANNE ZURAKOWSKI

Albion College
Albion, Michigan
Catherine E. Lamb, instructor

Susan Zurakowski is pursuing a double major in English and history at Albion College, although she is an accomplished musician and at one time considered music as the focus of her studies. She plays clarinet and flute and has received several awards for her work in both band and orchestra, including the John Philip Sousa Semper Fidelis Award for musical ability.

Born in 1963, Zurakowski grew up in rural Michigan in a family of writers and readers. Her father has worked as a journalist; her sister chose to devote herself to poetry. Her mother, an avid reader, encouraged her at a young age to keep a journal, and the daily practice of recording her thoughts and feelings has been, as Zurakowski notes, very helpful: "It keeps me limber. Since I write every day, I don't panic when I get a paper assignment." She credits her father with helping her to overcome the fear of failure when writing and to develop what she calls a writer's "thick skin" by accepting the fact that not every reader will respond positively to what she has written.

When asked to write an essay about some aspect of the mass media that influenced her, Zurakowski says she immediately knew that "four years of watching antiquated movies and collecting Clark Gable memorabilia would finally be of use."

For a more detailed study of Zurakowski's essay and the drafts that led to it, see pages 178–200.

Confessions of a Gable Groupie

"Just what do you see in him?" a friend inquires when he sees the Gable 1
paraphernalia that clutters my room. I look up at my favorite portrait, a still
from Gone With the Wind, and search for an answer. No, he wasn't particularly
good-looking. His ears jutted out from his head at forty-five-degree angles.
What's more, he had false teeth and was reputed to have one of the most
vulgar vocabularies in Hollywood. His screen image was that of a Hemingway
hero, a far cry from the sensitive male stars I usually admire. Why, then, do
I find myself fascinated by Clark Gable, the actor and the legend?

I first realized the impact Clark Gable had on me when I knew more Gable 2
movies than Top Forty tunes and could give anyone who would listen a detailed
account of his life, as well as a list and synopsis of his sixty-seven films. My
family and friends did not understand how I could voluntarily pass up a night
of roller-skating to spend the evening at my grandma's house, poring over her

ancient copies of *Photoplay* magazine. "Are you obsessed or something? You've already read it a million times!" was the exasperated complaint I got from my sister as she tried to divert my attention from the dog-eared pages of my Gable biography, *Long Live the King.*

From the launching of Gable's career in *A Free Soul,* where he slaps an 3 incredulous Norma Shearer's face, to his desertion of Scarlett O'Hara with the most famous parting shot in movie history, I am in cinema heaven. Only Gable could have carried off that last line of *Gone With the Wind*—"Frankly, my dear, I don't give a damn"—at a time when the use of profanity in films was explicitly banned.

Gable's rising popularity is to me as natural as the popularity of movies in 4 the thirties, which were an escape to a glitzy, glamour-filled world where the women were bedecked in mink and everyone lived happily ever after. Clark Gable films provided a more realistic escape. Although the "action and romance" formula was standard, Gable's approach was different. He was riveting as the owner of an Indonesian rubber plantation, a mutineer on a ship, a reporter, an aging cowboy, and an indigent gambler. Because he was neither rich nor cultivated in these roles, Gable's success appealed to people of the Depression era in a way that Robert Taylor's elegant savvy and Charles Boyer's Old World charm never could.

As the ideal role model, the ideal common man, Clark Gable set the 5 standards for middle-class America. People were glad, rather than horrified, when he slapped Norma Shearer in *A Free Soul*—he wasn't afraid to give that highfalutin lady what-for. Later, Gable virtually eliminated T-shirts from the American male wardrobe with his Oscar-winning performance in *It Happened One Night.* Rather risqué in 1934, the movie's "Walls of Jericho" scene, in which Gable partially disrobed, stunned the audience with the first on-screen flash of a bare chest. I can't remember the exact statistic, but T-shirt sales declined drastically within two months of the movie's release, a shock that Fruit of the Loom never quite recovered from.

Although best remembered as the quintessential Rhett Butler in *Gone With* 6 *the Wind,* Clark Gable typically starred in melodramas such as 1932's *Red Dust,* where he meets and is attracted to a seasoned woman, portrayed by Jean Harlow, with whom he shares a bawdy sense of humor and utter lack of gentility. Everything is dandy until halfway through the film, when he falls in love with an ordinary younger woman, depicted by Mary Astor. Gene Raymond, the unassuming sidekick, convinces Gable that he could never be happy with Astor's pallid charms. Gable sees the light, has a reconciliation with Harlow, and the two live happily—and probably illicitly—ever after, while the sidekick is left to comfort the deserted dame.

Such chauvinism and predictability would turn me against his films forever,   7
if not for the twinkling blue eyes, chiseled-in dimples, sardonically raised right
eyebrow, and the impression that Gable really *didn't* give a damn. And that
is enough for me.

Sure, I have heard all the arguments before, from "What a lack of credi-   8
bility" to "He was a stupid lummox who made it big on a fluke." These
dismissals are partially true, for nothing is less likely than a man marrying a
girl — two days after he meets her on a bus. And, in a candid explanation for
his success, Gable self-deprecatingly remarked, "This 'King' stuff is pure
bullshit . . . I'm just a lucky slob from Ohio [who] . . . had a lot of smart guys
helping me — that's all."[1] Yet this is all part of his attractiveness and a prime
example of the American "rags-to-riches" phenomenon.

"Well, what *do* you see in him?" a friend repeats impatiently, jolting me   9
back to reality. It isn't the answer he is looking for, but I shrug, noncommital.

"It's his ears. I have a thing for men with big ears." He leaves me to   10
contemplate my portrait, just as my sister bursts through the door.

"Hey Sue, you've just *got* to see that new Paul Newman movie — what a   11
hunk!" She sighs rapturously.

I glance once more at that cynically amused face, hat tipped over his brow,   12
and I laugh. "What?!" I say, with a smile. "And become obsessed, like you
are? NO thanks!"

[1]Lyn Tornabene, *Long Live the King: A Biography of Clark Gable* (New York: Putnam's, 1976),
p. 17.

QUESTIONS FOR READING AND REVISING

1. It is clear from the title that a Gable addict has written this essay. What
   evidence is there that Susan Zurakowski is writing with an informed passion?
   What details of her life confirm the intensity of her obsession?

2. How can you tell that Zurakowski is having fun writing about a subject that
   she cares about?

3. Describe the view of Gable that you get from this essay. In her introduction,
   Zurakowski writes that he was "a far cry from the sensitive male stars I usually
   admire." What was he like? Does this view confirm your own view?

4. Zurakowski confesses that she is a Gable groupie, but she also acknowledges
   the limitations of her idol in her introduction. What effect does this acknowl-
   edgment have on a reader? Does it strengthen or weaken Zurakowski's argument?

5. Are you convinced of Gable's charms by Zurakowski's essay? Evaluate how she builds her argument and explain why you agree or disagree with each of her major points.

6. Zurakowski shows us not only the impact Gable has had on her but also the appeal Gable had for people during the 1930s. How does this information serve Zurakowski's purpose? What is her purpose?

7. What attitude does Zurakowski assume her audience has about Gable? Is she writing to an audience that likes or dislikes Gable? Find evidence in the essay to show the audience she is writing to and how she is trying to appeal to this audience.

SUGGESTIONS FOR WRITING

1. Write an essay in which you analyze one of your addictions or obsessions.

2. Choose someone you admire and write an essay explaining this person's influence on you. What does this person represent to you? What kind of influence has this person had on you?

3. Like Zurakowski, we are all subject to "the magic of Hollywood." Is there some movie, director, or movie genre that you simply will not miss if it's showing on television or at the theater? What is its appeal for you? Even though you know the technique, formula, or dialogue by heart, what compels you to see the movie? Consider as many aspects of the film as you can — music, dialogue, acting, cinematography, costumes, and so on — to make your reader understand your enjoyment. Convince your reader that he or she is really missing out in not seeing your favorites.

TWO STUDENT WRITERS AT WORK

Part III

M OST PEOPLE WRITE without consciously thinking about what they are doing. There are as many writing habits as there are writers. Some people can write anywhere — riding on buses, waiting on lines, doodling on napkins in restaurants — while others need special conditions. Susan Zurakowski, for instance, reports: "I need to write in my room because if I try to write in the library or in a new place, I am likely to be distracted. I sit at my desk with several half-empty coffee cups, using a red pen and yellow legal paper, wearing an extremely disgruntled expression, and trying to make sense out of the piles of notes I write. Sometimes I get up and walk around the room, talking to myself as I try to figure out what I want to say."

This chapter observes Susan Zurakowski at work — getting started, writing, and revising — and considers writing from her point of view. Zurakowski talks about her concerns as she worked through her piles of notes and seven drafts to a final, prize-winning essay. Although all writers need to find the conditions and circumstances that work best for them and there are probably as many writing processes as there are writers, still we can learn a great deal about the stages of getting started, writing, and revising from studying how one writer made important decisions as she progressed through these stages.

Too often when a piece of writing is successful, readers do not have the opportunity to see how the essay was written; the writing carries readers along so that they are not concerned with the writer's process. The writing reads smoothly and logically and readers assume, if anything, that the writing must have flowed equally smoothly from the writer's pen. What readers don't see are the scratch-outs and the drafts, the decisions and conversations that went on in the writer's mind to produce such writing.

Zurakowski's notes and drafts show that a writer begins with fragments — notes to herself — and that ideas don't spring full-blown from a writer's mind and into clear, coherent prose. Rather, ideas tumble out in unformed, fragmented ways and are developed draft after draft as the writer makes decisions, evaluates those decisions, and adjusts her writing so that the new decisions are consistent with what she has written. What guides the writer in all these decisions are audience and purpose.

This chapter begins with a detailed look at the process by which Zurakowski wrote her essay "Confessions of a Gable Groupie." Then Annie Glaven's drafts for her essay "What Can You Do?" are given as an exercise. Studying these drafts of both Zurakowski and Glaven will show how writing evolves: beginning tentatively, growing, and becoming good writing. What comes through are the power and possibility of writing.

GETTING STARTED

In her freshman writing class, Susan Zurakowski was given the broad assignment to write on some aspect of the mass media that had influenced her. She reports that she knew right away she had a natural subject: Clark Gable. "I had been interested in Gable for six years and I was waiting for some kind of assignment for which I could write about him. When I received the assignment, I knew that years of watching antiquated movies and collecting Gable memorabilia would finally be of use."

Having a subject to write about is only the beginning for a writer. Zurakowski knew her subject—she knew she had a strong interest in writing about Gable—but she didn't know specifically what she had to say about him. She needed to get her thoughts down on paper to see what she knew. Zurakowski's method of getting started was brainstorming, a strategy that helps a writer think as quickly and as broadly as possible about a subject by writing down everything about the subject that springs to mind. Brainstorming usually takes the form of an unstructured list with the words or phrases written as quickly and as uncritically as possible. Brainstorming helps Zurakowski break the ice and get involved quickly with her subject. "One thought stimulates another and the more I brainstorm, the more I have to work with," she reports.

The following are copies of Zurakowski's brainstorming sheets for her essay "Confessions of a Gable Groupie."

ZURAKOWSKI'S BRAINSTORMING NOTES

```
--raised right eyebrow, cynical expression, mouth
  turned slightly down at one corner
--sexy, growl-voice
--slicked back hair, one strand constantly falling
  across forehead, 2 bottles of Brylcream or
  Quaker State
```

--big ears, "with those big ears, he looked like a
  sugar bowl"
--sense of flippancy, devil-may-care attitude
--macho image, calls all the women "baby"
--chiselled-in dimples
--"The King," makes the leading ladies swoon
--typical Gable theme: friendship with the bawdy,
  Jean Harlow-type characters (heart of gold),
  falls in love with the innocent and virginal-type
  characters (Mary Astor, Grace Kelly), has a sidekick (Spencer Tracy), gets in a fight over the
  innocent-type, sidekick makes him see the light,
  he realizes what wimps Mary & Grace are and winds
  up with the Harlow-type. (They live happily--
  illicitly--ever after, sidekick comforts the
  deserted dame)
--always wears a hat tipped over the brows
--rakish grin
--usually rural settings, except for the newspaper
  reporter movies and "It Happened One Night"
--recalcitrant women succumb to his charm
--complete lack of gentility
--predictable plots where he always wins
--optimistic themes, light-hearted comedies, "Man's-
  Man" image, no-nonsense practicality with flashes
  of whimsy, indomitable role model for the
  depression era

--starts out with small roles as a gangster who
  turns respectable

--big bruiser roles

--progresses to the newspaper-reporter roles where
  he falls in love with the women he's supposed to
  nail

--culmination in the 40's as the hero; war flicks;
  movies in the 50's as a gentleman; late 50's as
  an aging cowboy, writer, sailor who has to come
  to terms with his age

--finding out that "Clark Gable had false teeth?!!!?!"

--starting out with unquestioning admiration, reading
  several biographies and finding out about the
  "real" Clark Gable, realizing that he was flawed,
  admiring him more for it

--starts out interested, but cynical; sees Scarlett
  as she is, but still likes her; falls in love with
  her but has to hide it from her; admits his love
  at the end but walks away

--a pride that supercedes his emotions

--strength of character--"I wish I could care, but
  frankly, I don't give a damn"

--beats up Norma Shearer (stuck up, rich)

--Clark Gable movies are in large part survival
  movies that deal with problems of the Depression-
  era. They are, for the most part, optimistic
  and light-hearted.

```
--Other movies of the thirties and forties are

survival films, but deal more with the problems

themselves, rather than the individual, and how

he/she solves the problems.
```

Zurakowski spent one and a half hours brainstorming, asking herself questions and generating a lot of details and information. Her brainstorming sheets are rich with possibilities and information, and it is clear that she knows a lot about her subject. To an outside observer, these notes might look rather disorganized and idiosyncratic; yet this is how notes at this stage should look. The writer is writing the notes for herself, an audience of one, and it is important only that the writer can read and interpret her own notes. What outside observers can see in these notes, however, is that Zurakowski asked herself important questions as she brainstormed in order to see what she knew about her subject. She asked, for instance, What did Gable look like? And she wrote down his distinguishing features—his raised right eyebrow, cynical expression, slicked-back hair, big ears. Zurakowski let her mind roam; she brainstormed details about Gable's image and his influence on women, on the movies, on his time, and on Zurakowski herself. One thought suggested another.

These brainstorming notes offered Zurakowski the information with which to write a first draft. She had collected a stock of materials to work with, and this gave her the feeling that she had something worthwhile to write about. As she reports: "In these brainstorming sheets, I saw what I knew and where I was headed. I realized that I had a lot of material to work with, a real foundation of information, and this gave me a tremendous feeling of confidence in my subject."

Getting started is often the most difficult stage for writers. They stare at the blank page, waiting for inspiration, expecting to write a perfect opening sentence. Or they write something down, strike it out, crumple up the paper, mumble to themselves, "This isn't what I meant to say," and begin again and again. Having no sense of direction to guide them, they are forced to improvise, attempting to find ideas at the same time as they are developing and organizing them. The time spent in getting started is time well spent. Writers write with more confidence and ease if they have developed a focus for their first drafts. Such a focus shows writers where they are headed and leads them to a more developed and organized draft.

Zurakowski's brainstorming sheets offered her numerous details, but these details were unsorted and lacked a focus. She spent one hour reading and thinking about her notes, asking herself: What details seem most interesting? What details can be developed? How can the details be grouped to provide a focus? Zurakowski's next step was to pull together the best of her brainstorming by establishing a focus for her first draft. For Zurakowski, establishing a focus meant defining her audience and her purpose. Here are her notes to herself:

> *Audience:* My audience is a group of people who do not share my opinions about Gable — someone like my cousin who despises Gable or someone from my class who would have trouble understanding why I am obsessed with Gable. Since I am writing to an audience that does not share my opinions, I will have to avoid certain assumptions, such as that Gable was a great actor. I will also have to acknowledge and confront my audience's negative opinions about Gable.

> *Purpose:* The assignment is to show how Gable has influenced me, but I have brainstormed a lot of information about his influence on the movies. I think a larger focus would make the essay more interesting. I see my purpose as showing what a powerful and important person Gable was by showing his influence on me and on the movies.

A great deal of thinking and planning went into Zurakowski's decisions about audience and purpose. She might have decided to write to a different audience — a group of people, for instance, who are also obsessed with Gable — but that would have meant a different paper with an entirely different purpose. A clear purpose is achieved by considering possibilities, making decisions, and thinking about the needs and expectations of the intended audience.

WRITING

Having defined her audience and purpose, Zurakowski started to write her first draft. She reports: "As I wrote my first draft, I knew I had something to say that was worth reading. What was easy was writing my introduction since the question "Just what do you see in him?" has been asked so many times. It seemed a natural place to begin. What was difficult, and what is always difficult for me in writing first drafts, is accepting their imperfections. I try to write as much as possible to keep the momentum going. I don't want to worry about the mess or the mistakes since there is plenty of time later for these concerns."

Zurakowski's major concern as she wrote her first draft was to develop her ideas and to see if her writing was going in the direction she had planned. Her first draft gave her the chance to use the information she had collected in her notes and to see if she had accomplished her intentions. The following is Zurakowski's first draft.

ZURAKOWSKI'S FIRST DRAFT

Confessions of a Gable Groupie

"Just what do you see in him?" people inquire   1
when they see the Gable paraphernalia that clutters
my room. I look up at my favorite portrait, a still
from "Gone With the Wind," and search for an answer.
No, he wasn't particularly good-looking. His ears
jutted out from his head at 45° angles, causing him
to resemble a sugar bowl, and if the oil crisis had
been an issue in the thirties, he could have sold his
hair to the sheiks for more money than he made as
MGM's highest-paid star. What's more, he had false
teeth and was reputed to have one of the most vulgar
vocabularies in Hollywood. His screen image was that
of a slightly chauvinistic Hemingway hero, a far cry
from the Leslie Howard-type sensitivity that I
usually admire in movie stars. Why, then, do I find
myself fascinated by Clark Gable, the actor and the
legend?

I first realized the impact Clark Gable had on   2
me when I knew more Gable movies than top forty tunes
and could give anyone who would listen a detailed
account of his life, as well as a list and synopsis
of his 67 films. My friends could not understand why
I analyzed the television guide each week to hunt for
the Clark Gable movies, and were even more bewildered
when I announced that I was voluntarily passing up a

night of rollerskating to spend the evening at my
Grandma's, poring over her ancient copies of Photoplay magazine. Even my family was confused.
"You've already read it a million times!" was the
exasperated remark I got from my sister as she
futilely tried to divert my attention from the dog-
eared pages of my Gable biography, Long Live the King.
Five minutes later, when I was still reading, she
left in a huff, totally disgusted, and convinced
that I was insane.

None of these people are unkind or constitu-   3
tionally opposed to Clark Gable, yet they vehemently
reject my 3:00 am invitations to watch "It Happened
One Night" on channel 56's Late, Late Show. "What?
And become obsessed, like you are?" they reply.
"No thank you!" I don't mind, really. While I sit
in front of the television during the hours that
normal people sleep, I become part of the thirties
and I observe the rise of a legend. From the
launching of his career in "A Free Soul," where he
slaps an incredulous Norma Shearer's face, to his
desertion of Scarlett O'Hara with the most famous
parting shot in movie history, "Frankly, my dear, I
don't give a damn," I am in cinema heaven.

Only Gable could have carried off the last   4
line of "Gone With the Wind." The movie was released in 1939, at a time of strict enforcement of
the Hays Production Code, which explicitly banned

the use of profanity in films. But use it he did,
and the result was a magnification of his devil-may-
care charisma. Already bigger than life, Clark
Gable's lack of pretensions on screen further
endeared him to moviegoers. Although David O.
Selznick picked up the tab,[1] it was Clark Gable's
gain. From then on, he could do no wrong.

From the vantage point of restrospect, Clark   5
Gable's rising popularity in the thirties was to me
as natural as the popularity of movies themselves.
The movies, at that time, were an escape to a
glitzy, glamor-filled world where the women were
bedecked in mink, and everyone lived happily-ever-
after. Clark Gable films provided a more realistic
escape. Certainly, he invariably winds up with the
girl, and when "The End" flashes across the screen,
there is a sense of completion in knowing that "all's
well that ends well." Yet Clark Gable's approach to
these ends was different. He was capable of success
on an Indian rubber plantation, as a mutineer on a
ship, as a reporter, a pilot, an aging cowboy, and
an out-of-money gambler. Because he was neither
rich nor cultivated in these roles, Clark Gable's
success appealed to people of the Depression Era
in a way that Robert Taylor's or Charles Boyer's
never could. Clark Gable was the ideal role-model,
and his films the ideal inspiration, for here was a
man people felt comfortable in applauding. He was a

common man, dealing effectively with common problems.
They were glad, rather than horrified, that he slapped
Norma Shearer--he wasn't afraid to give that highfalutin' lady what-for. No wonder his films prompted
a household phrase of the thirties: "Who do you
think you are--Clark Gable?"

Although best remembered as the quintessential   6
Rhett Butler in "Gone With the Wind," Clark Gable
typically starred in melodramas, such as "Red Dust,"
where he meets and is attracted to a Jean Harlow-
type character with whom he shares a bawdy sense of
humor and total lack of gentility. Everything is
dandy until halfway through the film, when he falls
in love with a demure Mary Astor-type character, who
is responsible for his return to respectability. The
Spencer Tracy-type sidekick convinces him that he
could never be happy with the wimpy Astor; Gable sees
the light, has a reconciliation with Harlow, and the
two live happily--and probably illicitly--ever after,
while the sidekick is left to comfort the deserted
dame. Woven in between are a fistfight, a drunken-
rage sequence, and a rescue-the-wimp scene, all in
which Gable demonstrates his prowess and "man's man"
ability.

Such predictability and chauvinism would turn   7
me against his films forever, if not for the twinkling
blue eyes, chiselled-in dimples, sardonically raised
right eyebrow and the impression that Gable really

<u>didn't</u> give a damn. And that is enough for me.

Oh sure, I've heard all the arguments before,   8
from "what a lack of credibility" to "he was a
stupid, dumb lummox who made it big on a fluke."
These hold an element of truth, for nothing is
less likely than a man fighting a wild boar--and
winning. And, in a candid explanation for his
success, Gable self-deprecatingly remarked, "This
'King' stuff is pure bullshit. I'm just a lucky
slob from Ohio who . . . had a bunch of smart guys
helping me. That's all."[2] Yet this is all part
of his attractiveness, and a prime example of the
American "rags-to-riches" phenomenon. What could
be more appealing than the reality of tremendous
success--as the outgrowth of modest beginnings?
Considering the fact that Gable flicks grossed more
at the box office than any others, apparently nothing.

Even so, Clark Gable, the actor, was not excep-   9
tional; his range of performance was decidedly
limited. Throughout his film career, he rarely
deviated from the "tough guy" role. Still, the
image he projected was Gable and Hollywood at their
best; it epitomized the positive influence that the
movie industry could have on people. If Gable could
survive, so could they. Today, more than 50 years
after he was declared the King of Hollywood, Clark
Gable remains a movie legend and role-model for
middle-class America.

It isn't the answer they are looking for, but   10
I shrug noncommittally. "It's his ears. I have a
thing for men with big ears." Resignedly, they
leave me to contemplate my portrait, just as my
sister bursts through the door and interrupts my
reverie. "Hey Sue, you've just <u>got</u> to see that
new Christopher Reeve movie--what a <u>hunk</u>!" she sighs
rapturously. I glance once more up at that cynically
amused face, hat tipped over his brow, and I laugh.
"What?!" I say, with a smile. "And become obsessed,
like you are? No thanks!"

NOTES

1. David O. Selznick petitioned the Hays Com-
mittee to allow the use of the word "damn" in order
to keep with the original, Margaret Mitchell version
of the sequence. He was granted the use of the word,
but because Selznick was "technically violating an
article of the Production Code, he was fined $5000."
Roland Flamini, <u>The Filming of Gone With the Wind</u>
(London: Collier MacMillan Publishers, 1975), p. 320.

2. Lyn Tornabene, <u>Long Live the King: A</u>
<u>Biography of Clark Gable</u>. Quote taken from memory.

There is quite a jump between Zurakowski's rough, disorganized notes and this rough, but organized, first draft. Zurakowski referred to her notes as she wrote her draft, grouping details to establish her purpose. As she wrote, she found that some of the information from her notes, such as the history of Gable's career, was not useful. When she also found that she needed new information to define her ideas or to make a point, she went beyond her notes. New ideas came out in the writing of her first draft; one idea stimulated another, and new possibilities emerged as she wrote. Zurakowski was open and receptive, as writers need to be while writing a first draft, discovering new ideas and following their writing where it takes them. Zurakowski's first draft was a good beginning.

REVISING

Zurakowski put her manuscript aside for one day before beginning to revise her first draft. With time, she reports, she can gain the necessary distance to rethink what she has written and to see her writing more objectively. Zurakowski defines revision this way: "From experience, I know that most of the time 'writing' an essay is actually spent revising. Revision means to me isolating problems in my essay and working with them through a series of drafts. I read my draft to see what surprises, interests, or confuses me. Revising takes a lot of time and patience; my essays are finished only when I can walk away from my typewriter without feeling guilty."

Zurakowski's first concern as she read and reread her first draft was to see if she had accomplished her purpose for her intended audience. Two questions guided her reading at this point: Have I met my purpose? and Will my audience understand or care about what I have written? These guides of purpose and audience, which served as a directing force as she wrote her first draft, now guided Zurakowski as she revised.

Zurakowski describes her thinking during revision: "As I reread my draft, I felt that I had something interesting to write about, but I didn't think my draft was as effective or as persuasive as I knew it could be. The first problem was that I had assumed an unsympathetic audience, but I overdid it. I ended up, in places, showing Gable's limitations and insulting him. I knew this would never work. The second problem was with my purpose. My original purpose didn't work well for my audience. It didn't help to show Gable's influence on movies because it was too broad and unfocused. I needed to show Gable's influence on his own time—the 1930s—since Gable represented the message the movies of the thirties wanted to convey. I wanted to lift my audience out of the 1980s, out of their vision of what is important today, so that they could understand what Gable meant to people in the 1930s. Appreciating Gable's influence means appreciating what he meant to people in the 1930s."

To revise means, literally, to see again, and that is just what Zurakowski was able to do. While getting started, she could see her writing only as parts and pieces, but with an entire draft written, she could see from the perspective of the whole if her draft was consistent with her purpose. What Zurakowski saw was that she needed to refine her purpose to be more specific. By weaving together Gable's appeal during the 1930s with her own attraction to him in the 1980s, she would provide support for her own obsession with Gable and be more persuasive.

Zurakowski wrote and revised six more drafts before she was able to type a final draft and "walk away without feeling guilty." Her approach was, first, to satisfy her larger concern of establishing her purpose for her intended audience. Then she began to refine her writing, searching for a precise word or a more descriptive phrase, choosing between two examples, and rearranging sentences. It was through revising that Zurakowski achieved the qualities she wanted for her essay — interesting and persuasive writing.

As she moved from draft to draft, Zurakowski revised by adding, deleting, substituting, and reordering. These changes fall roughly in five categories: changing for purpose; changing for audience; checking effectiveness of each example; choosing between two examples; and changing for specificity and accuracy. Zurakowski's final draft, presented on the following pages, is a dramatic improvement over her first draft. The comments on the pages facing her essay, keyed by number, describe some of the major decisions and changes Zurakowski made as she revised her essay.

ZURAKOWSKI'S FINAL DRAFT

Confessions of a Gable Groupie

"Just what do you see in him?" a friend inquires 1
when he sees the Gable paraphernalia that clutters
my room. I look up at my favorite portrait, a still
from Gone With the Wind, and search for an answer.
No, he wasn't particularly good-looking. His ears
jutted out from his head at forty-five-degree angles. 2
What's more, he had false teeth and was reputed to
have one of the most vulgar vocabularies in Hollywood. His screen image was that of a Hemingway
hero, a far cry from the sensitive male stars I
usually admire. Why, then, do I find myself fascinated by Clark Gable, the actor and the legend?

I first realized the impact Clark Gable had on
me when I knew more Gable movies than Top Forty
tunes and could give anyone who would listen a detailed account of his life, as well as a list and
synopsis of his sixty-seven films. My family and 3
friends did not understand how I could voluntarily
pass up a night of roller-skating to spend the
evening at my grandma's house, poring over her
ancient copies of Photoplay magazine. "Are you
obsessed or something? You've already read it a
million times!" was the exasperated complaint I got
from my sister as she tried to divert my attention
from the dog-eared pages of my Gable biography,
Long Live the King.

CHANGING FOR
AUDIENCE

1. In her early drafts, Zurakowski wrote "people inquire" but changed this to "a friend inquires." She explains: "The conversation becomes more personal and more persuasive if the audience feels there really is someone who is asking this question."

CHANGING FOR
AUDIENCE

2. Zurakowski decided to delete two details here: "causing him to resemble a sugar bowl" and "if the oil crisis had been an issue in the thirties, he could have sold his hair to the Sheiks for more money than he made as MGM's highest-paid star." Zurakowski explains: "I wanted to acknowledge Gable's limitations because my audience would be ready to do this if I didn't, but my intention wasn't to insult him. These details went too far, and I had already made the point about his looks."

CHOOSING BETWEEN
TWO EXAMPLES

3. Zurakowski dropped the example "My friends could not understand why I analyzed the television guide each week to hunt for Clark Gable movies." She explains: "It was a choice between this example and the 'poring over ancient copies of *Photoplay* magazine' example. I decided the *Photoplay* example was more effective for my audience since not many people do this, whereas most people look through *TV Guide.* The *Photoplay* example conveys my obsession with Gable more effectively."

From the launching of Gable's career in A Free
Soul, where he slaps an incredulous Norma Shearer's
face, to his desertion of Scarlett O'Hara with the
most famous parting shot in movie history, I am in
cinema heaven. Only Gable could have carried off
that last line of Gone With the Wind--"Frankly, my
dear, I don't give a damn"--at a time when the use
of profanity in films was explicitly banned.   4

Gable's rising popularity is to me as natural
as the popularity of movies in the thirties, which
were an escape to a glitzy, glamour-filled world
where the women were bedecked in mink and everyone
lived happily ever after. Clark Gable films provided a more realistic escape. Although the "action   5
and romance" formula was standard, Gable's approach
was different. He was riveting as the owner of an   6
Indonesian rubber plantation, a mutineer on a ship,
a reporter, an aging cowboy, and an indigent gambler.
Because he was neither rich nor cultivated in these
roles, Gable's success appealed to people of the
Depression era in a way that Robert Taylor's elegant   7
savvy and Charles Boyer's Old World charm never
could.

As the ideal role model, the ideal common man,   8
Clark Gable set the standards for middle-class America.
People were glad, rather than horrified, when he
slapped Norma Shearer in A Free Soul--he wasn't afraid
to give that highfalutin lady what-for. Later, Gable

CHANGING FOR
PURPOSE

4. Zurakowski dropped almost the entire fourth paragraph of the first draft, her discussion of Gable's ability to carry off the line, "Frankly, my dear, I don't give a damn." She explains: "I refined my purpose and realized that these sentences were off the point since they illustrated Gable's effect on the movies. They said nothing about his effect on me or on the 1930s and only served to distract my readers from my purpose."

CHECKING
EFFECTIVENESS OF
EACH EXAMPLE

5. Zurakowski dropped the sentence "Certainly he invariably winds up with the girl, and when The End flashes across the screen, there is a sense of completion in knowing that 'all's well that ends well.'" She explains: "This example would not be effective for my audience since it describes a formula that could be applied to most romantic movies. Realizing this, I added the opening phrase 'Although the "action and romance formula" was standard.'"

CHANGING FOR
SPECIFICITY

6. Zurakowski substituted two phrases: She changed "capable of success on an Indian rubber plantation" to "riveting as the owner of an Indonesian rubber plantation." And she changed the phrase "out-of-money gambler" to "indigent gambler."

CHANGING FOR
AUDIENCE

7. Zurakowski added the phrases "elegant savvy" and "Old World charm" to describe Robert Taylor and Charles Boyer because she decided that her audience, being unfamiliar with movies of the 1930s, might not know who these actors were and might need more information.

CHANGING FOR
PURPOSE

8. Zurakowski added the phrase "the ideal common man" because this helped her reinforce her purpose of showing Gable's appeal for people in the 1930s.

virtually eliminated T-shirts from the American   9
male wardrobe with his Oscar-winning performance in
It Happened One Night. Rather risqué in 1934, the
movie's "Walls of Jericho" scene, in which Gable
partially disrobed, stunned the audience with the
first on-screen flash of a bare chest. I can't
remember the exact statistic, but T-shirt sales
declined drastically within two months of the movie's
release, a shock that Fruit of the Loom never quite
recovered from.

Although best remembered as the quintessential
Rhett Butler in Gone With the Wind, Clark Gable
typically starred in melodramas such as 1932's Red
Dust, where he meets and is attracted to a seasoned
woman, portrayed by Jean Harlow, with whom he shares
a bawdy sense of humor and utter lack of gentility.
Everything is dandy until halfway through the film,
when he falls in love with an ordinary younger woman,
depicted by Mary Astor. Gene Raymond, the unassuming   10
sidekick, convinces Gable that he could never be happy
with Astor's pallid charms. Gable sees the light, has
a reconciliation with Harlow, and the two live happily
--and probably illicitly--ever after, while the sidekick is left to comfort the deserted dame.   11

Such chauvinism and predictability would turn me
against his films forever, if not for the twinkling
blue eyes, chiseled-in dimples, sardonically raised
eyebrow, and the impression that Gable really didn't

CHANGING FOR
PURPOSE

9. Zurakowski decided to add this example about Gable eliminating T-shirts from the American male wardrobe. She dropped the example "His films prompted a household phrase of the thirties: 'Who do you think you are — Clark Gable?' " She explains: "It would have been excessive to use two examples here. Since my purpose was to show Gable's influence during the 1930s, I decided the T-shirt example was more effective because it showed more influence."

CHANGING FOR
ACCURACY

10. Zurakowski had written "The Spencer Tracy–type sidekick," but she changed this to "Gene Raymond, the unassuming sidekick" because the former had been a mistake.

CHANGING FOR
AUDIENCE

11. Zurakowski dropped the sentence "Woven in between are a fistfight, a drunken rage sequence, and a rescue the wimp scene, all in which Gable demonstrates his prowess and 'Man's Man' ability." She explains: "This sentence would have taken my audience's sympathy away and would have created the wrong response at this point in my essay. Mentioning the fistfight and drunken rage would only confirm my audience's negative opinions."

give a damn. And that is enough for me.

Sure, I have heard all the arguments before,   12
from "What a lack of credibility" to "He was a
stupid lummox who made it big on a fluke." These
dismissals are partially true, for nothing is less
likely than a man marrying a girl--two days after he
meets her on a bus. And, in a candid explanation for
his success, Gable self-deprecatingly remarked, "This
'King' stuff is pure bullshit . . . I'm just a lucky
slob from Ohio [who] . . . had a lot of smart guys
helping me--that's all."[1] Yet this is all part of
his attractiveness and a prime example of the American "rags-to-riches" phenomenon.

"Well, what <u>do</u> you see in him?" a friend repeats   13
impatiently, jolting me back to reality. It isn't
the answer he is looking for, but I shrug, noncom-
mittal.

It's his ears. I have a thing for men with big
ears." He leaves me to contemplate my portrait, just
as my sister bursts through the door.

"Hey Sue, you've just <u>got</u> to see that new Paul   14
Newman movie--what a hunk!" She sighs rapturously.

I glance once more at that cynically amused face,
hat tipped over his brow, and I laugh. "What?!" I
say, with a smile. "And become obsessed, like you are?
NO thanks!"

CHECKING
EFFECTIVENESS OF
EACH EXAMPLE

12. Zurakowski decided to delete the example "nothing is less likely than a man fighting a wild boar and winning." Instead, she added the phrase "nothing is less likely than a man marrying a girl two days after he meets her on a bus." She decided that this example was more realistic and thus would be more effective.

CHANGING FOR
PURPOSE AND AUDIENCE

13. Zurakowski decided to drop an entire paragraph in which she illustrated Gable's limitations. Before dropping the paragraph, she tried in successive drafts to rewrite it. For instance, as she rewrote the paragraph in her fourth draft she added these new sentences: "Today, more than fifty years after he was declared King of Hollywood, Clark Gable remains a movie legend and prototype for such actors as Magnum P.I.'s Tom Selleck, whom *TV Guide* has dubbed 'The Clark Gable of the 80s.' Indeed, he is carrying on the tradition in true Gable style, complete with mustache, dimples, and charismatic appeal. Whether or not he makes an article of clothing extinct remains to be seen." As Zurakowski explains: "I revised this paragraph more than any other paragraph in my essay before finally deciding to drop it. Since I liked the paragraph so much, it took me several drafts before I realized that the paragraph, even with the Magnum example added, didn't say anything about Gable's influence on me or about his influence in the thirties. The paragraph was too general and took my readers away from understanding why Gable has influenced me."

CHECKING
EFFECTIVENESS OF
EACH EXAMPLE

14. Zurakowski had written "Christopher Reeve movie," but she changed it to "Paul Newman movie." She decided that Reeve was not an effective example because he was too much like Gable. She explains: "Paul Newman represents something different from Gable, a different type of actor, and he might be someone whom my audience is obsessed with. If so, they will understand my obsession with Gable better."

Zurakowski wrote about Gable with an informed passion and had some fun writing about a subject she cared strongly about. Through revising she was able to achieve a more focused and effective essay as she questioned and changed what needed to be developed. Changes, whether small or large, were not made in isolation, but rather as a way to establish her purpose for her intended audience. As we learn from Zurakowski, the best reason for putting anything down on paper is that you can then see it, understand it, and know how to change it. In revising, Zurakowski brought her ideas and her imagination together to produce a lively, readable, and persuasive essay.

EXERCISE:
THREE DRAFTS BY ANNIE GLAVEN

Annie Glaven was given the assignment to write an essay using examples. She reports that she chose to use the examples most familiar to her from her own life: "I wanted to clarify some of the misconceptions people have about what it is like to be handicapped and to reaffirm my own ability to do anything. Being handicapped has not excluded me from being an active participant in the mainstream of society."

Glaven writes out of her own deeply felt experiences and understanding. She reports that she was more involved with this essay than with any other essay she has ever written and that she spent a tremendous amount of time writing and revising the essay. She wrote seven drafts before she was able to type a final draft and call her essay finished. This exercise looks at Glaven's first, fourth, and final drafts to understand the changes and decisions Glaven made as she developed her essay.

GLAVEN'S FIRST DRAFT

What Can You Do?

I am approached quite often by people who are　　1
curious about my handicap. For the most part, because the questions are so common, I feel as if I
should carry a tape recorder that I can press start,
and it will play beep! this is a recording and continue with my monologue. However, there have been
times when the tape recorder would have been of
little value since the questions were quite out of
the ordinary.

Once, when a woman asked me about my leg, and I　　2
mechanically reiterated the story, she went on to
tell me about her brother's son who was severely
retarded. I fidgeted in my seat, and burned with
the desire to scream, "they didn't amputate my
brains."

Not so long ago, I was sitting in the hospital　　3
conference room with two other women waiting to
receive a report. One of the women introduced herself and she said she didn't remember ever seeing me
before. I said that I had worked with her once, and
she must remember well; a light must have shone. She
blurted to the other woman, "Oh, she's the little
girl with the wooden leg." I found it hard to be
still, and play the stereotyped game of being deaf
as well as an amputee.

Another question asked of me once that actually   4
started me laughing was, "Do they really make your
legs out of trees?" When I had composed myself
enough to answer I simply said, "Only parts of trees."

Perhaps the question that pained me most and   5
made me bleed inside was when a person once asked,
"What can you do?" I was unable to respond to that
question well. It was as if everything that I had
struggled to do, or adapted to was rendered meaningless. The countless times I picked myself up from
the pavement while learning to ride a bike. The
times that I tried to be as confident as the girl
with the smooth gait and nice wiggle when approaching
a boy. The relay races I ran in second grade on
crutches--still trying to win. How could I have
possibly asked this person "What can't I do."

Questions on Glaven's First Draft

1. Glaven's first draft was rough, but it provided her with a good place to begin. Describe the strengths and weaknesses of Glaven's first draft.

2. What do you see as Glaven's purpose in writing this essay? Did she achieve her purpose in this draft?

3. Who is Glaven's audience? What assumptions did she make about her audience in this draft? What additional information does her audience need to understand her purpose?

4. Glaven's draft has a series of examples. How does she order these examples?

5. How effective is Glaven's last paragraph? Does she answer the question, "What can you do?" in the body of the essay?

GLAVEN'S FOURTH DRAFT

What Can You Do?

I am approached quite often by people who are   1
curious about my handicap. Because the questions
are so common I feel as if I should carry a tape
recorder that I can press start, and it will play,
"Beep! This is a recording," and continue with,
"I had my right leg amputated when I was five due
to osteogenic sarcoma." However, there have been
times when the tape recorder would have been of
little value since the questions asked were extraordinary.

I have found that the single motive behind a   2
child's question is based simply on the need for
knowledge; sometimes, this means for them to understand something different from themselves. For me
it is imperative to offer factual information regarding my handicap. The following two examples
characterize a child's need for such knowledge.

A question actually prompting my laughter was   3
once asked by a serious young girl who wanted to
know, "Do they really make your legs out of trees?"
After successfully masking my amusement I answered,
"They only use parts of trees."

While completing a ski run down the Needle, at   4
Haystack Mt. in Vermont, I decided to break for
lunch. I glided over to the ski rack at the base of
the lodge, bent over to release the binding of my ski

and replace my outriggers--adaptive poles with
crutches, when I felt a tug on my ski pants. There
stood a pint sized boy muffled to the ears who asked,
"What happened to your leg? Are you all right?"
Smiling, I answered that my leg had been sick and it
had to be removed so I could continue to live. At
this point, his father spotted him and yelled, "Come
eat your lunch." While waddling away the child murmured, "I'm glad you're O.K." I relished a question
not shrouded by sophistication and one filled with
genuine concern.

Far from the innocence of a child's curiosity   5
there is a large group of people who are unable to
see that people mislabeled handicapped do accomplish
everyday events, as well as more significant tasks
based solely on their own merit. As in my case,
appealing to peoples' sentiment is not always beneficial nor is it synonymous with success.

Once when a woman asked me about my leg, and I   6
mechanically reiterated the story, she went on to
tell me about her brother's son who was retarded.
The not so subtle comparisons between her nephew's
handicap and my own caused me to fidget in my seat
and want to scream, "They amputated my leg, not my
brains."

One day, as a junior in high school, I walked   7
into home room and reflected back to the previous
night at the harvest dance when I was crowned

homecoming queen. A girlfriend of many years
sauntered over to me and offered her congratulations. In a hushed tone, she then asked if I felt
I was selected because of my leg. Initially, I
wanted to scream NO! But then, recalling my own
first thought, I answered, that yes I had considered
the same idea when first nominated, but had decided
that whether I won or lost the casting vote wouldn't
be dependent upon my leg. She quickly followed
this up with, "Well, I'm glad you feel like this.
I'm sure you're right." My friend through tone and
expression conveyed her disbelief in the fairness of
the decision. I wondered how many others felt
similarly and felt robbed of my chance to feel pride.

In my senior year of high school I was president 8
of the ski club and we took a ski trip to Mt. Sunapee
in New Hampshire. We arrived at the rental shop with
ample time for everyone to be fitted with the appropriate size skiis, boots, and poles and still be on
the slopes when the chair lifts opened. After helping
thirty kids learn to step into their bindings and
snap on their safety straps I guided the courageous
skiers over to the bunny hill and the less brave over
to the instructor's line up. Because I have an above
the knee amputation, in order to avoid injury, I don't
wear my prosthesis when I ski; instead, I ski with one
ski and outriggers--Canadian crutches with ski tips
welded to the ends. After I stepped into my own

binding and grabbed my outriggers, a group of my
closest friends and I traversed over to the chair
lift that leads to the mountain's summit. A
woman stopped short in front of us, and looking at
me, screeched, "Jesus Christ, now I've seen everything. What the hell are you trying to prove?"
My friends were quicker than I to defend me. They
asked her to join me in a run down the Wild Goose,
the racing trail, if she thought she could handle
it. The woman, unable to handle my friends or their
challenge, snowplowed over to another chair lift.
I heartily thanked my friends, who continued to stew
over the incident, and secretly wished for the opportunity to ski with that woman. I wanted her to know
that there was more to me than just being handicapped.

    Since my amputation I have answered a battery of 9
questions; their connotations fall into four categories: serious, amusing, derogatory, and supportive.
The question that pained me most and provoked the
most thought was when a person once asked, "What can
you do?" I contemplated the question then and have
since. Immediately, I felt compelled to make a pact
with myself to never retreat from any experience or
challenge because of my handicap or to be influenced
by the prejudices of others, regarding my handicap.
I was unable to respond to this question well at the
time. It was as if the countless times that I had
picked myself up from the pavement while learning to

ride a bike, the relay races I ran in second grade
on crutches--still trying to win--the times I tried
to be as confident as the girl with the smooth gait
and nice wiggle when approaching a boy were rendered
meaningless. Today, the integrity of the contract I
made with myself remains intact and if I were asked
the same question now I would answer, "What can't
I do!"

Questions on Glaven's Fourth Draft

1. Glaven's fourth draft was still rough, but it was more detailed and organized than her first draft. What are the major differences between the first and fourth drafts? What did Glaven accomplish in her fourth draft?

2. Why did Glaven drop the example about sitting in the conference room with the woman who blurted out, "Oh, she's the little girl with the wooden leg" (paragraph 3)? Why do you think she decided to add three new examples? What are the strengths of the examples she added?

3. Glaven structured her fourth draft by categorizing people's responses to her handicap by the type of questions they ask. Why did she decide to use this structure to organize her draft? How does this structure support her purpose?

4. How specifically has Glaven strengthened her purpose in her fourth draft?

5. How does this draft more successfully answer the question posed in Glaven's last paragraph, "What can you do?"

GLAVEN'S FINAL DRAFT

What Can You Do?

I am approached quite often by people who are   1
curious about my handicap. Because the questions
are so common, I should carry a tape recorder that
will play, "Beep! This is a recording," and continue with, "I had my right leg amputated when I was
five due to osteogenic sarcoma." However, there
have been times when the tape recorder would have
been of little value since the questions asked were
extraordinary.

The primary motive behind children's questions   2
is simply the need for knowledge. It is imperative
to offer factual information regarding my handicap.
The following two examples characterize a child's
need for such knowledge. A serious young girl once
wanted to know, "Do they really make your legs out
of trees?" After successfully masking my amusement
I answered, "They only use parts of trees."

One day while completing a ski run down the   3
Needle, at Haystack Mountain in Vermont, I decided
to break for lunch. I glided over to the ski rack at
the base of the lodge and bent over to release the
binding of my ski and replace my outriggers (adaptive
poles with crutches) when I felt a tug on my ski
pants. There stood a pint-sized boy muffled to the
ears who asked, "What happened to your leg? Are you
all right?" Smiling, I said that my leg had been sick

and it had to be removed so I could continue to
live. At this point, his father spotted him and
yelled, "Come eat your lunch." As he waddled
away, the child murmured, "I'm glad you're O.K."
The child's unsophisticated question and his
genuine concern touched me.

Unlike children, many adults are unable to see   4
that people mislabeled handicapped do accomplish
everyday events as well as more significant tasks·.
Once when a woman asked me about my leg and I
mechanically reiterated the story, she went on to
tell me about her brother's son who was retarded.
The not so subtle comparisons between her nephew's
handicap and my own caused me to fidget and want to
scream, "They amputated my leg, not my brains!"

One day, as a junior in high school, I walked   5
into homeroom and reflected back to the previous
night at the harvest dance when I was crowned homecoming queen. A good friend came over to offer her
congratulations. In a hushed tone she then asked if
I felt I was selected because of my leg. Initially,
I wanted to scream, "No!" But then, recalling my
own first thought, I replied that yes, I had considered
the same idea when first nominated but had resolved
that whether I won or lost, the deciding vote wouldn't
be dependent upon my leg. She quickly reacted with,
"Well, I'm glad you feel like this; I'm sure you're
right." From her tone and expression, I knew my

friend questioned the fairness of the decision.
Feeling robbed of my chance to feel proud, I
wondered how many others felt similarly.

In my senior year of high school when I was   6
president of the Ski Club, thirty members, two
chaperones and I took a ski trip to Mt. Sunapee in
New Hampshire. We arrived at the rental shop with
ample time for everyone to be fitted with the
necessary ski equipment and still be on the slopes
when the chair lifts opened. After helping everyone learn to step into their bindings and snap on
their safety straps, I guided the braver skiers over
to the bunny hill and the less brave over to the
instructor's lineup. Because I have an above-the-
knee amputation, in order to avoid injury I don't
wear my prosthesis when I ski; instead, I ski with
one ski and outriggers—Canadian crutches with ski
tips welded to the ends. After I stepped into my
own binding and grabbed my outriggers, a group of
my closest friends and I traversed over to the chair
lift that leads to the mountain's summit. A woman
stopped in front of us, and, looking at me, yelled,
"Jesus Christ! Now I've seen everything! What the
hell are you trying to prove?" My friends were
quicker than I to defend me. One challenged her to
join me in a run down the Wild Goose, the racing
trail, if she thought she could handle it. Embarrassed,
the woman snowplowed over to another chair lift. I

heartily thanked my friends, who continued to stew
over the incident. A few minutes later on the chair
lift, alone in my thoughts, I was saddened that
once again I had been looked at as limited.

Since my amputation I have answered a grab bag   7
of questions. The question that pained and provoked
me the most was from a woman who asked, "What can you
do?" I was unable to respond to this question well
at that time. It was as if the countless times that
I picked myself up from the pavement while learning
to ride a bike, the relay races in second grade on
crutches, still trying to win, the times I tried to
be as confident as the girl with the smooth gait and
nice wiggle when approaching a boy were rendered
meaningless. The question compelled me to make a
pact with myself never to retreat from any experience
or challenge because of my handicap or to be influenced
by the prejudice of others. Today, the integrity of
the contract I made with myself remains intact, and
if I were asked the same question now I would answer,
"What can't I do!"

Questions on Glaven's Final Draft

1. Glaven's final draft is polished and readable. What are the major differences between the fourth and final drafts? What did Glaven accomplish in her final draft?

2. In her final draft, Glaven dropped paragraph 5 as it appeared in her fourth draft. Why do you think she decided to drop this paragraph? Is her essay stronger without this paragraph? Explain.

3. Why do you think Glaven dropped paragraph 8 as it appeared in her fourth draft? What would have been the effect if she had kept the paragraph?

4. The last four sentences of paragraph 9 were dropped after the fourth draft. Why are the paragraph and the essay stronger because of this change?

5. In paragraph 10 of the fourth draft, Glaven categorized and labeled the questions she has been asked. She dropped these labels in the final draft. Why might it have been important for her to label the questions when she was writing her fourth draft? Why do you think she eventually decided to drop the labels?

6. After studying these three drafts of Glaven's essay, summarize what Glaven has achieved in revising.

PEER EDITORS
AT WORK

Part IV

THE PREVIOUS CHAPTER examined the composing process from the writer's point of view. A student writer, Susan Zurakowski, reconstructed the different procedures she used to help her get started, write, and then revise a successful essay. This chapter studies the composing process from both the writer's and the reader's points of view by focusing on how writers can work with their peers to improve each other's essays. When applied to student writing, the term *peer editors* refers to students who read carefully, write diligently, and talk informatively about the drafts of other students' essays. Like their professional counterparts (see "The Professional Editor at Work," pages 251 – 286), peer editors serve as supportive readers ready to understand a writer's purpose and able to assist the writer in achieving that purpose. In such circumstances, a writer senses the immediacy of an audience — of peers willing to read his or her work thoughtfully and to offer detailed comments on how effectively a particular draft expresses the writer's intentions. Peer editors can provide writers with both specific praise and practical advice about how to strengthen the successful features of an essay and repair its flaws. And by responding to and evaluating their peers' work, writers are better able to write, read, revise, and edit their own essays.

Peer editors and writers can work one on one, in small groups, or within the class as a whole to help each other get started, draft, revise, and edit essays that will satisfy themselves and their course requirements. Although the principles and procedures of peer editing can be applied to any stage of the composing process, peer editing usually works best after writers have produced a first draft of their essays, when they can benefit most from detailed and supportive responses to what they have written. By working collaboratively with peer editors, writers are not limited to their own perspective on the composing process; they can see how other writers — the peer editors — would deal with exactly the same circumstances and challenges in writing.

This chapter examines the most effective techniques peer editors can use when responding to the writing of other students. The chapter presents an example of peer editing: Several students offer detailed responses to and recommendations for how Charlotte Russell might improve her essay "Logging: Then and Now." The chapter then considers in general terms how writers might both work most productively with the responses of peer editors and plan more effective revisions based on the peer editors' comments and recommendations. Then, more specifically, the chapter presents Charlotte Russell's work on a revision of her essay and includes Russell's explanations of how and why she incorporated, modified, and occasionally rejected the peer editors' suggestions. A newly revised draft of Russell's essay follows, along with several peer editing exercises — in which students can apply the principles and procedures of peer editing first to Barbara Howell's "Survival and the Pig" and then to their own writing.

THE PEER EDITOR'S RESPONSE TO WRITING

The most effective peer editor is an interested and sensitive reader. To be a sympathetic and helpful critic of another student's writing, the peer editor should be willing to work diligently to understand the writer's purpose and to offer thoughtful and specific advice about how the writer might best achieve that purpose. The peer editor needs to be interested in helping other students to write better — not by suggesting ways to avoid errors but by assisting them to articulate fully their ideas.

When approaching another student's writing, the peer editor should think, talk, and write about it seriously and respectfully. Any writer will respond more energetically and appreciatively to criticism — be it positive or negative — that has been tactfully worded. Judicious comments also signal that the peer editor is genuinely interested in helping another writer improve; the most helpful comments are the most specific, direct, and encouraging. The peer editor who says simply that he or she "liked" or "disliked" an essay doesn't help a writer understand either the specific strengths or the weaknesses of the essay. But noting, for example, that the writer has emphasized a particular point by developing a striking metaphor in the third sentence of the second paragraph makes that achievement more appreciable — and the skill more repeatable — for both the writer and the peer editor. And it is the ability to repeat success that makes writing so satisfying and enduring an intellectual enterprise.

Peer editors can respond in innumerable ways to another student's writing. The most typical and widely used strategies for peer editing fall into two categories: specific comments made in the margin of the essay and a general statement made usually at the end of the essay. The specific and general comments most often serve two functions: to describe what the writer has actually said in the essay and to evaluate the specific strengths and weaknesses of what the writer has written.

Perhaps the most valuable service a peer editor can perform for a writer is to return a clear and, at least initially, nonjudgmental description of what the writer has written. One of the best ways to do that is to write as many specific observations as possible about the essay directly on the manuscript. In peer editing, an *observation* is a statement about which there can be no disagreement. In this sense, an observation is concrete, limited, verifiable, and often fairly obvious. It is also nonjudgmental. The purpose of the peer editor's observations is to help the writer understand and appreciate a reader's perceptions of what the writer has actually written. The observation might address, for example, fundamental problems in logic and organization: "You mention the same point about the effects of nuclear weapons in paragraphs 4 and 7." Or a seemingly obvious observation such as "I notice that you begin the first five sentences in your essay with 'It is' and 'There are' " may lead the writer to infer that he or she ought to reread the essay with an eye on varying its verbs and sentence structure. But the decision to do so remains where it belongs — solely with the writer.

Evaluative comments shift the emphasis from describing what the essay says to assessing its specific strengths and weaknesses and to suggesting particular revisions. In making evaluative comments, the peer editor writes detailed marginal notations about such elements of composition as the writer's word choice, tone, use of examples, logic, and organization. The peer editor identifies both what the writer does well and what he or she needs to spend more time on. The more honest the peer editor's assessments are, the more helpful the peer editor will be.

A particularly useful kind of evaluation is for the peer editor to summarize as succinctly as possible the controlling idea of the essay and to note how fully the writer develops that idea in each paragraph. The aim of this evaluation is to assist the writer in expressing, clarifying, and developing completely the main point of the essay as well as the assertions in each paragraph that support it.

The peer editor usually writes a general evaluation at the end of the essay, based on the specific marginal notations made throughout the paper. The peer editor's goal in this general evaluation is a balanced overview of the essay's strengths and weaknesses, not simply a summary of its flaws. The peer editor also includes suggestions to help the writer develop a detailed and achievable plan for revision. These suggestions should be selective rather than exhaustive and should help the writer set clear priorities for revising. These general comments are also the most appropriate place for the peer editor to review the essay with an eye on helping the writer make it as succinct, engaging, and elegant as possible. These are also quite likely the last suggestions the writer can draw on before revising the essay and submitting it to the instructor for an additional reading and a grade.

Student writers who are also peer editors will be both practiced writers and practiced readers, for the skills of writing and reading are truly integrated. What peer editors learn about the interaction between reading and writing will help them a great deal when they turn to their own writing. For the many contributions that the peer editor makes to the eventual success of another student's essay, the peer editor earns the respect of the writer who has been helped and benefits from that writer's advice when the peer editor turns his or her attention back to crafting an essay.

PEER EDITING CHARLOTTE RUSSELL'S ESSAY

To demonstrate how a writer can improve an already strong essay with the help of peer editors, this section presents several peer editors' responses to Charlotte Russell's essay "Logging: Then and Now." We have chosen this essay because of its ambition and complexity. Russell writes knowledgeably, respectfully, and critically of logging in the Pacific Northwest, where, as she reports, legend has it that "the trees are as tall as a skyscraper and so wide that twenty men couldn't encircle one." This is an area where, as she says, "the majority of people eat, breathe, and sleep logging."

Charlotte Russell explains that the "seed" of her essay can be traced to rare films that she viewed about old logging methods, conversations in which old-timers swapped tall tales and dramatic stories about logging, as well as her own experiences walking through the majestic and serene forest that borders her home in Oregon. But she realized that this peaceful world of "wooden mono-liths" and "breathtaking beauty" is now threatened by the chain saws and behemoth "Cats" of the modern logging industry.

With this stark contrast in mind, Russell set out to convey her sense that "the forest had a chance in 1880 to survive; it doesn't now. My goal was simply to express my sadness, my anger, my frustrations, and my respect as succinctly as I could."

Near the end of the spring 1983 quarter, we invited students in a writing class at the University of California at San Diego to respond as peer editors to Charlotte Russell's essay. At that time, the students — David Caldwell, Angela Didio, Jo-Ellen Fisherkeller, and Dan Martin — had accumulated nearly ten weeks' worth of peer editing experience. These students read and responded to Charlotte Russell's essay as though she were a member of their class. Then Russell responded in writing to the peer editors' comments, and she planned and wrote a revision based on their suggestions.

Here are both the specific marginal notations that the peer editors made on Charlotte Russell's essay and their general comments at the end of the essay. Read the essay as it appears on pages 120–124 without any comments on it. Then reread it as it appears below, this second time considering the peer editors' responses to it.

RUSSELL'S EDITED ESSAY

Logging: Then and Now

Logging in the Northwest in the 1880s was
quiet and methodical compared to the noisy,
mechanical drone of the highly technical logging
characteristic of the 1980s.   It was by painstaking and tedious maneuvers that men and animals
were able to drag fifteen thousand board feet of
timber out of the forest.   Today, with the aid of
modern equipment, loggers can move millions of
board feet of timber in a short period of time.   In
1880, water was the method for transporting the
logs to the sawmills, so only timber which was easily
accessible to the shoreline was cut.   Nowadays,
machines make it possible for men to reach far inland and cut from the steep terrain common to the
Northwest.

The mammoth firs and cedars growing a hundred   2
years ago were so large that often twenty men with
outstretched arms could not encircle one.   It
wasn't a single man brandishing a motorized chain
saw that felled one of these giants; instead, two
men would usually spend eight days chopping, hacking,
and sawing a chunk out, using their axes and cross-
cut saw until finally, with a tremendous roar that

Marginal handwritten annotations:

I understand your contrast between "quiet" and "noisy," but the differences between "methodical" and "mechanical" aren't clear enough. (DM)

Do you need the phrase "It was"? (DM)

Do "quiet" and "methodical" balance "painstaking" and "tedious"? (DC)

Can you be more specific? (JF)

Can water be a "method"? (DM)

You create the sense that new logging methods are more efficient. Is that what you intended? (I don't think so.) (DM)

You balance the two parts of the comparison nicely here. (DC)

You don't establish your own attitude toward logging in the first paragraph. (AD)

Your tone here is neutral. Will it continue to be? (DC)

This sentence is more than 50 words long. (JF)

echoed through the pristine forest, the virgin

This adjective confused me. "Pristine" sounds too dainty for huge, strong trees. (JF)

tree would fall heavily to the ground, crushing

everything in its path. Back at the stump, the

choppers would refill the bottle of kerosene that

hung inverted from their cross-cut saw and select

another tree.

Shouldn't the sentences on kerosene be in the same paragraph? Also, describe the function of the kerosene before telling about the "choppers" who "refill" it. (DC)

    Periodically, the men would check this bottle   3

of kerosene because not enough kerosene dripping

down over the cross cut would create drag from the

You change the structure of your contrast here. In the first paragraph, you included both sides (old and new), but here you describe only the old. (JF)

sticky pitch. Pitch settled in the first ten to

Should you explain "drag"? Is "pitch" like sap? (DM)

twelve feet of the tree, which made sawing at this

level impossible. A method they used for getting

above this pitch line was a springboard, a flat

board with a metal hook on the end of it. They

would jam this board into a notch they had made

with their axes at about ten to twelve feet above

If loggers can get above "the pitch line," why do they need kerosene? Besides, isn't this an unnecessary detail? (DM)

the ground, each man having a springboard on his

You make it easy for us to see the men at work here.

side of the tree. They would then "spring" onto

You give us a great deal of information. (DC)

this board and continue with their cross cut.

You do not name the other 2 reasons. (DM)

Sometimes there was a third reason for the saw

dragging, but that was probably due to one of the

loggers falling asleep, rather than to a dull saw.

That was called "riding the saw," and because cross

Isn't this idea different from the second one in the sentence? If so, then shouldn't you start a new sentence? (AD)

cutting required precision teamwork, if one man

didn't pull his own weight, he was quickly fired.

Once the sawyers were through, the buckers 4

would come to saw the logs to their desired size.

Couldn't you cut these two words without damaging your sentence? (AD)

Their job wasn't an easy one because they usually

had to stand at tortuous angles balanced between

What is the reference for this word? (JF)

several logs. After they were out of the way, the

swampers would raise and flatten one side of the

A reader inexperienced in logging would get lost in this jargon. The overdescription hurts the balance and purpose of your essay: to contrast "then" and "now." (DM)

You use the verb "to be" in the first four sentences of this paragraph. (AD)

log, bevel one end so it wouldn't catch on the

skids, and plow them out of the ground. Skids were

roads made out of hand-hewn fir logs approximately

ten to twelve feet long. One half their diameter

would be embedded in the ground about nine feet

apart, so a twenty-foot log would have a bearing on

two skids. Young men, about thirteen years old,

would run ahead of the train of logs with a swab

You use lots of details and make the loggers' work come alive. (DC)

and bucket of grease, liberally greasing each skid.

Another skid, called a "brow skid," was constructed

You describe the skids well. I can see how this part of logging works. (JF)

at the landing for transferring the logs to the

water. In one week, an average of nine hundred

Your tone changes here. You use such words as "easy," "torturous," "grueling," "hazardous," and "lucky." You no longer seem neutral. (AD)

cords was cut and dragged slowly by a team of six-

teen oxen to the landing. For this grueling and

hazardous work the logger was paid $1.00 a day for

You repeat the word "day" here. (DM)

a twelve-hour day. After putting in his twelve

hours, the logger would trudge wearily back to camp,

where he would make his home for the next six

months. The ones that could walk back to camp were

Why not include the pay scale for the 1980s? (DM)

Does this mean he won't work for another 6 months? (JF)

The image of the lucky ~~ones, because accidents~~ : *accidents* in the 1880s *Wouldn't it*
"ticks on a   *be simpler to*
dog" supports were as common as ticks on a dog. Many a logger *say it this way?*
your point   *(AD)*
well. (JF) would walk past a dead man propped up against a

Your details stump, awaiting removal at the end of the day to a *There is a dramatic,*
make this picture   *jolting*
of logging freshly dug grave back at camp.   *immediacy in*
clear. (JF)   *this sentence. (DC)*

Camp consisted of a group of seven to ten) *The word "camp"*
                                             makes a good
hastily built shacks. Twenty-five loggers were *transition between*
                                                 paragraphs. (DM)
housed in each one, and at 6:00 p.m. they would

all be inside peeling off their soaked clothes and *You don't*
                                                    explain why
soggy boots, hanging them above a crackling fire *their clothes*
                                                  were "soaked"
in the wood stove. It was the bullcook's job to *and their boots*
                                                  "soggy." (AD)
You sound get the fires started in each cabin and feed these
more relaxed
here. Try to starving loggers. He was the most respected man
maintain
this voice in the camp. At his signal, the men would quietly *What does this*
throughout   *paragraph have*
your essay. (AD) filter into the dining hall and, at another signal, *to do with*
                                                                 cutting down
sit down to eat. There never seemed to be enough *trees? (JF)*

food, no matter how high the bullcook heaped each

plate, but eventually every man would begin to

The verbs
you use here stretch, rub his satisfied belly, and wander back
are lively. (JF) *You use alliteration in this sentence. (DM)*
to his cabin for a smoke, a story, or a song before *Aren't there*
                                                      two ideas in this
the kerosene lamp was extinguished.   *one sentence? If*
                                                      so, shouldn't you
This first   *separate them*
sentence talks The logging camps disappeared long ago. The *into two*
about the   *sentences? (AD)*
logging camps, ringing of the axes and the yells of the bull-
but the rest
of the puncher as he prodded the tired oxen to the landing
paragraph
does not have been replaced by the mechanical whine of the *Well-balanced*
(AD)   *contrast. (JF)*

gasoline-powered chain saw and the noise and smell
of diesel-driven yarders. Instead of taking days
to fell a tree, it now takes minutes. The image

Why do you describe the old loggers as "dumb"? What did they do that makes people call them "dumb"? (DC)

of the "dumb country logger" has been transfigured

You mention this image, but you never describe it in any way. (DM)

into a new breed of professionals. It takes highly

skilled men to run the complex machinery used in

logging today. Millions of dollars' worth of equip-

ment are at stake, so the boss is very careful

about whom he hires. Accidents are rare now, but

should they occur, a helicopter would be summoned

This sentence doesn't seem to lead naturally to the next one. Maybe you should drop it or start a new paragraph. (JF)

with a two-way radio for immediate removal of the

injured. Cats, shovels, and skylines using various

cables or lines are rigged to help log on steep

terrain or in other inaccessible areas. These

Is your point that modern logging is wasteful? Or is it more efficient in terms of time? The image is either confused or inconsistent. (AD)

metal beasts use more fuel and spare parts in one

day than the whole team of oxen ate in feed in one

month. Myriad gauges, dials, and complicated

whistle signals must be memorized by the yarder

engineer, who is in charge of the lines that pull

the logs out of the forest. From the yarder, the

lines are strung to a D.A. cat with a C frame built

What is a "C frame"? (DC)

on. From this line, another line, called a

"carriage," drops down and pulls the log in place.

This whole apparatus is called a "skyline."

Besides the yarder engineer, there's the   7

[margin note, top left (DM):] Too many technical terms here. Does the reader really need to know all this? (DM)

hooktender, the rigging slinger, the choke setter,

and the chaser. The hooktender is the head man

and oversees the entire logging operation. He's

got to be able to splice a line quickly and make

sure all the other lines are properly attached. He

[margin note, right (DM):] What "lines"? Attached to what? Do you really need this sentence? (DM)

does whatever is necessary to keep the logging

operation running smoothly. The rigging slinger is

the man who sets the carriage in motion while

simultaneously checking the quality of the logs.

The choke setter then slips a line around the log

and cinches it through an eye, much as the choker

collar on a dog works. The chaser is the man who

removes the log from the landing with the aid of a

shovel attached to another yarder and loads it on a

logging truck destined for the mills. These five

men now do the job that used to take thirty. It's

a new era of logging--fast and efficient. This new

technology of man and machines has now been refined

[margin note, left (AD):] Although you define the terms, you still make me realize how unfamiliar they are. Do you want to create that effect? Your essay might be more effective if you left out most of these terms. Some are necessary, but many more seem distracting. (AD)

[margin note, right (DM):] Can you make this sentence simpler? (DM)

to a science that can rape an entire forest of its

[margin note, right (AD):] These last two sentences seem like the heart of your essay. If they are, why don't you make these points earlier? (AD)

trees in days. The loggers, however, like to think

of themselves as the gardeners of the forest, har-

vesting a crop of ripe timber.

[margin note, left (DM):] You use "rape" to express your attitude toward the new technology. (DM)

It took a lot of strength and stamina to be a

logger in the 1880s. Nothing was easy. Each tree

posed a new challenge and was conquered only through

[margin note, left (DM):] You shift your focus suddenly between these two paragraphs. (DM)

[margin note, right (AD):] Too many technical terms in this long paragraph. I lost interest. These terms do to the reader what modern loggers do to the forest. I think this paragraph puts the reader off. (AD)

sheer will, determination, and muscle.   Today, the

Is it romantic because it is obsolete? (DM)

loggers have taken this legacy for granted.   Sadly,

much of the <u>romance</u> that was a part of logging has

vanished and, like the virgin-growth timber, will

never return.

"Sadly"? Is it sad that loggers are no longer paid $1.00 a day and that they can escape injury more easily? (JF)

What are you mourning? The vanishing style of logging? The vanishing forest? Both? (DC)

This paragraph seems tacked on. How is it tied to the ideas in the previous paragraph? (DC)

You use the word "romance" to talk about the old ways, but you also say that it is "grueling" and "hazardous." What is the "romance"? (JF)

General Comments at the End of the Essay

The four peer editors added these general comments, in addition to their marginal notes, to the end of Russell's essay.

DAVID CALDWELL   —I notice the following structure in your essay:

—in paragraph one you talk about old and modern logging

—in paragraph two you talk about old and modern logging

—in paragraph three you talk about old logging

—in paragraph four you talk about old logging

—in paragraph five you talk about old logging

—in paragraph six you talk about old and modern logging

—in paragraph seven you talk about modern logging

—in paragraph eight you talk about old and modern logging

—As a sheer comparison of methods, modern logging is clearly superior. But I think you are saying something more, yet you don't bring that point out enough.

—You seen to have a clear understanding of your subject, and you seem to care about your ideas. Let that show more. But I'm still not sure whether it's the romance of old-time logging that you miss or whether you're angry at what modern technology has done by making nature so easy to destroy.

ANGELA DIDIO   —Your first paragraph creates the impression that there will be a comparison in this essay. Yet, while some paragraphs do compare logging in the 1880's and 1980's, others do not. For example, your focus in the first paragraph on straight comparison shifts quickly to the difficult logging techniques of the old days. Before the conclusion, another contrast is drawn to show that modern technology makes logging easier. Your thesis seems to be that the old ways of logging are harder and more admirable, but the first paragraph does not suggest this—the conclusion does. In effect, your first paragraph doesn't prepare your reader for your conclusion. You don't simply show the differences between the old and the new methods of logging, you also imply that the old is better than the new. Maybe you should rethink your introduction to prepare your audience for your point of view.

JO-ELLEN FISHERKELLER   —I really liked your informative tone and all of the details you gave us. From your detailed description of the loggers' "grueling" job, I got more of a sense of relief for those men when modern technology made their work easier. You bring up the grandeur and the power of the forest only indirectly, and the intention of the modern loggers seems no different from that of the "old" loggers. Why shouldn't the present method exist, or how should it be changed?

Reading your essay gives me the sense that the old loggers had more dignity and earned more respect for their awesome task than the modern loggers. But if modern loggers think they are high tech gardeners, how did the "old" loggers regard their work? Their job is described in detail, but what kind of men were they? What did they think of their work?

DAN MARTIN

— You use many specific examples to back up the points you make, yet you don't always define all of the logging terms you use. In this sense, I think your essay could be improved if you would concentrate more on who your audience is. If you want to give people who don't know much about logging a clear sense of what logging was like in the "pristine" forest, then you should eliminate most of the jargon in your essay. You could then also develop your sense of the majesty of the forest, the immense size of the trees, and many similar points. You could then also spend more time on the sweat, hardship, and dignity of 19th century loggers. Your ideas about the "rape" of the forest and the modern "gardeners" could best be developed into a separate essay.

As I read this version, I'm just not sure what your purpose is. Is this an anti-logging paper? an anti-technology paper? an anti-progress paper?

— You contrast several aspects of logging in the 1880s and 1980s: "romance" vs. "rape"; humans vs. machines in the forest; personal vs. technical dimensions of logging, etc. It seems as though each of these could be developed into a separate essay.

— Your last paragraph is very short.

Questions on Russell's Edited Essay

1. Reread the general statements of the peer editors at the end of Charlotte Russell's essay. On which aspects of the essay does David Caldwell focus his attention? Angela Didio? Jo-Ellen Fisherkeller? Dan Martin? What overall advice does each offer? Which peer editors add new ideas in their general comments? What specific changes in focus, tone, and word choice do you notice

between the peer editors' general concluding statements and their marginal comments? Which parts of the essay does each regard as most successful? Least successful? Why?

2. Review the peer editors' detailed marginal notations. Which of these comments are observations (statements about which there can be no disagreement)? Which are evaluations that try to summarize the main idea of the essay and then show the relation between each paragraph and this idea? Which offer recommendations for revising?

3. Examine Jo-Ellen Fisherkeller's comments at the end of the essay. What is her attitude toward logging "then and now" and toward Charlotte Russell's attitude about that subject?

4. List the points that the peer editors agree on. On what points do they disagree? On what points do you agree with the peer editors' responses to Charlotte Russell's essay? On what points do you disagree with them?

5. Reread Dan Martin's final comments. Sketch out what Charlotte Russell would need to do in a revision to respond adequately to what he says. Then reread Angela Didio's concluding statement. In what specific ways might Charlotte Russell's plan for revision be altered by what Angela Didio says?

THE WRITER'S RESPONSE TO PEER EDITING

The writer who benefits most from peer editing is the one who listens most attentively to what the peer editors have to say about an essay and then examines with them the implications of their observations and recommendations. But peer editing — like the process of writing — is a skill that takes time and frequent practice to develop. So the writer and the peer editors need at least occasionally to remind each other that even the best-intentioned efforts at peer editing — and especially the first few tries at it — may not bring immediate improvement in each other's writing. There are few quick fixes in the world of ideas.

The writer who is about to work with peer editors can anticipate receiving a good deal of generous and supportive criticism from readers who are familiar with — and sympathetic to — the writer's purpose. And the ever-present fact that there is a real audience who will read and respond to what the writer has written may well be all the reassurance the writer needs that writing is worth the effort involved, especially when the writer faces moments — as nearly every writer does — when ideas seem hard to discover and when energy and interest in writing seem to falter.

To make the best possible use of the peer editors' responses and advice, the writer needs to listen thoughtfully to their observations and recommendations and to take advantage of these responses in writing a final draft. By listening purposefully, the writer is less likely to be distracted from examining the strengths and weaknesses of an essay by a peer editor's poorly phrased comment or ill-advised judgment.

When done rigorously, peer editing is as much a writing exercise as a reading exercise. When peer editors are searching quickly for the best way to convey their responses to an essay, they too may occasionally slip into awkward or even inappropriate phrasing. But such moments, however uninstructive they may appear at first glance, are opportunities for the writer to reciprocate by helping the peer editors express themselves more effectively. Sometimes the peer editors' comments may not be entirely clear, and in such cases the writer should not hesitate to press for clarification. This process often results in a dialogue in which the writer has a chance to explain more fully his or her purpose or sense of audience and the peer editors have an opportunity to clarify and develop some of their comments and suggestions. But whatever the particulars of such a dialogue, writing is clearly the source — and the result — of productive conversation.

Writing should be at the center of peer editing. The writer leaves a peer editing session with more than impressions of the peer editors' responses. The writer carries away — and later can evaluate and act on — the peer editors' detailed written responses to an essay, responses that have been amplified in the writer's discussion with the peer editors. Having all of the peer editors' comments in writing not only makes particular points of the discussion recoverable later but also enables the writer to spend time after the discussion evaluating the comments and developing priorities for revision.

A writer whose work has the benefit of peer editing develops the ability to evaluate the reactions of many different readers, each of whom may read the essay in a slightly different way. But the writer ought to pay special attention to any comments about the strengths and weaknesses of the essay that have been pointed out by more than one peer editor. In each instance, the writer has to decide what to change and what to retain in a new draft. The peer editors can help, but the authority and the responsibility for those decisions remain the writer's.

Discussing and then evaluating the comments of the peer editors should help the writer develop a clear sense of how to improve the essay. The writer's plan for revision should include the peer editors' recommendations that the writer has decided to accept, along with the writer's own ideas about how to reinforce the essay's strengths and eliminate its weaknesses. The peer editing process encourages a writer to treat an essay as a work-in-progress, to understand his or her specific strengths and shortcomings as a writer, and eventually to produce stronger writing at every phase of the composing process.

ONE WRITER'S RESPONSE TO PEER EDITING

In this section we present Charlotte Russell's responses to the peer editing of David Caldwell, Angela Didio, Jo-Ellen Fisherkeller, and Dan Martin. Charlotte Russell's comments explain her decisions to include, adapt, and sometimes reject the peer editors' recommendations. Following her comments is the revised version of her essay that she prepared using the peer editors' reactions and advice.

The following are Charlotte Russell's responses to the peer editors' observations and recommendations, grouped according to the principal issues raised by the peer editors.

ON HER PURPOSE
IN WRITING

The idea to write about the eventual loss of this pristine forest was always in the back of my head, but I needed to make it an interesting topic for readers. Man versus Nature is a common subject of many authors, so I felt it would be a safe theme. I wanted to strike a common chord that would actively involve my audience in the story (even if they lived in Kenmore Square in Boston, where trees are a rarity). My wanting to preserve that forest would be like someone wanting to preserve the little church in the middle of downtown Government Square or a little covered bridge somewhere or a natural canyon or some other nostalgic refuge. Everyone could relate to this idea. So I considered the audience, the lasting impression I wanted, even the pace of the essay. Knowing all of this was the easiest part. Putting it all down so it flowed right was another matter.

In the essay I am mourning both the vanishing style of logging and the disappearance of the forest. I was asked to write a comparison/contrast essay, and I didn't want to get argumentative, except perhaps slightly so in the last paragraph.

One of the peer editors asked me to explain just exactly what I was explaining. I wish I could label it more clearly. I wanted of course to contrast logging in the 1880s and

1980s, but I also used the logging contrast to help bring out my philosophy, which has a lot to do with how our society today views things. There's always an *immediacy* about everything. *Instant* mashed potatoes, *instant* pudding, *instant* this or that, or *quick* this or that. Immediate gratification is "in" today, and the word "rape" epitomizes today's mentality. We do something today without thinking about its repercussions for tomorrow. It takes only a few minutes with a chain saw to wipe out a tree that has been growing for a hundred years. And the loggers don't take one tree by itself. They "clear-cut" a forest forty acres at a time. It turns my stomach to drive past a barren hill that has been clear-cut by loggers. Are my kids going to see a tree over twenty years old when they grow up? I don't know. The trees used to be awesome. Today, they are mighty. Tomorrow, if they are here at all, they'll be ordinary in size and inferior in quality — and like everything else "efficiently" mass-produced.

ON HER COMPARISON/
CONTRAST STRUCTURE

I realized that an imbalance existed in my essay (comparing the 1880s and the 1980s) when I saw the peer editors' comments. I really appreciated David Caldwell's summary enumerating exactly what I talked about in each paragraph. This helped me to see more clearly how I structured the essay. (I never thought of doing this myself.) From this vantage point, I can now clearly see that I talked about old and new logging in the first two and last two paragraphs and that I concentrated in the middle paragraphs on old-time logging (which is what I wanted to stress anyway).

I realize that despite trying to be fair and to explain both sides of logging, I got bogged down in the details of describing the mechanized "beasts." Personally, I don't see how describing these machines helped the reader form an opinion for or against logging in the 1980s. Finally, I was under a two-thousand-word restriction, so I chose to stress logging in the 1880s because it was more interesting and challenging.

ON THE FUNCTION
AND STRUCTURE
OF PARTICULAR
PARAGRAPHS

Angela Didio said I should prepare my readers in the first paragraph for my conclusion. Why? The reason the first paragraph is seemingly neutral is simply to introduce the subject and to attract a general audience for my essay (from loggers to environmentalists). If I had stressed my point of view in the first paragraph, I would have limited my audience even more than I did.

Paragraph 5 was special because in it I tried to capture some of the flavor of camp life, which was an integral part of logging in those days. My instructor insisted that I explain the loggers' camp life, and I feel it added more than just interesting information to the essay. The image of the "dumb country logger" was a quote from a man who owns a logging company and who has been logging for a long time. It's a common saying in Oregon. In those days, anyone who was "smart" (and I say that tongue-in-cheek) was a lawyer, a doctor, *anything* but a logger. You'd have to be nuts or dumb to work twelve hours for $1.00, risking your life cutting down or bucking huge trees in the rain or snow, but rarely in the sunshine. And this also answers another peer editor's question concerning the wet clothes hanging above the wood stove. I invite that person to visit the Pacific Northwest in the summertime for a frolic in our "dry" season. There's another saying up here: "Oregonians don't tan, they rust!"

I noted Dan Martin's comment about the last paragraph's being short, and I expanded it.

ON HER USE
OF JARGON

I chose to use the special terminology of logging to lend authenticity, realism, clarity, and interest to the essay. I assumed the other jargon would be understood by readers. I was amazed, therefore, that one of the peer editors didn't know what "pitch" was or that "pristine" means "in its earliest period or state" or "having its original purity." Assuming too much is a weakness of mine, and one I continue to work on.

In response to Dan Martin's comment about jargon in paragraph 4, let me say that the audience I had in mind would know what a "yarder" is, and if they didn't, then the brief explanations of these pieces of equipment would give them authenticity and realism. In other words, if the reader got lost in the descriptions it wouldn't matter because that information wasn't essential to forming an opinion about my subject. The reader still would be able to gather that there was an awful lot of equipment up there moving lots of timber around. And I was hopeful that the reader would get a sense of the noise and smell of diesel-eating machines.

ON SPECIFIC WORD
CHOICES

"Methodical" can mean something done in a painstaking way, and logging in the 1880s was certainly done that way.

I contrasted this to logging in the 1980s, which is done in a "mechanical" way, with machines doing the lifting, pulling, stacking, etc. It may be mentally tedious, but it isn't "painstaking." In this respect, "methodical" stands in contrast to "mechanical." When you have machines to help you, it's more mental anguish than physical stress.

Choosing the words "rape" and "romance" was intentional, and I was pleased that most of the peer editors caught it.

ON PEER EDITING

On the whole, I felt that the comments were quite helpful and informative. They made it easier for me to see clearly what I had said. Peer editing is a valuable tool for the novice writer, and I learned a great deal about the way I write.

I revised the essay according to the comments that were duplicated by the peer editors. I rejected those comments that would have required a totally revised essay. In my revision, I answered such questions as "Is pitch like sap?" I changed verb tenses and rearranged some sentences, hoping that this would reduce some confusion. I deleted other things in the essay that caused problems (not only to the peer editors but also to me). The most dramatic change is the expansion of the last paragraph. Several peer editors commented that the essay ended too abruptly. Although I liked the way I had originally written it, I could see their point, and I used their response to my advantage as a writer. I put more of myself into this paragraph — as some peer editors asked for. About the only thing that remains the same is the philosophy underlying the essay—and the title.

Now that you have had the opportunity to read Charlotte Russell's responses to the observations and recommendations of the peer editors, examine the revised version of her essay, which she prepared after considering the peer editors' reactions and advice.

RUSSELL'S REVISED ESSAY

Logging: Then and Now

Logging in the Northwest in the 1880s was   1
quiet and methodical compared to the noisy, mechanical drone of the highly technical logging which
characterizes the 1980s. Painstaking and tedious
maneuvers in the 1880s enabled men and animals to
drag 15,000 board feet of timber out of the forest.
Today, with the aid of modern equipment, loggers
move millions of board feet. A hundred years ago,
rivers were mainly used to transport logs to the
sawmills, so only timber which was easily accessible
to the river's shoreline was cut. Nowadays, machines
have made it possible for men to reach far inland
and cut timber from the steep terrain common to the
Northwest. Hundreds of lone truck drivers now transport the freshly cut logs to the mills instead of
the slow, sometimes unpredictable river. These men,
however, must make several trips, back and forth, in
one day, and it's not unusual for them to drive a
hundred miles one way.

The mammoth firs and cedars growing in the 1880s   2
were so large that often twenty men with outstretched
arms could not encircle one. A single man brandishing
a motorized chain saw didn't fell one of these giants;
instead, two men would usually spend eight days
chopping, hacking, and sawing a chunk out with their
axes and cross-cut saws. Finally, with a tremendous

roar that echoed through the pristine forest, the virgin tree would fall heavily to the ground, crushing anything in its path. Back at the stump, the men would check the bottle of kerosene that hung from their cross-cut saw and select another tree. Periodically the men checked this bottle of kerosene that hung inverted over their cross cut because as it dripped slowly down the blade, it would provide the lubrication necessary to prevent drag from the "pitch," or sap.

In these large trees, pitch settled in the first ten to twelve feet, so the men would get above this concentration of sap with the aid of a "springboard." The springboard was a flat board with a metal hook on the end, and they would jam it into a notch they had made with their axes above this "pitch line." Each man would have a springboard on his side of the tree. The men would "spring" or jump onto the board and continue with their cross cut. Besides pitch, the saw might drag from another reason. Sometimes a partner would fall asleep or "ride the saw," which meant he would let the other man do all the sawing. Because this strenuous job required precision teamwork, the man that was caught not "pulling his own weight" would be fired on the spot. Once these "sawyers" were through, the "buckers" would come to saw the logs to their desired size.

The buckers' job wasn't an easy one, as they   4
usually had to stand at tortuous angles balanced
between several logs. It was common practice in
the 1880s to fell several cedars and firs before the
buckers came in. The trees would fall in a hap-
hazard, crisscrossing pyramid of logs, making the
buckers' job extremely dangerous. Poised at
various positions then, these men would get the logs
ready for the "swampers." The swampers had many
jobs, one of which was to raise and flatten one side
of the log, beveling it (which made it look like a
big pencil) so it wouldn't catch on the "skids" and
plow them out of the ground. Skids were roads made
out of hewn fir logs approximately ten to twelve
feet long. Half the log's diameter was embedded in
the ground about nine feet apart, so a twenty-foot
log would have a bearing on two skids and wouldn't
be in danger of shifting and burying its nose in the
ground. Young men about thirteen years old would
run ahead of this train of logs with a swab and a
bucket of grease to grease each skid. Another skid,
called a "brow skid," was constructed at the landing
and used for transferring the logs to the water. In
one week, an average of nine hundred cords were cut
and dragged slowly by a team of sixteen oxen to the
landing. The logger was paid $1.00 for every twelve
hours he put in. It was a grueling and hazardous job.
Each night for the next six months the logger would

trudge wearily back to camp. In the morning, the
loggers began the process all over again.

Camp consisted of seven to ten hastily slapped
together shacks; each shack housed about twenty-five   5
loggers. At 6:00 p.m. they were inside peeling off
their soaked clothes and soggy boots to hang them on
one of several hooks above a crackling fire in the
wood stove. The "bullcook" got the fires started in
each cabin and then left to cook the meals. He was
the most respected man in the camp. At his signal,
the hungry men would quietly filter in to the dining
hall, and at another signal they would eat. There
never seemed to be enough food no matter how much
the bullcook fixed, but eventually every man would
begin to stretch, rub his belly, and wander back to
his cabin for a smoke, a story, or a song before
the kerosene lamp was extinguished.

The logging camps have long ago disappeared.   6
The ringing of the axes and the yells of the "bullpuncher" as he prodded the oxen to the landing have
been replaced by the mechanical whine of the gasoline-powered chain saw and the noise and smell of
the diesel-driven yarders. Instead of days to fell
a tree, it now takes minutes. The image of the
"dumb country logger" has been transfigured into a
new breed of professionals. It takes highly skilled
men to run the complex machinery used today.
Millions of dollars' worth of equipment are at stake,

so the boss is careful who he hires. Accidents in
the 1880s were as common as ticks on a dog. Many a
logger would walk past a dead man propped up against
a stump awaiting removal at the end of the day.
Today, many logging operations have the help of
helicopters to transport the injured. "Cats,"
"shovels," and various cable rigging called "skylines" now help to log on steep terrain or inaccessible areas. These metal beasts use more fuel and
spare parts in one day than the whole team of oxen
ate in one month. Myriad gauges, dials, and complicated whistle signals must be memorized by the
yarder engineer. Besides him, there's the "hooktender," the "rigging slinger," the "choke setter,"
and the "chaser." These five men now do the job
that used to take thirty. It's a new era of logging:
fast and efficient. This new technology of man and
machines has now been refined to a science that can
rape an entire forest of its trees in days. The
loggers, however, like to think of themselves as
"gardeners" harvesting a crop of ripe timber.

        It took a lot of strength and stamina to be a   7
logger in the 1880s. Nothing came easy. Each
massive tree posed a new challenge and was conquered
only through sheer will, determination, and muscle.
Modern loggers have taken this legacy for granted.
Unlike their ancestors, the loggers today have many
modern conveyances which take them to, and aid them

in, cutting down the timber. At the rate this modern technology is ravaging the forests, the only timber our future generations will see will be what they look at out their car window at a tree farm. Logging methods in the 1880s gave the forest time to renew itself; that's not possible or economically efficient today. And so it would seem that more than just the romance of old-time logging has vanished and, like the virgin-growth timber, will never return.

Questions on Russell's Revision

1. In her responses to the peer editing (pages 234–235), Charlotte Russell discusses some of her plans for revising her essay. What did she decide to focus on in her revision? Which points in her response does she accomplish most successfully? Point to specific words and phrases in her responses and in her revision to support your answer.

2. Which of Charlotte Russell's responses to the peer editors' comments do you agree with? Which do you disagree with? Why? Which points in Russell's plan for revision would you like to see expanded? Dropped? Altered slightly? Why?

3. Which aspects of Russell's essay could benefit from additional attention and revision? Why? Point to specific places where she could make further changes, and indicate what those changes might be.

4. Charlotte Russell says that she put more of herself into the last paragraph. How has she done that, and with what effect?

5. Write as many observations as you can about the specific differences between Charlotte Russell's original essay (pages 120–124) and her revised essay. In what specific ways has she improved it? In what ways is her purpose clearer? How is her comparison/contrast better balanced? How does each paragraph relate more clearly to the main point of the essay? How does she consider more carefully her audience's knowledge of logging? How does her choice of words reflect a different consideration for her audience than in the original essay? Point to specific words and phrases in the essay to support your response.

PRACTICING PEER EDITING

In this section we have an opportunity to practice applying the principles and procedures of peer editing to Barbara Howell's "Survival and the Pig" and then to their own writing.

The following checklist points out many of the concerns that peer editors should keep in mind as they work on an essay. Your instructor may add others.

1. *Purpose.* What is the writer trying to do in the essay? What is the main idea, the essay's controlling idea or overriding point? What is the intention or the promise that the essay states or implies? Where and how well does the writer act on that intention or promise? What specific examples, ideas, or information would help clarify and reinforce the writer's purpose?

2. *Organization.* How is the essay organized? What is its basic structure? Comment on the logic and effectiveness of the sequence of paragraphs. How well does each paragraph support and develop the essay's main idea? In

which paragraphs is the main idea most effectively supported by details and examples?

3. *Choice of words.* Is the language of the essay primarily abstract or concrete? If it is abstract, do you understand what each abstraction means? Does the writer use special terminology or colloquial terms? How effective is such language? How does it support the writer's purpose?

4. *Point of view.* Point of view is the point or perspective from which the essay is written or the story is told. From what perspective does the writer approach the subject of the essay? Is he or she neutral, distant, or highly involved in the subject? Where is this point of view stated or implied? Does the writer maintain the point of view consistently throughout the essay? Point to places where the writer's point of view is most clearly stated, where it seems uncertain, and where it is consistent or inconsistent.

5. *Audience.* Characterize the audience that the writer seemed to have in mind when writing the essay. What does the writer expect the audience to know about the subject? Point to specific words and phrases that reveal the writer's assumptions about the audience's knowledge of the subject.

From your own experience and your study of peer editors at work, what other aspects of composition should peer editors attend to as they read another student's writing? Prepare sets of questions for each aspect.

Exercises in Peer Editing

1. Apply the principles of peer editing to "Survival and the Pig" by Barbara Howell (pages 245–249), following the peer editing procedures outlined in this chapter. Read the essay several times, writing your observations, evaluations, and recommendations in the margin.

   — Write as many observations as you can about the essay. (Remember, an observation is a statement about which there can be no disagreement.)

   — Summarize the essay's main idea and note how the writer supports and develops that idea in each paragraph.

   — Identify both the specific strengths and weaknesses of the essay. In this respect, pay particular attention to Barbara Howell's sentence structure and variety, her verb tenses and voice, her paragraph transitions, and her concluding paragraph.

   — Prepare a general statement at the end of Howell's essay, noting the essay's overall strengths and weaknesses and offering some specific recommendations for revision.

After you have completed your work as a peer editor on "Survival and the

Pig," write Barbara Howell a letter in which you analyze the strengths and weaknesses of her essay and offer her as much reasonable, practical, and detailed advice as you can about what she might do to improve her essay in another draft.

2. Your own writing is the focus for this exercise. Prepare a draft of an essay according to your instructor's directions. Then review the various peer editing activities described on pages 217–220. Bring your essay to class and present it to your peer editors. After you have received their written observations and recommendations on the essay, along with their assessment of its specific strengths and weaknesses and their recommendations for improving it, prepare a detailed plan for revising your essay. Consult with your peer editors about your plans for revision, and then draft a new version of the essay.

3. Review the peer editing process. Based on your experiences with it, write an essay in which you offer a clear sense of what you think you have learned about writing and reading as a result of these peer editing exercises. How has peer editing helped you improve your writing? In what specific ways has it strengthened your reading? What new insights have you developed about the processes of writing and reading? How, specifically, will peer editing affect the ways in which you will prepare your next essay? What do you see as the limitations of peer editing? How would you suggest improving or extending the peer editing process? Be as specific as possible. The emphasis in your essay should reflect either your reservations about or your enthusiasm for peer editing.

HOWELL'S ESSAY

Survival and the Pig

The pig jumped up! He tried to run away as   1
blood squirted everywhere. Tackling the pig, I
sat upon him with knife in hand. Soon I had control and could make the slit at the throat bigger,
letting the blood gush out more freely. The blood
ran out steadily with every last heartbeat.

The scene described above was a typical be-   2
ginning for a pig-killing ritual that I watched
every winter until I was old enough to take part in
the process myself. Being a farm girl from a rural
community in Blackshear, Georgia, I witnessed and
participated in this annual ritual until I left my
family's small farm four years ago. The process of
the pig killing was very important for the whole
family. The pig is a symbol of wealth and security;
and rightly so, for there is nothing, I mean nothing,
wasted from the slaughter of a pig. Every part is
eaten or used in some manner or fashion. Also, a
pig can be sold for ready cash if hard times hit,
and since the winter always seems the worst for
family finances, the animal can be like money in the
bank.

The pig killings were always done in the cold   3
months: November, December, January, and February.
So November and December were the best months for my
family; these months insured fresh pork on Thanksgiving

and Christmas. Since the pigs were killed, cleaned,
and cut up outside, the temperature had to be at
least forty degrees; fresh pork spoils very fast.
Another problem the cold abated was the blowflies
that are so populous in the summer months. Only a
few flies would be left by November; these you
could destroy before they deposited their eggs or
maggots on the meat. Cold weather, then, had many
values as well as faults.

The cold weather signified something else be-   4
sides the season for the butchering of animals and
for the celebration of the holidays. The crops that
we had struggled over all spring, summer, and fall
had been harvested and stored away or sold. The
fields where the tobacco, corn, and sweet potatoes
had grown were burnt to the ground. Then the
beautiful black, sandy soil was plowed under. The
dirt would lie idle, neither giving up any of her
stature nor taking away any of ours. She was left
alone to replenish her fertility. The winter had
come.

Yet the idealism of farming would slip out of   5
my mind when the first squeal of a harassed pig
would reach my ears. Then I would know it was time
for my part in the process. My first job was to
clean out the boilerhouse. The eighty-gallon cast-
iron boiler had to be washed out with lye soap, then
rinsed out thoroughly. Dipping the water out with a

lard can took an awfully long time. The boiler had
been built off the ground with fire bricks as its
base. It looked like a built-in barbecue stand
that is frequently seen at beaches and national
parks, but with a big kettle built in the middle.
I constructed a fire under the boiler, then poured
forty gallons of water in. As soon as the water
started to boil, I pulled the fire out of the
boiler's furnace. The water would boil for a long
time then. I ran to the house to tell everyone
that we were ready. We would all go to the pen to
kill the pig and drag him back to the boilerhouse.

We would arrive at the pigpen just minutes   6
after the water started to boil. My daddy and
Uncle Rass would catch the pig and tie his legs up.
Daddy would grab his ears and hold his head slightly
off the ground, so that my uncle Rass could shove a
tub under the pig's neck. I always made the incision into the pig's throat. We would then wait
five or ten minutes until all the blood dripped out
and the heart stopped beating. My mamma would then
take the blood-filled tub back to the house to make
blood pudding and sausage.

After we made sure that Mamma got into the   7
house with her heavy load, we would begin. Dragging
the 150-pound pig to the boilerhouse was not easy.
Daylight would be just peeking out when we would
string the pig up by his hind legs. The rope would

be attached to a movable pulley at the top of the
boilerhouse. Then we would place a two-by-four
across the boiler and position the pig in the
middle of the board. Slowly we would let his upper
body slide into the simmering water. But this was
only for a few minutes to loosen the hair. The
stench from the freshly killed pig was stifling.
The air was so cold, clean, and brisk that it would
tingle my nose as ginger ale does, but now neither
I nor the dogs would want any part of this dead
animal.

    Then the pig would be ready. We would lift him   8
out of the water and steady his body on the board.
With dull butter knives and cold, naked hands we
would scrape and pluck the hairy bristles off the
pig, paying close attention to the head.

    Soon Mamma would come out and inspect our work.   9
"The pig is clean enough to cut up," she would yell.
On getting approval, we would move the pig from the
boilerhouse to the open shed. A big number-ten
galvanized washtub (used by the children to take
baths) would be placed under his head. With a knife,
my daddy cut the pig from his tail down the middle of
his stomach, laying open the wound. The innards
would fall out neatly; next Daddy would cut the head
off and place it in the tub also.

    It was now my mamma's job to go through the tub
and pick out what would be needed. It seemed nothing   10

was wasted. The brain was taken from the head to
be scrambled with eggs and pickled. Then the head
was cooked until tender to make hog's head cheese.
Mamma would make a stew with dumplings out of the
liver, heart, and lung. The intestines were
cleaned and readied to fill with sausage. Nothing
was wasted.

As Mamma would work feverishly on her task,   11
Daddy would finish cutting up the carcass. All of
the meat but one shoulder and the feet would be
taken to the abattoir to be cured.

Throughout all these procedures I cannot think   12
of any one thing that was thrown away, except maybe
the bristles, which sometimes were saved for the
making of brooms. Nothing at the time of the
slaughter seemed more important than the pig. He
was our security for the long winter months when the
fields yielded no crops.

Now as I look back on the pig-killing process,   13
it conjures up vivid memories of a more simplistic
lifestyle, a lifestyle that I seem to have lost
either to the fast pace of modern society or to time
itself. The past sense of security I felt that can
never be retrieved in this life, at least not as I am
leading it now. For age has brought complexity that
will not allow me to return to the golden days of my
memories.

THE PROFESSIONAL
EDITOR
AT WORK

Part V

I N THE LAST TWO CHAPTERS we have seen how students revise their work, first on their own and then with the help of peer editors. In this chapter we have the opportunity to see a professional editor, Jane Aaron, make suggestions for revision as she shapes the essays by Bruce Adams and John Thatcher as if for publication in a magazine.

Observing a professional editor at work teaches several lessons about the place of revision in the composing process. First, all writing, even good writing, can be improved. Good writing takes time, effort, and patience, and often requires further revision, or editing, even after a "final" draft. Second, professional editing provides a model of close and careful reading that we can translate to our reading of our own and other writers' work. The job of the professional editor is to provide an objective view; by standing in for the audience, the editor shows the writer whether he or she has communicated effectively with that audience. Aaron's editing of Adams's and Thatcher's essays shows how a revised sentence or paragraph, a change in emphasis or tone can allow the writer's intentions to become even clearer to their readers. We see the power and possibility of revising as Adams's and Thatcher's essays move from strong essays to polished pieces.

Third, observing the professional editing process also shows what happens when a piece of writing goes public. For those who publish their work, whether in a commercial magazine or the school paper, editing is the final step of the composing process. As readers we are not aware of this stage — of the extensive editing that goes on — because the printed page does not reveal how each piece of writing was created. We see only the polished words and are not privy to the suggestions and changes, the additions and deletions that constitute the important work of editing.

Because the interaction between a professional editor and a writer demonstrates vividly the very process a writer must follow in preparing a final draft, we invited Jane Aaron, a professional editor, to edit the essays of Bruce Adams and John Thatcher. In fifteen years as a professional editor, Jane Aaron has worked with authors of magazine articles, of books for general audiences, and of college textbooks in almost every discipline, including freshman composition. She is the editor of *The Compact Reader*, an anthology of essays for composition courses, and the contributing editor to *The Little, Brown Handbook*, a best-selling composition textbook.

Our editing procedure was similar to the standard editing process used by most professional publications. Aaron edited Adams's and Thatcher's essays by making some changes, suggesting others, and questioning the writers in places about their meaning and intended effect. With the edited versions of their essays, she sent them a covering letter in which she explained her general response to their essays and offered an analysis to support her comments on their manuscripts. The students were asked not only to revise their essays using Aaron's suggestions but also to describe how they felt to have their work professionally edited. Before reading the edited versions of these essays, read the unedited essays as they appear on pages 19–22 for Adams and pages 146–150 for Thatcher. Then look at the questions that follow the revised version of each essay.

We begin this chapter with Jane Aaron's description of an editor at work.

A PROFESSIONAL EDITOR
DESCRIBES HER WORK

In their comments on being edited (pages 264 and 278), Bruce Adams and John Thatcher describe initial feelings of insecurity and indignation that would sound familiar to any editor. Like most writers who have poured themselves into their work, they had good reason to believe that their essays were suc-cessful. And indeed they were. But, like most manuscripts received by pub-lishers, the essays also had the potential to be better—clearer, more convinc-ing, more enjoyable for readers.

An editor is a kind of messenger between writer and reader, representing each to the other. On the one hand, the editor helps the writer state his or her message as effectively as possible. On the other hand, the editor represents the typical reader for whom the piece of writing is intended, anticipating his or her needs for information, clarity, and readability. At the practical level this dual representation works itself out in one process, as the editor helps shape the writer's work for the reader's maximum understanding and enjoy-ment.

The goal of the editing process is thus to preserve all the strengths of the manuscript while removing whatever impedes communication between writer and reader. Such a broad goal can encompass any feature of the work, including development, organization, emphasis, pace, specificity, conciseness, consis-tency, and accuracy. The process is not predictable, however, for each writer's purpose is unique, and the barriers to clear, effective expression are many. From one writer's work to another's, or even from one paragraph to the next in the same work, fresh problems arise to demand fresh solutions. And always the solutions must be conceived in the context of the writer's intentions and the reader's needs.

In order to understand the writer's intentions, diagnose the weaknesses of the manuscript, and conceive appropriate solutions, the editor may read the work as closely and as often as the writer has. Usually the first reading is a quick one to get the gist of the author's ideas and the sound of the author's voice. Then slower readings follow, during which the editor notes any problems in organization, gaps in the development of ideas, shifts in tone, or unnecessary repetitions. These readings require a kind of peripheral vision of the mind, an ability to recall the entire work while concentrating on a bit of it in order to see the connection—or lack of connection—between the part and the whole.

The actual editing is the most time-consuming part of the process, as the editor tries to resolve the larger problems and also weighs every sentence against the author's intentions and the reader's likely response. It is during this stage that the dialogue between editor and writer occurs. The writer's part in the dialogue consists of the words on the page. The editor's consists of changes, questions, comments, and suggestions, either on the manuscript, in the margins, or on separate sheets of paper. Sometimes the editor changes the manuscript without explanation if the need for change seems obvious enough; most corrections of grammatical, spelling, and typographical errors fall into this category. Sometimes the editor explains changes that reflect interpretations of the author's meaning. And sometimes the editor relies solely on suggestions or questions if the meaning cannot be safely assumed or if passages seem to require rewriting that the author is best equipped to handle. (All three approaches appear on Mr. Adams's and Mr. Thatcher's essays.) The explanations and suggestions may be lengthy, seemingly out of proportion to the problem being addressed, so that the author will understand why the manuscript is not clear or what impairs its readability. An editor quickly learns that a simple comment like "Not clear" usually prompts the natural response "It's clear to me"—and no revision.

When the editing is completed, the editor returns the manuscript to the author with a covering letter that includes a general response to the piece— both strengths and any overall weaknesses that will provide some context for the specific comments on the manuscript. (See the letters on pages 257 and 271.) Usually the author's revision is the final round in the process, as it was with Mr. Adams's and Mr. Thatcher's essays. But occasionally the editor may negotiate last-minute changes with the author before the manuscript is set in type.

Editing requires a certain amount of mind-reading, to discern the writer's intentions, as well as a sense of the possible solutions, an ear for language, and a firm grounding in the conventions of grammar, punctuation, mechanics, and spelling. It also requires an ability to work "silently," suspending one's own ideas instead of pushing them on the author. Of course, editors sometimes overstep their bounds. Beyond grammar and spelling, few matters in writing are clear-cut: almost everything is a question of choice, of judgment, and judgment calls are endlessly debatable. Although authors have the final word, the good ones, from an editor's standpoint, will always suspend their initial feelings of insecurity and indignation to engage in the debate. By that criterion alone, Mr. Adams and Mr. Thatcher are excellent authors.

BRUCE ADAMS, "EMERGENCY ROOM"

What follows is Jane Aaron's editing of Bruce Adams's essay. We begin with Aaron's letter to Adams and her editing of the essay. We then see Adams's comments on Aaron's editing and the essay as he revised it in response to her comments.

EDITOR TO AUTHOR:
JANE AARON'S LETTER TO BRUCE ADAMS

Dear Mr. Adams:

The attached suggestions for your essay are intended to help you make a very strong piece of writing even stronger. Your narrative is gripping: the pace, details, and first-person point of view make the reader experience the situation as if he or she were actually there in your shoes. But occasionally an inconsistency, an inappropriate image, or a rough passage breaks the spell. In a less compelling essay these spots might go unnoticed; in your essay they briefly interfere with the reader's intense concentration.

I have written suggestions and questions in the essay's margins and have made some changes when showing seemed clearer than telling. I hope you agree that with these revisions the essay would hold the reader even more firmly from first word to last. Of course, the final decisions on revision rest with you.

Sincerely,
Jane E. Aaron

ADAMS'S EDITED ESSAY

Emergency Room

By looking out the window of the ambulance,   1

I can see we are getting close to the hospital.

As we speed by the familiar buildings, the flashing

emergency lights turn them into hundreds of freeze-

frame photographs. The strobe lights turn everything

that their light falls on a monotone hue of either   *Presumably, the siren is a continuous sound, so it's*

red or blue. <u>The siren's only rival is the screaming</u>   *difficult to capture how the*

<u>of my patient, which pierces the air like an explosion</u>   *patient's scream, rivaling the siren,*

<u>in the night.</u> I struggle for balance while crouched   *is like an explosion. Also, is "explosion"*

on the floor as the vehicle makes a sharp turn into   *the right word? It conveys sudden,*

the parking lot. Finally, the ambulance jerks to   *loud sound at odds*

a stop. I know that we have arrived at our   *with reader's imagination of siren or scream.*

destination, the emergency department.

The pain in my hands grows worse as the time   2

goes by. The amount of pressure I have had to put

on the subclavian artery to stop the bleeding is

causing my hands to cramp. Suddenly, my mind is

diverted from the pain as the rear doors fly open

note apparent contradiction here between your hotness and your coolness just a couple of minutes later (next ¶). and the cool night air rushes in <u>chilling the sweat</u>

<u>on my face.</u> The doctor looks at me. I shake my

head. This patient is probably going to die no

matter what we do. Most of his life-sustaining

blood lies in the parking lot of an east-side bar

The image of a strike or blow seems inconsistent with a gunshot, since presumably neither the assailant nor the gun actually hit the victim. Try for a more appropriate image?

where he was shot. With the swiftness of a cobra

strike, his assailant struck the fatal blow with *jumps the gun— we don't know yet that the injury is fatal.*

a sawed-off shotgun. Where once were an arm and

chest wall there are now grotesque fragments of

human form.

As I stand up, I feel the warm sensation of   3

liquid running down my pant leg into my shoe. For

the first time I realize that I am covered with

warm, sticky blood. We wheel the patient from the

awk. repetition

ambulance onto the ~~ambulance~~ loading dock. The

(see first page)

heat lamps overhead radiate a soothing warmth against

the cool, humid night air. The calloused police

officers look on casually at the action passing

before them. They have seen all this too many times

to be shocked or even curious.

My adrenalin is peaking as we hit the   4

malfunctioning electric doors with a crash. As

the three of us enter the emergency department,

we turn sharply into room two: the crisis room.

The humming white lights are almost blinding after

the darkness of the night. The room is lined with

people in statue-like poses in anticipation of our

arrival. As we position the patient onto the hard

table, I notice that the once screaming man is now

silent and motionless.

A crash shatters the silence as an over-eager   5
intern knocks over a mayo stand, scattering the
once-sterile surgical instruments onto the floor.
The charge nurse just rolls her eyes as she bends
over to ~~begin~~ picking up the instruments. The body
is quickly enveloped by a group of surgeons. A
sterile and gloved surgeon signals to me and
simultaneously I withdraw my paralyzed hand as he
reapplies pressure to the damaged artery. The once-
quiet room is now a <u>flurry of activity</u> with blood   *This phrase has become almost a cliché; and, in any event, you go on to describe sounds more than activity.*
pressure cuffs squeezing, electrocardiogram indicators
beeping, and oxygen outlets hissing. The attending
emergency room physician stands with his arms folded
watching the ~~orchestration of~~ activity. He gives
his nod of approval to the <u>chief surgeon</u> as he walks
toward the head of the table. *(same person?)*

The <u>chief resident of thoracic surgery</u> is now   6
standing directly beside the table; ~~He~~ carefully   *change avoids "He... He..." in two successive sentences*
surveys^{ing} the damage done by the shotgun. He quickly
helpful to add this since so much was made of its toppling, above   turns toward the _{now-upright} mayo stand, ~~and~~ grabs a bottle of   *change conveys quickness better than "and..." "and..." of original*
betadine solution, and pours ~~it~~ *the solution* over the entire   *"it" seems to refer to "bottle"*
chest. The betadine turns the flesh orange as the
excess spills onto the floor, staining the surgeon's
tennis shoes. The charge nurse adjusts the overhead
light which illuminates the surgical field. The

"carefully"
used
above; surgeon squints as he looks at the skin in the
seems →
unnecessary reflection of the overhead light. He turns again to the
here
mayo stand and ~~carefully~~ picks up the shining

stainless steel scalpel. With his left hand he
With his right hand, *OK? clearer*
palpates the chest wall. Precisely but quickly,

he cuts the skin between the protruding ribs. As

the blade slices through the skin, the skin separates

without help. The normally yellow fat globules,

turned orange by the betadine, balloon from the

incision. With his second pass of the blade, ~~a~~
note popping
repeated below—
I'd cut here ~~popping sound is made as~~ he enters the pleura of
the passive
construction the inner chest wall. Blood ~~spurts out with a~~ *gushes out,* *"spurts" and "forceful"*
is a bit awkward *are contained in*
anyway) ~~forceful gush,~~ covering the surgeon's gown and *"gushes"*

gloves as he separates the two sections of the rib

cage. The charge nurse hands him the rib spreaders

with a slap.
The surgeon   7
problems with ~~He~~ deftly inserts the apparatus into the
images in the
original: separation between the two ribs. ~~He manipulates~~
"machine-like
precision" is ~~the spreaders with machine-like precision. The~~
hackneyed and
is taken care ~~cartilage of the ribs pops like the knuckles of~~
of, anyway, *he* *-is the ribs*
by "deftly" ~~a boastful schoolboy~~ as ~~they are~~ spread to form
in preceding *the cartilage makes a popping*
sentence; an unnatural opening into the man's chest. The *sound.*
"knuckles of surgeon reaches his gloved hand into the ~~cavernous~~ *adjective*
boastful *unnecessary*
schoolboy," opening and works his way past the ribs, clotted *given previous*
though fresh, *sentence*
yanks the blood, and lung tissue to the heart. He carefully
reader out of
the emergency
room to the
playground

palpates the organ. It is flaccid and void of

life's blood. He shakes his head as he examines

and then

the heart further, ~~He~~ grimaces as he feels the

changes here to →
break up "He...
He... He..."
pattern a bit the large puncture wound in the posterior aspect of

the left ventricle. He instinctively reaches for

the cardiac patches and sutures but stops short

as he realizes the damage is too extensive for

repair. He looks at the ~~emergency room~~ attending

physician as if to ask a question. The attending

just shrugs his shoulders and sighs. There is a

minor point,
but there moment of stillness as the surgeon removes his hand
was no
sense of
nonstillness from the man's chest and pronounces the time of
before—that is,
nothing moved death.
but the surgeon's
arm and face,
no one spoke.   The feeling is just coming back to my hands   8

as I attempt to write my trip report. My clothes

are wet with blood and smell like a slaughter house.

My legs are beginning to itch from the combination

of dried sweat and blood. My mind drifts as I think

of how much we can do for some patients and how

little we can do for others. I ask the unanswerable

question of why some people die as others live.

All we can do as paramedics is give each patient

our all.

    I look toward the emergency room doors to see   9

my partner coming toward me. He calls my name and

[right margin handwritten note:]
Here you shift
point-of-view
from yours to the
surgeon's—that is,
you are relating
what the surgeon
feels, not what
you see. Can you
let the surgeon's
actions (his
shaking head, his
grimace, perhaps
more on his motions)
convey what he's
finding inside the
body?

motions toward the ambulance. ~~He says we have~~
~~another call waiting for us.~~ "The natives must
be restless tonight," he says. "We have another
shooting."

The quotation is an effective ending, but this sentence detracts from it because it's so similar.

THE AUTHOR RESPONDS:
COMMENTARY FROM BRUCE ADAMS

I thought Ms. Aaron's comments were extraordinary. As a novice writer, I knew I needed some fine tuning. As an interested third party, she helped me draw my essay together to make it stronger. Her comments on shifting tense and story congruency were very helpful. I knew that she was trying to make my story the best it could be.

Initially, I had trouble with the idea of being edited because it was difficult to see the mistakes which I let slide through the final revision process. However, once my ego healed, I was able to look at her comments and use them to put the finishing touches on my essay.

Ms. Aaron's comments were helpful in seeing that the story as a whole must be congruent. Ideas must follow through, tenses must be similar, and images illustrated in the story must be clear and to the point. Her comments showed me how to tie one aspect of the story to another, how to relate a certain event to another event to build some depth into the story.

In general, I used most of Ms. Aaron's suggestions. I didn't have the feeling that she was giving me actual replacements for my mistakes. I felt that she gave me a general idea to focus on and expected me to take it from there. The most difficult part of revising the essay using her comments was trying to keep the story my own. When someone has a lot of input in your work, you become a little insecure in your own ability. However, if you reassure yourself that this is a professional decision, and not a personal one, things will go smoothly from there.

ADAMS'S REVISED ESSAY

Emergency Room

By looking out the window of the ambulance, I   1
can see we are getting close to the hospital. As
we speed by the familiar buildings, the flashing
emergency lights turn them into hundreds of freeze-
frame photographs. The strobe lights turn everything their light falls on a monotone hue of either
red or blue. The siren's only rival is the screaming of my patient, which pierces the air in irregular
explosive bursts. I struggle for balance while
crouched on the floor as the vehicle makes a sharp
turn into the parking lot. Finally, the ambulance
jerks to a stop. I know that we have arrived at
our destination, the emergency room.

The pain in my hands grows worse as the time   2
goes by. The amount of pressure I have had to put
on the subclavian artery to stop the bleeding is
causing my hands to cramp. Suddenly, my mind is
diverted from the pain as the rear doors fly open
and the cool night air rushes in, chilling the sweat
on my face. The doctor looks at me. I shake my
head. This patient is probably going to die no
matter what we do. Most of his life-sustaining
blood lies in the parking lot of an east-side bar
where he was shot. A meaningless argument ended
with the devastating force of a sawed-off shotgun.

Where once were an arm and chest wall there are
now grotesque fragments of human form.

As I stand up, I feel the warm sensation of   3
liquid running down my pant leg into my shoe. For
the first time I realize that I am covered with
warm, sticky blood. We wheel the patient from the
ambulance onto the ambulance loading dock. The heat
lamps overhead radiate an uncomfortable warmth
against my already overheated body. The calloused
police officers look on casually at the action
passing before them. They have seen this too many
times to be shocked or even curious.

My adrenaline is peaking as we hit the mal-   4
functioning electric doors with a crash. As the
three of us enter the emergency department, we turn
sharply into room two: the crisis room. The humming
white lights are almost blinding after the darkness
of the night. The room is lined with people in
statue-like poses in anticipation of our arrival.
As we position the patient onto the hard table, I
notice the once-screaming man is now silent and
motionless.

A crash shatters the silence as an over-eager   5
intern knocks over a mayo stand, scattering the once-
sterile surgical instruments onto the floor. The
charge nurse just rolls her eyes as she bends over to
pick up the instruments. The body is quickly enveloped by a group of surgeons. A sterile and gloved

surgeon signals to me and simultaneously I withdraw
my paralyzed hand as he reapplies pressure to the
damaged artery. The once-quiet room is now filled
with the clatter of blood pressure cuffs crackling,
electrocardiogram indicators beeping, and oxygen
outlets hissing. The attending emergency room
physician stands with his arms folded watching the
activity. He gives his nod of approval to the
senior surgical resident as he walks toward the
head of the table.

The senior surgical resident is now standing   6
directly beside the table, carefully surveying the
damage done by the shotgun. He quickly turns toward
the now-upright mayo stand, grabs a bottle of betadine solution, and pours the solution over the
entire chest. The betadine turns the flesh orange
as the excess spills onto the floor, staining the
surgeon's tennis shoes. The charge nurse adjusts
the overhead light which illuminates the surgical
field. The surgeon squints as he looks at the skin
in the reflection of the overhead light. He turns
again to the mayo stand and picks up the shining
stainless steel scalpel. With his left hand he palpates the chest wall. With his right hand, precisely but quickly, he cuts the skin between the
protruding ribs. As the blade slices through the
skin, the skin separates without help. The normally
yellow fat globules, turned orange by the betadine,

balloon from the incision. With his second pass of
the blade, he enters the pleura of the inner chest
wall. Blood gushes out, covering the surgeon's
gown and gloves as he separates the two sections of
the rib cage. The charge nurse hands him the rib
spreaders with a slap.

    The surgeon deftly inserts the apparatus into   7
the separation between the two ribs. As he spreads
the ribs to form an unnatural opening into the man's
chest, the cartilage snaps loudly. The surgeon
reaches his gloved hand into the opening and works
his way past the ribs, clotted blood, and lung
tissue to the heart. He carefully palpates the
organ. A squish is heard as the surgeon manipulates
the flaccid heart. He shakes his head as he examines the heart further and suddenly grimaces as he
tells of a large puncture wound in the posterior
aspect of the left ventricle. The surgeon instinctively reaches for the cardiac patches and sutures
but stops short as he admits the damage is too extensive for repair. He looks at the attending
physician as if to ask a question. The attending
just shrugs his shoulders and sighs. Everyone's
eyes are on the surgeon as he removes his hand from
the man's chest and pronounces the time of death.

    The feeling is just coming back to my hands as   8
I attempt to write my trip report. My clothes are
wet with blood and smell like a slaughter house.

My legs are beginning to itch from the combination of dried sweat and blood. My mind drifts as I think of how much we can do for some patients and how little we can do for others. I ask the unanswerable question of why some people die as others live. All we can do as paramedics is give each patient our all.

I look toward the emergency room doors to see   9
my partner coming toward me. He calls my name and motions toward the ambulance. "The natives must be restless tonight," he says. "We have another shooting."

Questions on Adams's Essay

1. Jane Aaron wrote to Bruce Adams: "I hope you agree that with these revisions the essay would hold the reader even more firmly from first word to last. Of course, the final decisions on revision rest with you." Adams responded in his commentary: "The most difficult part of revising the essay using [Ms. Aaron's] comments was trying to keep the story my own." Do you feel that Adams was successful in keeping his story his own? Give specific instances.

2. How does Aaron describe the purpose of Adams's essay? Do you agree with her description?

3. Aaron writes: "The pace, details, and first-person point of view make the reader experience the situation as if he or she were actually there in your shoes." Did you feel this involvement while reading the essay? Choose particular passages and explain how pace, details, and point of view contributed to holding your interest.

4. Aaron lists three types of changes she makes on manuscripts: changes without explanation; changes that she explains; and changes that she suggests but leaves for the author to make. Find examples of all three types in Aaron's editing of Adams's essay. For the last type of change, do you agree that the change was better left to the author?

5. In her letter to Adams, Aaron mentions problems with inconsistency (paragraphs 2 and 3) and rough passages (paragraph 6). Do you agree with her? Why or why not? Does Adams's revised essay need further revision?

6. Study paragraph 7 of Adams's original essay with Aaron's comments. Do you agree with Aaron's comments? Why or why not? Then look at paragraph 7 of Adams's revised essay. Has Adams taken all of Aaron's suggestions? What has he accepted and what has he rejected? Describe the differences between the original and revised essays. What further revisions would you suggest?

7. In Adams's original essay, look at the sentence in paragraph 5 beginning "The once-quiet room is now a flurry of activity." Do you agree with Aaron's comments about this sentence? Does the phrase "a flurry of activity" add anything to the sentence? Is Adams's revision an improvement? If so, how? If not, what further revision would you suggest?

8. One of Aaron's editing strategies is to strengthen passages by cutting a word or sentence. Find such places and explain why the sentence or paragraph is stronger with these deletions.

9. Which of Aaron's comments did you find most helpful? What did you learn about reading and writing from studying Aaron's comments on Adams's essay?

10. Imagine that you are a professional editor preparing Adams's essay for publication. Are there any more changes that you would suggest? Annotate Adams's revised essay, as Aaron did with the original essay, explaining the changes you think are necessary and offering possible solutions. Write a letter to Adams describing the strengths of his revision and what still needs to be done.

JOHN THATCHER, "ON KILLING THE MAN"

This section continues with Aaron's editing of John Thatcher's essay. Again we see Aaron's letter to Thatcher and her editing of the essay, followed by Thatcher's comments and his revised essay.

EDITOR TO AUTHOR:
JANE AARON'S LETTER TO JOHN THATCHER

Dear Mr. Thatcher:

Your essay is insightful and moving. It is also quite complex, so many of the attached suggestions for revising it are necessarily complex as well. The second half of the essay—the detailed narration of the raccoon experience —is fast-paced and powerful. It is effective in itself, but it is even more dramatic because of the build-up it receives in the first half of the essay. I imagine that this earlier section was difficult to write. It combines an explanation of trapping with an expression of your initial, conventional feelings about trapping—all in an ironic tone that keeps hinting, "This is not the full story; something important is going to happen." As complicated as this first half is, some passages understandably succeed less well than others. As you will see, several of my comments concern the sequencing of information, some shifts away from the first person ("I"), and an inconsistency in tone. In both halves of the essay, I have also queried other passages and made occasional changes for clarity and emphasis.

I hope that all my suggested revisions interpret your intentions accurately and that you agree they will strengthen the essay's capacity first to suspend and then to move the reader. The decisions on whether and how to implement the suggestions are, of course, yours to make.

Sincerely,
Jane E. Aaron

THATCHER'S EDITED ESSAY

On Killing the Man

I wanted to trap! All of the other boys did.   1

Certainly that was reason enough for me. And what

about the stacks of money to be made through this

time-honored trade? Why, boys had been known to

make a small fortune in one season. Boys ~~that~~ *who*

verbs
shift from
past to
present tense

wished to become young men required inordinate

amounts of money, and for those ~~that~~ *who* liv*e* ^*d* out of

town, on a farm with a woods and small creek,

trapping during the winter ~~is~~ *was* a most convenient

means to an end: ~~The end being, in most cases,~~

a colon seems to
emphasize the ear's
importance just as
effectively as the
sentence fragment
and eliminates
repetition ("end...
end") and an
apparent contradiction
("an end... in most cases).

the all-important automobile. So I began trapping

in the winter of my seventeenth year. I felt as if

I were pleasing generations of woodsmen; the

pioneer spirit raged in my blood. I would soon be

a man. ~~Whose man?~~

The reader doesn't yet understand the
implications of this question, and it is
repeated more effectively later. OK to cut?

This paragraph
is hard to read
because most
sentences do
not have
human actors
as subjects (see
underlining)
and few
sentence subjects
pick up either
the subject or
the object of
the preceding
sentence (thus
forcing readers

One goes about trapping in this manner. At   2

the very outset one acquires a "trapping" state of

mind. This entails several steps. The purchase of

as many traps as one might need is first. A pair

of rubber gloves, waterproof boots, and the grubbiest

clothes capable of withstanding human use come next

to outfit the trapper for his adventure. A library

of books must be read, and preferably someone with

to refocus their attention on each new sentence). The problem may occur
because you start with "one" as the subject of the first two sentences
and then (naturally) want to avoid it. Why not rewrite the
paragraph using the first person ("I")? That would make you
the actor (removing the unnecessary distance between you and the
paragraph content), and it would probably smooth the flow of
sentences almost automatically.

experience is needed to educate the novice. The
decision has to be made on just what kind of
animals to go after, what sort of bait to use, and
where to place the traps for highest yield.
Finally, the trapper needs a heavy stick. Often a
trap set to drown the animal once caught fails to
do so. Then it is necessary to club the animal and
drown him. A blow with a club will not damage a
pelt the way a gunshot would. A club is a most
necessary piece of equipment for the trapper.

Properly outfitted and informed,

So I set out on my wilderness adventure. My

On each foray,

booted feet scarred the frosted grass. The traps
slung over my shoulder tolled a death knell as they
slapped against my back, and the oaken club rapped
a steady drumbeat on my thigh. I had my chance to
become a man, a real man in the old sense of the
word. I was the French voyageur trapping lands no
white man had ever seen before. I was Dan'l Boone
about to catch my famous coonskin cap. I was the
Hudson Bay Company trapper, trading axes and blankets
with the Indians and sending beaver pelts to London
for a gentleman's top hat. I was my father too. I
was he and he was me as the two of us set out together for the great woods. This was truly the way
men should live.

[Right margin annotation:] Your later explanations of what animals you were trying to catch (p. 3, 1st paragraph) and how / why you set traps in water (p. 4, middle) would be more helpful here. Assuming that the raccoon experience was your first clubbing, you might also indicate that your knowledge of how a club was used was secondhand. That would set up the transition on p. 4.

[Left margin annotation:] I gather from later paragraphs that you went trapping several times (at least), but this paragraph seems to describe a single experience and so leads the reader to expect a continued emphasis on one experience. Could you reword the first couple of sentences as suggested or in some other way to indicate that you did this more than once?

[Right margin annotation:] these images give a real sense of your feelings at the time

I moved this sentence from the end of the paragraph because it seems a better transition from the previous paragraph and a better lead-in to what follows. OK?

~~I~~ I soon learned that becoming a man is a most difficult
~~The actual work of trapping can be completed~~
task, and enjoying the work is even harder.
~~only after the trapper has suffered as much as~~

~~possible.~~ It is cold, tedious, backbreaking,   *Placing the "fun" view before your view would emphasize your view more.*

finger- and toe-numbing, infuriating torture often

described as exciting and fun by someone who really

enjoys trapping. In my case the traps were mostly

set in the water. This is done in the hopes of

See p. 2, top: move information there? (The next sentence will then need a new beginning.)

catching muskrats, raccoons, and possibly a mink or

two. It is also done to enhance the feeling of al-

ready numb fingers by immersing them in freezing

If you accept moving this sentence to the beginning of the paragraph, these 2 paragraphs could be combined. A new transition would be needed; for instance: "and catching the animal does not finish the work: it must be skinned by cutting [etc.]"

water. ~~It is a most difficult task becoming a man,~~

~~even more difficult to enjoy doing it.~~

Once the animal is caught, it must be skinned.

This involves cutting the pelt away from the body,

scraping off the fatty deposits from the underside,

and stretching the skin on a board until it is dry.

single pelt requires a substantial effort

All in all, a ~~great amount of work~~ for a twenty-five-

return

dollar ~~pelt.~~ Twenty-five dollars, that is, if the

pelt is large for a raccoon, if it is in good con-

(shift in person)

dition, and if the dealer ~~you go to~~ is a generous

The two sentence fragments here made reading difficult. I've suggested one way to work them into one complete sentence.

It isn't clear here whether you felt the sense of accomplishment and satisfaction. If you did, then perhaps you should say so directly. The reversal in your attitude when you kill the raccoon would then be that much more dramatic.

man. But who can deny the sense of accomplishment

a man feels when he sells his pelts? Only he can

of

know the great satisfaction ~~felt by~~ outsmarting

by

small animals ~~through~~ catching and killing them in

a man feels

traps they could not smell or see. What joy ~~is felt~~

4

5

when ~~a man can say~~ he has beaten nature with only

his quick mind, traps of spring steel, rubberized

gloves that leave no betraying scent, scientifically

tested lures and baits, and clever sets that catch

and hold

the animals ~~and sink them to their deaths as they~~

~~struggle to get away~~ while water fills their small,

gasping lungs.

But often the novice does not succeed in

making a "water set" that quickly drowns the animal.

One cold morning I stayed home from school,

and though sick with a cold I checked my trapline

like any humane trapper. [My "water sets" had not

worked the night before. I walked in the direction

of a trap anchored to a fallen log that was in-

tended to encourage a trapped animal to escape by

swimming across the creek and thus drown itself.]

As I neared the trap I immediately saw that it had

been disturbed, but didn't see an animal. "Drowned,"

I thought. When I was very close to the set, I

realized the animal was not drowned and underwater;

hopelessly entangled around a limb of the log was a

large male raccoon, *still alive.*

Now I had a problem. The raccoon must be

knocked senseless and drowned. The club that hung

suddenly

around my wrist had grown very heavy, ~~all of a sudden~~

(Handwritten annotations in margins, including: "The heavy sarcasm in these 2 sentences seems to jump the gun on the powerful raccoon experience...", "This is an excellent transition, but can you make it more personal...", "I suggest deleting these 2 sentences...", "OK to add this so the point is unmistakably clear?")

8

and my stomach knotted at the thought of what I

had to do. I was torn between wanting to absolve

wanting to do what I had worked so hard to come to and

myself by setting him free (although I knew he

the raccoon

would suffer a horrible death) ~~and doing what it~~

← *Occasionally, it seems necessary to repeat "raccoon" instead of using a pronoun.*

~~was I had worked so hard to come to.~~ I wanted to

I suggest reversing the conflict-ing emotions in this sentence (as shown) for 2 reasons: (1) the sentence is easier to read if the longer part comes second; and (2) the next sentence starts with "I wanted to be a man," so the 2 sentences are now parallel in content.

be a man, but also wanted to run away from what I'd

done and cry into my mother's breast. My hand,

however, was forced by my earlier actions, and now

I had to take this creature's life to end the suf-

fering I had caused it. The bile rose in my throat

as I raised the club.

    At that moment I knew what an awful thing it   9

is to be hated, violently hated by another living

The sentence would be even easier to read if you phrased the inserted emotion more clearly—per-haps "wanting to achieve what I had worked for"?

The raccoon

thing. ~~He~~ looked at me and not at the club. He looked

at me with his trap-torn flesh bleeding away his

fear, leaving only raging hate. ~~He barely paused in~~

barely let up

his screamed hiss as the club came down, again and

← *rewording focuses attention on the hiss— ok?*

again, on his skull. I didn't kill him well because

because

he was my first murder, and ~~the~~ hot tears ~~that burst~~

~~from me~~ blinded my eyes, making the blows poorly

The tears seem to be a second reason for killing poorly— hence changes —ok?

aimed.

    Once the hideous screaming stopped and the   10

despising, damning eyes rolled back into their

the raccoon.

sockets, I drowned ~~him~~. As I watched the water

fill him up and the bubbles and blood float up from

his nostrils, I wondered if I was now the man I
had wanted to be. Whose man? I decided then that
the boy who was responsible for this wretched thing
was not ready to be a man because he had aspired to
be someone else and not himself. I knew then that

Rewording seems more emphatic. I would never do this despicable thing again, and ~~never have~~ ~~since~~. To reach manhood is a wonderful

Perhaps start a new paragraph here to set off your reflections on the incident from the incident itself?

a more precise word is needed here because "thing" appears in the 2 preceding sentences with a different meaning. "achievement" perhaps? thing, but ~~this~~ *it* happens only when the man can look at himself and recognize what he sees. A boy must kill "the man," the one he has dreamed for himself, ~~in his head,~~ in order to let out the one inside ~~that~~ *who*

This sentence is complicated, and fewer words help make it more readable. patiently ~~bides his time~~ *waits* until the boy ~~is ready to~~ *can*

accept what he is. It makes a significant event to
make the change. In my case it took the murder of

neither of these sentences seems necessary. you make the points clearly and concretely in the surrounding material. an animal. Life is not always clean and bloodless. If I could have killed my "man" with a swift rapier thrust I would have done it. Instead I ~~am left with~~ *remember*

The last sentence, especially, seems a weaker ending than the sentence preceding it. ~~the memory of~~ blow after blow on a tiny head. I still see the bared teeth and still hear the wild snarling. My "man" died especially hard in bloody frothing waters. I have learned from that and will

never forget.

THE AUTHOR RESPONDS:
COMMENTARY FROM JOHN THATCHER

When I read Ms. Aaron's comments, I was at the same time greatly flattered and scared to death of her changes. I had never been edited by someone who edits other people's work for a living. I didn't know where to start. Somewhere in my mind I thought I should play the temperamental young author and fight the suggestions of the mad-slashing editor who wanted me to compromise my writing. Once I started, however, I found all of Ms. Aaron's comments helpful, clear, and perfectly logical. Ms. Aaron helped me polish my essay so that it is now meaningful to anyone who may read it.

It has been a bad practice of mine to feel mild indignation while being edited. In the past I thought I personally was being edited, not the thing I'd written. After this experience I have learned that I am not being told that I am inadequate but that my writing isn't as good as it might be. It's not a good idea to treat one's writing as if it were carved in stone. Now I welcome an outside opinion to point out something I might have missed. Often I am too close to my writing and miss many things that could be strengthened.

From studying Ms. Aaron's comments, I learned that I need to treat writing as a craft. My writing has always been an outlet for great emotion with little conscious thought toward form, balance, timing, and the things that make writing aesthetic. I also discovered that in order to create the desired effect on my reader, I need to be careful with correct introduction of information, suspense, and climax. I feel that too often I have been bowling my reader over with emotion and often have not been clear in an effort to be a better writer. Writing is like building a house of cards; you've got to be patient and careful.

Before I began rewriting I decided that I would accept most of Ms. Aaron's suggested changes. I knew they were all in my best interest, and the only disagreement arose where a word or short phrase that I liked was being deleted. When I was through rewriting I was surprised that my essay was not an empty shell as I had feared. The suggested changes even inspired some new thoughts. My essay is now more polished and satisfying. I knew it had rough edges; I just needed Ms. Aaron to show me where they were.

THATCHER'S REVISED ESSAY

On Killing the Man

I wanted to trap! All of the other boys did. 1
Certainly that was reason enough for me. And what
about the stacks of money to be made through this
time-honored trade? Why, boys had been known to
make a small fortune in one season. Boys who
wished to become young men required inordinate
amounts of money, and for those who lived out of
town, on a farm with a woods and small creek,
trapping during the winter was a most convenient
means to an end: the all-important automobile.
So I began trapping in the winter of my seventeenth
year. I felt as if I were pleasing generations of
woodsmen; the pioneer spirit raged in my blood. I
would soon be a man.

I went about trapping in this manner. At the 2
very outset I acquired a "trapping" state of mind.
This entailed several steps. I purchased the traps
I thought I would need first. Next, to outfit myself for my trapping adventures I collected a pair
of rubber gloves, waterproof boots, and the grubbiest clothes capable of withstanding human use. I
read a library of books and was educated by an experienced trapper, my father. I then made the decision on just what kinds of animals to seek, what
sort of bait to use, and where to place my traps for
highest yield. Finally, I found a heavy stick: a

souvenir Indian war club from Cherokee, North
Carolina. I had decided to set my traps in the
water. I had hoped to catch water animals such
as muskrats, raccoons, and possibly a mink or two.
My traps were anchored to something heavy on the
bank to encourage trapped animals to swim away from
their torment, into deeper water, where they would
drown from the weight of the trap pulling them down.
The club was a precautionary measure to stun and
drown animals that might inconveniently choose not
to follow my plan. I knew my club would not damage
a pelt the way a gunshot would. My club was my most
necessary piece of equipment as I began my passage
into manhood.

With a storehouse of woodland lore and all the 3
trappings, as it were, dangling from me, I set out
early every morning on my wilderness adventures.
The brilliantly cold eye of the winter sun looked on
morosely each brittle dawn as my booted feet scarred
the frosted grass. The traps slung over my shoulder
tolled a death knell as they slapped against my
back, and the hickory club rapped a muffled drumbeat
on my thigh. I had my chance to become a man, a
real man in the old sense of the word. I was the
French voyageur trapping lands no white man had ever
seen before. I was Dan'l Boone about to catch my
famous coonskin cap. I was the Hudson Bay Company
Trapper, trading axes and blankets with the Indians

and sending beaver pelts to London for a gentleman's
top hat. I was my father too. I was he and he was
I as the two of us set out together for the great
woods. This was truly the way men should live.

I soon learned that becoming a man is a most   4
difficult task, and enjoying the work is even
harder. What someone who really enjoys trapping
would call exciting and fun was for me cold,
tedious, backbreaking, finger- and toe-numbing,
infuriating torture, and my "water-set" traps served
only to enhance the feeling of my already numb
fingers by immersing them in freezing water. And
once you've been successful in catching an animal,
your work begins again. The animal's pelt must be
cut away from its body. The layer of subcutaneous
fat must be scraped from the underside, and the
skin must be stretched on a board designed for the
purpose and left to dry. All in all, a single pelt
requires a substantial effort for a twenty-five-
dollar return--twenty-five dollars, that is, if the
pelt is large for a raccoon, if it is in good condition, and if the dealer is a generous man. But I
believed a man could feel no greater sense of
accomplishment than when he sold his pelts. I
wanted to know the great satisfaction of outsmarting
animals by catching them in traps they could not
smell or see. I wanted to know the joy a man must
feel when he has beaten nature with only his quick

mind, traps of spring steel, rubberized gloves that
leave no betraying scent, and scientifically
tested lures and baits. I wanted my water sets to
succeed in catching, holding, and drowning my prey.

Being a novice, I had not counted on the possi-   5
bility that my water sets might fail to pull down a
captured animal while water filled its small, gasping
lungs.

One cold morning I stayed home from school, and   6
though sick with a cold I ran my trapline like any
humane trapper. As I neared the last trap on my
line, a water set anchored to a fallen log, I immediately saw that it had been disturbed. But I didn't
see an animal. "Drowned," I thought. When I was
very close to the set, I realized the animal was not
drowned and underwater; hopelessly entangled around
a limb of the log was a large male raccoon, very
much alive.

Now I had a problem. The raccoon must be   7
knocked senseless and drowned. The club that hung
from a thong on my wrist had suddenly grown very
heavy, and my stomach knotted at the thought of what
I had to do. I was torn between wanting to do what
I had worked so hard to come to and wanting to absolve myself by setting the raccoon free (although
I knew he would suffer a horrible death). I wanted
to be a man, but I also wanted to run away from
what I'd done and cry into my mother's breast. My

hand, however, was foreced by my earlier actions, and now I had to take this creature's life to end the suffering I had caused it. The bile rose in my throat as I raised the club over my head.

At that moment I knew what an awful thing it is to be hated, violently hated by another living thing. The raccoon looked at me and not at the club. He looked at me with his trap-torn flesh bleeding away his fear, leaving only white, raging hate. His screamed hiss barely let up as the club came down, again and again, on his skull. I didn't kill him well because he was my first murder and because hot tears blinded my eyes, making the blows poorly aimed.   9

Once that hideous screaming stopped and the despising, damning eyes rolled back into their sockets, I drowned the raccoon. As I watched the water fill him up and the bubbles and blood float up from his nostrils, I wondered if I was now the man I wanted to be. Whose man? I decided then that the boy who was responsible for this wretched thing was not ready to be a man because he had aspired to be someone else and not himself. I knew then that I would never do this despicable thing again, and I never have.   10

To reach manhood is a natural progression, but it happens only when the new man can look at himself and recognize what he sees. A boy must kill

8

"the man," the one he has dreamed for himself,
in order to free the one inside who patiently bides
his time until the boy can accept what he is. It
takes a significant event to make the change. In my
case it took the murder of an animal. If I could
have killed my "man" with a swift rapier thrust I
would have done it. Instead I remember blow after
blow on a small head. I still see the bared teeth
and still hear the wild snarling. My "man" died
especially hard in bloody frothing waters.

Questions on Thatcher's Essay

1. John Thatcher remarked in his response to Jane Aaron's editing: "It has been a bad practice of mine to feel mild indignation while being edited. In the past I thought I personally was being edited, not the thing I'd written." What is it about the process of editing that makes writers feel indignant? Why do writers need the outside opinion that an editor can provide?

2. In her letter, Aaron states Thatcher's intention as she sees it. Do you agree with her evaluation? Do her suggested changes maintain this intention?

3. In his response, Thatcher says that his revised essay is "not an empty shell" but that Aaron's suggestions "inspired some new thoughts" and the essay "is now more polished and satisfying." Do you agree? How does Thatcher keep his enthusiasm for and involvement with his subject in revising?

4. Aaron shows Thatcher that some passages in his essay succeed less well than others. From her comments, decide which passages in the essay she thinks are most successful and which are least successful. Do you agree with her?

5. Locate Aaron's comments in the first part of the essay that ask Thatcher to rewrite a paragraph or sentence using the first-person pronoun ("I") rather than the third person ("one" or "he"). Why do these comments help Thatcher's purpose?

6. In her letter, Aaron mentions problems with "sequencing of information." Which of her specific comments deal with this problem? How did she think Thatcher should revise the essay? Did Thatcher make the changes she asked for?

7. Aaron questions Thatcher's inconsistency in tone. In paragraph 5 in particular she feels that Thatcher's sarcasm anticipates too early the narrative that follows. Do you agree with her? Why or why not? Has Thatcher answered her criticism in his revision? Has he toned down the sarcasm? Is the revision more effective here than the original? Can you suggest other ways of revising?

8. Aaron likes the images Thatcher uses in paragraph 3 because they give a sense of his feelings at the time. Do you agree that they are successful? Why are they important for making the narrative more meaningful?

9. Aaron made occasional changes, as she says, for "clarity and emphasis." Find places where her changes make Thatcher's meaning clearer. Why does her rewording make the meaning clearer in each case? How has she improved the emphasis? What has been emphasized more effectively in the revised essay?

10. Study paragraph 2 of Thatcher's original essay, with Aaron's comments. Do you agree with Aaron's comments? Why? Then look at paragraph 2 of Thatcher's revised essay. Has he used all of Aaron's suggestions? What has he accepted and what has he rejected? Describe the differences between the original and revised essays. What further revisions would you suggest?

11. Which of Aaron's comments did you find most helpful? What did you learn about reading and writing from studying Aaron's comments on Thatcher's essay?

12. Imagine that you are a professional editor preparing Thatcher's essay for publication. Are there any more changes that you would suggest? Annotate Thatcher's revised essay, as Aaron did with the original essay, explaining the changes you think are necessary and offering possible solutions. Also write a letter to Thatcher telling him what the strengths of his revision are and what still needs to be done.

RHETORICAL
ARRANGEMENT

Research Writing

Boxerman, "Not So Fast, Milton Friedman!" p. 35
Cohen, "The Matter of Maids and Mops," p. 47
Klein, "Saturday Morning Sexism," p. 87
C. Thompson, "To Search Is to Grow," p. 151

To the Student:

We are running the Bedford Prizes in Student Writing again and will publish the winners in a new edition of *Student Writers at Work*. To help us in our planning, we need to know what you think of the current edition.

Please take a few minutes to complete this questionnaire and send it to Bedford Books of St. Martin's Press, 165 Marlborough St., Boston, MA 02116. We promise to listen to what you have to say. Thanks.

School _____

School location (city, state) _____

Course title _____

Instructor's name _____

1. Did you find it valuable to read other students' writing? _____

_____

_____

2. Did you like hearing what other students say about their writing? _____

_____

_____

3. Did you also read writing by students in your own class? _____

4. Did your teacher assign essays by professional writers? _____

5. What other textbooks did you use with *Student Writers at Work*? _____

_____

Please evaluate the essays.	Liked a lot	Okay	Didn't like	Didn't read
Adams, "Emergency Room"	___	___	___	___
Barrus, "Todd"	___	___	___	___
Bean, "Bitter Sitter"	___	___	___	___
Boxerman, "Not So Fast, Milton Friedman!"	___	___	___	___

	Liked a lot	Okay	Didn't like	Didn't read
Buchanan, "Dancing Grandma"	___	___	___	___
Cohen, "The Matter of Maids and Mops"	___	___	___	___
Dietrich, "The Teapot Whistles"	___	___	___	___
Egnor, "A Life of Quiet Desperation"	___	___	___	___
Emminger, "The Exhibition"	___	___	___	___
Gardinier, "The Advantage of Disadvantage"	___	___	___	___
Glaven, "What Can You Do?"	___	___	___	___
Hill, "Returning Home"	___	___	___	___
Hollingsworth, "Zero Planting"	___	___	___	___
Howell, "Survival and the Pig"	___	___	___	___
Klein, "Saturday Morning Sexism"	___	___	___	___
Landmann, "The House"	___	___	___	___
Menter, "Home Is Where the Heart Is"	___	___	___	___
Morgan, "Man's Moral Bankruptcy"	___	___	___	___
Moss, "Bronc Busting vs. Equine Education"	___	___	___	___
Rolls, "Lady Diana: He Married the Wrong Woman"	___	___	___	___
Russell, "Logging: Then and Now"	___	___	___	___
Saukko, "How to Poison the Earth"	___	___	___	___
Scannell, "Locks and Tresses"	___	___	___	___
Seilsopour, "I Forgot the Words to the National Anthem"	___	___	___	___
Senturia, "At Home in America"	___	___	___	___
Tennant, "A Stranger's Eyes"	___	___	___	___
Thatcher, "On Killing the Man"	___	___	___	___
C. Thompson, "To Search Is to Grow"	___	___	___	___
J. Thompson, "A Frozen Night"	___	___	___	___
Turner, "El amor y la muerte: An Interpretation"	___	___	___	___
Zurakowski, "Confessions of a Gable Groupie"	___	___	___	___

Please also evaluate the other sections of the book.

	Liked a lot	Okay	Didn't like	Didn't read
Part I: Students on Writing	—	—	—	—

Comments: _____

_____

| Part III: Two Student Writers at Work | — | — | — | — |

Comments: _____

_____

| Part IV: Peer Editors at Work | — | — | — | — |

Comments: _____

_____

| Part V: The Professional Editor at Work | — | — | — | — |

Comments: _____

_____

Any general comments or suggestions? _____

_____

_____

Name _____

Mailing address _____

_____

Date _____